The Three Nephites

The Three Nephites

Saints, Service, and Supernatural Legend

JULIE SWALLOW,
CHRISTOPHER JAMES BLYTHE,
ERIC A. ELIASON, and JILL TERRY RUDY

Manufactured in the United States of America
1 2 3 4 5 C P 5 4 3 2 1
♾ This book is printed on acid-free paper.

Publication of this book was supported in part by a
grant from the L. J. and Mary C. Skaggs Folklore Fund.

Cataloging data available from the Library of Congress

LCCN 2025010535
ISBN 978-0-252-04683-4 (cloth : alk.)
ISBN 978-0-252-08892-6 (paper : alk.)
ISBN 978-0-252-04836-4 (ebook)

For William A. Wilson, without whose teaching and collection this book would not be possible

Contents

Acknowledgments

The publication of this book feels like nothing short of a miracle. It could never have come to fruition without help and support from many individuals. There are so many people to thank, and while not all of them can be placed here, it's important to publicly acknowledge some of them. I'd like to dedicate this book to the following individuals:

Scott Howell, who encouraged the work and allowed people in the front office of Brigham Young University's Salt Lake Center (BYU SLC) to help during their quiet times. And thank you to the front office staff who combed through thousands of stories, including Kelly Lau, Beihe (Sunny) Le, Vashti Musig, Mercedes Ng, Sarah Tengan, and Ellie Whitlock.

Amy Bernards, BYU SLC's fantastic librarian, who helped with research and documentation.

Stirling Miller, who created charts, formatted stories, and did countless spreadsheet searches.

Steve Taggart, whose miraculous phone call changed my perspective.

Glorianna Tillemann-Dick, who moved in next door and turned out to be the best neighbor and editor a girl could wish for.

Jessica Green, my calm, insightful colleague and friend, who made all things feel possible and offered to read drafts whenever I felt stuck.

Christine Blythe, archivist extraordinaire and all-around lovely human being, who provided research assistance and a listening ear.

Denise Jamsa, Bert's daughter and good friend, who generously shared her interviews with her father.

The BYU Faculty Publishing Center and the fantastic students who helped with this project over the years: Emily Strong, Aaron Green, and Gabriela Welling.

Jill, Eric, and Chris, not only for your written contributions but also for your hard work, mentorship, meeting attendance, patience, humor, and encouragement. This could not have happened without you.

Alison Syring and everyone at University of Illinois Press.

My family, the greatest miracle of all: my parents, Charles and Lynne Swallow; my daughters Isabella, Caroleine, and Phia, who listened to me talk about this project for *years* and frequently offered helpful editorial suggestions. My love for you is beyond the power of expression; and, of course, to Stephen James, *mein unsterblicher Geliebter*.

Finally, this book is dedicated to Bert, who trusted a former graduate student with a project of this scale after she had stepped away from academia. And, to Phil Synder, who unknowingly served as a proxy for Bert's voice when I needed it most.

Thank you all.

—Julie Swallow

Authors' Note

Many of the stories in this book have been edited for readability and length. If you are interested in seeing the original version of any stories contained here, the documents will be available in the near future through Brigham Young University. The number following each story in this book corresponds to the number in the collection, making it easy for readers who are interested to find the original version.

The Three Nephites

Prologue

JULIE SWALLOW

A tale similar to the following is responsible for one man's academic passion and the publication of this book:

> Brother and Sister Handy were driving from Burley to Idaho Falls, Idaho, where they planned to do temple work. Although they had never before picked up a hitchhiker, they stopped out in the desert for a nicely dressed gentleman, whom they thought to be a businessman. The man got into the back seat of their two-door sedan and then began to question them. He asked them where they were going, and how often they went. He also asked several questions about the Church. He then asked if they had a two year's supply of food. When they answered negatively, he stressed how important it was and admonished them to get it as quickly as possible. When Sister Handy turned to speak further with him, he was gone. Although the area was clear for miles around, the man was nowhere to be seen.
>
> —Lynn Slaugh. Sister of Brother Handy. Time the story occurred: 1960. Collected by Carolyn Roberts in 1962. #0078.

On a rainy night in 1960, William "Bert" Wilson was story swapping with friends as they drove to Salt Lake City, Utah, when he heard of the disappearing passenger urging drivers to gather two years of food storage; he understood the unnamed stranger to be one of the Three Nephites. Bert later wrote of the experience: "I believed the story, partly because of the mood in the car that night, but primarily because I had grown up with stories of Nephite visits and found this account compatible with my past experience."[1]

This is a book of miracles. Certainly, it's an extensive academic treatment of immortal wanderers colloquially named the Three Nephites among members of the Church of Jesus Christ of Latter-day Saints, but it is also the realization of one man's passion project. Over the course of his famed career, the world's preeminent Latter-day Saint (LDS) folklorist, William A. Wilson—or "Bert," as he was known among friends, colleagues, and students[2]—collected fifteen hundred stories of encounters with the Three Nephites. Now, years after his death, his story collection, which represents decades of work, is finally receiving the academic exploration he had hoped for.

Bert was raised in a house next to the train tracks in rural, Depression-era Idaho, and few could have anticipated Bert would become a renowned academic. Yet his work on Finnish and religious lore came to be heralded as groundbreaking within its field. In sharp contrast to his other successes, Bert's presentations on the Three Nephites received a mixed response: Some in his academic community felt they were too tainted by his religious leanings, while those within his faith found his approach too secular, bordering on sacrilegious. Even Bert struggled at certain points with his writings on the three travelers, fearing he had misrepresented his own culture by overemphasizing their significance. However, he remained committed to the project.

Bert's tenacity can be traced to his upbringing. His mother, Lucille Green Wilson, read to her children every night, instilling a love of language in Bert that would manifest itself in his later years as he carried books with him to his railroad and farm jobs, reading during any downtime.[3] Being a reader didn't translate into being a stand-out student though. He was a class clown, and he wasn't particularly interested in going to college. Undaunted by his lack of enthusiasm, his mother traveled from Idaho to Nephi, Utah, where Bert was working on the railroad, and made sure he was registered at Brigham Young University (BYU).

He brought a drinking and smoking habit with him to college, but after waking up on the ground, hungover and bruised from falling off a horse, Bert decided to change his ways, giving up alcohol entirely. Around the same time, his hometown bishop asked him to think about serving a mission, which would require him to kick his lingering tobacco habit. Several failed attempts to do so brought him to his knees in supplication. Upon asking God to help him stop smoking, he recalls, "I opened up a package of cigarettes . . . lit up one cigarette—and it was the nastiest thing I ever tasted in my entire life. And I just scrunched up the whole package of cigarettes and threw them away, and that was the last cigarette I ever smoked."[4] This privately held miracle not only confirmed Bert's faith but also made him receptive to the stories of those with similar experiences.[5]

While serving his two-and-a-half-year mission in Finland, Bert was introduced to *The Kalevala*—the national epic of the Finns. The poem would form and propel much of his academic career. After becoming the first college graduate in his family, Bert continued at BYU for a master's degree before heading to Indiana University (IU) to pursue a PhD in Uralic studies and the folklore program. "Finnish Matters" brought Bert to Indiana, but folklore changed his worldview.[6]

At IU, Bert met Richard M. Dorson, a man so influential in folklore circles that he was described by some as the "father of American Folklore" or, more colorfully, as a scholar "doing for folklore what Kinsey did for sex."[7] Dorson was thrilled to have a Latter-day Saint in his program and encouraged him to study his own culture.[8] Under Dorson's tutelage, Bert expanded his understanding of what folklore entails; he could find it in his own faith community, his own workplace, and in his own family. His life circumstances well positioned him to pursue his academic interests. Through his own efforts and those of his many students, Bert eventually amassed thousands of stories that give insight into the Latter-day Saint experience: missionary stories, pioneer stories, traditions specific to Latter-day Saints, and even jokes. He wrote eloquently about how folklore functions in Latter-day Saint culture, reflecting members' outlooks, motivations, and aspirations. He made sure all of these stories were organized and accessible in archives that are widely used today by folklore scholars and other interested individuals.

During his doctorate studies, Bert's fascination with Three Nephites stories flourished. Earlier in his career, Bert had felt that "folklore" was something *other* people had. However, his research into these stories taught him that he carried his own folkloric traditions that should be both respected and analyzed. Previous scholars dismissed Three Nephites stories as relics of an unsophisticated pioneer era, but Bert affectionately referred to them as his "companions." He felt they deserved a book-length analysis and, consequently, decided not to place his vast Nephite collection into the BYU archive he created, choosing instead to hold on to them until a dedicated volume could be completed.

Bert was a busy man. He edited journals, wrote books, spoke at academic conferences and community events, and served in many leadership roles. He was a devoted husband and father, as well as a mentor to students and faculty. Still, it was not Bert's schedule but rather the scope of his Three Nephites project—combined with a fastidious attention to detail and his own developing attitudes about the stories contained therein—that delayed its completion for over three decades.

I came to this project in 1992, during my time as Bert's graduate assistant. I worked with Bert's wife, Hannele, to provide structure and insight into his extensive collection. We went through each story, noting any mention of the Three Nephites' physical appearance, behavior, and characteristics. It wasn't a simple task—when Bert first started collecting stories in the mid-1960s, he didn't gather too many details about who was telling the story, where it was learned, or when and why it was told. But by the 1990s, as folklorists turned their attention to the "performance" of folklore, Bert began including more contextual data about each story: biographical information about the storyteller and the listener, details about the storytelling event, and whether the story was a firsthand experience or something heard from a friend of a friend. He was particularly interested in how the teller and the listener felt about the story. This contextual information was captured on worksheets, created by Hannele and me, that were appended to each story. Because Bert was constantly refining these details, Hannele and I had to start over each time an additional data point was added.[9]

Bert knew there was almost no consistency in the physical descriptions of the Three Nephites. They were men, yes, but they appeared both old and young, spiffy and shabby, light-skinned and dark-skinned. The Three Nephites from the stories he collected spent the bulk of their time engaged in missionary work, genealogy/temple work, and humanitarian service. Having immortal emissaries engage in these activities validated church programs, creating a sense of security about one's decisions to participate in the LDS faith, inspiring members to participate in the same activities, and confirming the existence of a loving God.[10] The way the Three Nephites continued to strengthen contemporary Latter-day Saints was one of many broader insights Bert gleaned from his eclectic collection.

Bert's research contradicted earlier Three Nephites scholars who believed these stories would remain within the Intermountain West; his initial collecting endeavors while in Indiana disproved that theory. Additionally, many folklorists had suggested that these stories were destined for extinction, calling them remnants of the church's relatively uneducated and culturally isolated pioneer past. They predicted that as modern members assimilated into mainstream culture, they would disappear. Significantly, previous scholars, such as Richard Dorson, Wayland Hand, Hector Lee, and Austin and Alta Fife, were either not a part of the Latter-day Saint faith or participated more culturally than spiritually. As an active Latter-day Saint, Bert knew that a belief in the Book of Mormon implied a belief in the Three Nephites. Because the story is embedded in LDS scripture, many members accept the possibility that the Three Nephites could offer modern-day assistance to someone, even if that possibility is remote, thus ensuring the ongoing survival of the stories. Bert's dual participation in the world of scholarship and the world of believing churchgoers enabled him to appreciate the stories from several angles and to understand why they were likely to remain a part of Latter-day Saint lore. In the essay "Freeways, Parking Lots, and Ice Cream Stands: Three Nephites in Contemporary Mormon Culture," he beautifully articulates how his identity as both scholar and believer directs his attention to different aspects of these stories:

> As a folklorist interested in human behavior, I am, to be sure, more concerned with the influence of the stories on the lives of those who believe and tell them than I am with the validity of the stories themselves; and as a literary scholar, intrigued by the struggle for human souls revealed in the Nephite drama, I am more concerned with the artistic tensions developed by the actors in that drama than I am with the historical accuracy of the narratives. But as a Latter-day Saint who believe[s] in the Book of Mormon, I also believe that the Three Nephites may do what the Book of Mormon says they can do. Having read hundreds of Nephite accounts, and having compared them with each other, with Mormon folklore in general, and with supernatural legends outside Mormon tradition, I can discount many of the narratives. But I can't discount them all.[11]

Bert's understanding of the place of the Three Nephites within Latter-day Saint culture enabled him to prove what he knew intuitively: The Three Nephites stories take place all over the globe and evolve with changing times. In the late 1800s, the Three Nephites saved pioneers crossing the desert in wagons or rescued a horseback rider stuck on a slippery shale precipice; in stories told after the arrival of the automobile, they provide roadside assistance or pull people from the wreckage of a car crash. The wanderers may have applied "tobacco boiled in lard for a caked breast of [a] nursing mother" in stories from early church history, but stories told after the 1960s indicate that the Three Nephites have also modernized: They know CPR and they demonstrate paramedical and surgical skills.[12] Regardless of when the event takes place, the Three Nephites offer blessings, either formally with oil and the laying on of hands or by simply speaking of good things to come.[13]

Bert's deeply held belief in the gospel led him to worry that his focus on supernatural legends gave a distorted view of the Latter-day Saint community. Taken out of context, Three Nephites stories may give the impression that Latter-day Saints believe "that all one needs to do to get out of a tight situation is pray for help and an angel will pop up from behind some cloud to solve all his or her problems."[14] The stories, isolated from those who practice the religion, made Latter-day Saints seem "*me*-centered"—focused solely on how God could help them. In stark contrast, Bert saw his tradition as "*other-*

centered," with church members spending a great deal of time, money, and energy on the well-being of those around them.[15] He was concerned that the Three Nephites stories overshadowed the stories of "intense service willingly given by members" and worried that he had been complicit in creating a distorted view of Latter-day Saints.[16] He likewise felt that folklorists too often focus on religious beliefs rather than religious daily practice, skewing the types of stories collected. Scholars gravitate to supernatural stories because they are more compelling than stories about daily quiet service.

Technically, Bert retired from BYU in 1996. But he never stopped working. His wrestle with his "companions"—and the concern that his lifelong study of them was more of a hindrance than a help to the faith community he strove so tirelessly to serve—continued. In a 1998 academic presentation, he decried the scholarly focus on the flashy elements of religious practices and urged scholars to turn their attention to the fundamental lived experience of practitioners. He spoke eloquently of daily acts of service rendered by the faithful who are living their beliefs and gave examples of stories he had heard over his lifetime. These are the types of stories most commonly shared by LDS Church members, and they are the most reflective of how they spend their time:

> Stories of . . . service tell of Relief Society women in a local congregation taking turns sitting with the ill or dying; of a railroad worker during the great depression who divided half his shift with another worker so each could earn enough money to feed his family; . . . of a financially strapped church member in Finland who rode his bicycle across town early in the morning to clear a frail widow's walkway after each snow storm; of a church member who, upon finding a drunk man lying in his own vomit, picked him up, cleaned him up, took him to a hotel, and arranged his night's lodging.[17]

Bert emphasized that stories like these aren't unique to Latter-day Saints; there are many good people in the world doing good deeds. But such stories, told among members of the LDS faith, are the best illustration of how Latter-day Saints live their religion. He wanted folklorists to pay closer attention to them: "Though more pedestrian in character than dramatic supernatural tales, these stories take us much closer to the core of Mormon moral and humane values than the supernatural stories ever will. In studying Mormon folklore, we neglect them at our peril."

His gentle criticism wasn't reserved for folklore scholars. He was also concerned about how those within his faith community approached these supernatural stories. In 1995, he published an article in *Brigham Young Maga-*

zine, whose readership is almost exclusively made up of Latter-day Saints. In it, he acknowledged that many of the stories appeal to him, and he would like to believe they are true. In fact, he does believe some are true. But he warns that it is dangerous to base one's faith in them. Faith should be placed in doctrine alone. He quotes LDS Church president Harold B. Lee: "It never ceases to amaze me how gullible some of our Church members are in broadcasting sensational stories, or dreams, or visions."[18] While the article itself was warm, funny, and insightful, many readers missed those elements and simply felt attacked because they saw a beloved family story classified as mere "folklore."

Despite his obvious ongoing frustration with the Three Nephites stories, Bert could never completely abandon them. He continued to mull over the project, rethinking how he would organize and discuss such a large collection. Our painstakingly revised worksheets were lost in an office move, and the information they detailed was never entered into a database to facilitate further analysis as he had hoped. However, we had gotten all fifteen hundred stories digitized.

In 2006, Bert bequeathed the flash drive with the entire story collection to me and asked me to try to recreate the worksheet in spreadsheet form. As his health declined, he asked me to complete the project myself. When he died in 2016, I felt the full weight of that request.

I found myself behaving similarly to my mentor, working and reworking, building up and picking apart my materials over the years. I created three versions of the data worksheet, each time adding a few more details. I went through the collection of stories multiple times, noting such things as the gender of the collector and storyteller; the time of collection and time of story; where the story was learned; where the story collection took place and where the story itself took place; and any details about the Three Nephites' appearance, behavior, and predilections. I was able to enlist the help of some dedicated BYU student employees during their downtime at work. They combed through the stories several more times, looking for anything I missed and patiently starting over if I added a story or a worksheet detail. After several years at this task, the long-hoped-for data visualization could finally be realized. Once that aspect of the project was completed, I selected what I felt were the best stories to represent the key themes presented in the following chapters.

Organizing a book of this scope was one of the many tasks that slowed Bert's progress. During some of our last discussions, he had been toying with the idea of dividing the book into four sections that mirrored the fourfold mission of the church: Proclaim the Gospel, Perfect the Saints, Redeem the

Dead, and Care for the Poor and Needy.[19] However, this proved problematic. The institutional church had been moving away from that phrasing of their mission for several years. Additionally, many of the stories intersect with several of these categories. Does a story about a starving missionary who miraculously receives a food delivery from one of the three wanderers fit under Proclaim the Gospel or Care for the Poor and Needy? All organizational structures I considered had some flaws, but I finally settled on the following: After an introduction that provides information about who the Three Nephites are and why they are of interest to folklore studies, the book consists of five chapters, each providing a brief academic introduction to the stories included in that section: (1) "Vanishing Hitchhiker" Nephites addresses that once-popular story cycle, (2) "The Worldwide End of the World" considers the Three Nephites as harbingers of the Second Coming, (3) "Proclaiming-the-Gospel Stories" examines the interactions of the Three Nephites with missionaries, (4) "Mix-ups, High Jinks, and Jokes" explores Three Nephites stories that are intended to get laughs, and (5) "That Your Joy Might Be Full" analyzes the types of service the Three Nephites render and reflects on the connection to the Latter-day Saint injunction to be "anxiously engaged" in service to others.[20] The epilogue ties the book together and points to potential areas for further research.

Certainly, readers can jump over the introduction and chapter essays and just enjoy some great stories, but I'm convinced that taking the time to read the included background and analysis will enrich your experience. And for those hoping to explore even further, all the stories in Bert's collection, as well as the many Three Nephites stories that have been submitted since Bert stopped collecting, will eventually be made public through Brigham Young University after the publication of this book.

Bert could have written this book alone; I could not. Consequently, I invited Christopher Blythe, Eric Eliason, and Jill Terry Rudy to join the project. Together we have created a book dedicated to Bert's legacy. Like me, Jill was one of Bert's students; she knows Bert's scholarship better than anyone, having worked with him on a compilation of his writings titled *The Marrow of Human Experience: Essays on Folklore*. Jill and Eric eventually became Bert's colleagues in the English department at BYU. Although Christopher never met Bert, his academic trajectory was influenced by Bert's writings. Bert frequently served as a guest lecturer on the Three Nephites in Eric's folklore classes. Knowing most of Bert's writings on the Three Nephites were scattered across yellow legal pads that could never be deciphered, Eric took copious notes. His Three Nephites lecture notes provide insight into Bert's thinking.

Personally, I have scoured the collection multiple times, working with Bert as he agonized over how to write about such a vast collection. Eric, Jill, and I are tradition bearers, carrying much of Bert's Three Nephites analysis in our heads. But this is a feature of our work and not a bug. Folklorists frequently study material that has moved from the oral tradition into written form. It seems fitting that some of Bert's scholarship may have experienced a similar transformation.

Even with our collective experience and expertise, we acknowledge that we aren't Bert. We don't write as eloquently, and we can't say how his thoughts might have continued to evolve. Knowing that, we have still made every attempt to honor who he was and how we understood him to approach his field of study. He would not have wanted a book about the Three Nephites written in the 2020s to rely on a story collection that ended in 1998. Consequently, we added about 100 recently collected stories, taking the total story collection to 1,686 stories and confirming that the Three Nephites still make contemporary appearances in people's lives and in their storytelling sessions. We also believe that Bert would have been deeply gratified by the results of the data analysis. The Three Nephites are, first and foremost, engaged in humanitarian service. In many ways, these stories serve as both a blueprint for a life of religious devotion and a reflection of the lives of the millions of Latter-day Saints who often engage in service that borders on the superhuman. When seen in that light, these stories do provide what Bert had hoped: "a better understanding and appreciation of what [Latter-day Saints] feel and believe most deeply."[21]

Author's Note: This is the general formatting for the tags to the stories in this book:

> [Storyteller's name], [age]. [Profession] from [where they were from]. [Estimated time of event]. [*Context about belief*]. Collected by [collector's name] in [year the story was collected]. #[story number].

If any of the information is missing, it was not included in the story submission.

Introduction

JULIE SWALLOW

Story origins can rarely be pinpointed. But Three Nephites stories stem directly from the Book of Mormon, part of the scriptural canon of the Church of Jesus Christ of Latter-day Saints. The introduction to the Book of Mormon describes the book as:

> A volume of holy scripture, a record of God's dealings with ancient inhabitants of the Americas and contains the fulness of the everlasting gospel. . . . The record gives an account of two great civilizations. One came from Jerusalem in 600 B.C. and afterward separated into two nations, known as the Nephites and the Lamanites.

The climax of the narrative is Christ's visitation to the American continent after his death and resurrection. During Christ's brief visit, he called twelve apostles among the Nephites, just as he had in Israel. Before ascending again to heaven, he asked the Nephite apostles what they would like him to do for them. Nine of the men asked to "speedily come unto thee in thy kingdom."[1] However, three of them desired to receive the same thing John the Beloved was granted: to "tarry in the flesh" in order to bring souls to Christ until his Second Coming.[2] The Book of Mormon account states: "And they are as the angels of God, and can show themselves unto whatsoever man it seemeth them good. Therefore, great and marvelous works shall be wrought by them, before the great and coming day [of judgment]."[3]

This scriptural account indicates that the three were "caught up into the heavens" and "a change [was] wrought upon their bodies."[4] Jeffrey R. Holland, writing while a member of the First Quorum of the Seventy, wrote the following about the change made to their bodies:[5]

> Mormon called this change upon the Three Nephites a "transfiguration," and they did have a transfiguring experience. However, the more traditional understanding of the status of these three is that they were "translated" beings. A person who is transfigured is one who is temporarily taken into a higher, heavenly experience, as were Peter, James, and John, and then returned to a normal telestial status . . . These Three Nephites, as part of their translation experience, were also transfigured, caught up into heaven, where they saw and heard unspeakable things.[6]

According to Holland, the Three Nephites are "mortal" but in a "terrestrial condition."[7] The distinction between "telestial" and "terrestrial" is important here. Some LDS authorities suggest that the earth transformed when Adam and Eve were cast out of the Garden of Eden, falling from its higher *terrestrial* state to its current *telestial* existence.[8] Holland is suggesting that although the Three Nephites are mortal, their bodies exist in a state that is somewhere between an earthly and heavenly one. Eventually, when Christ comes a second time, the Three Nephites will experience "an instantaneous, deathlike transition."[9] Their current terrestrial state explains why it is that they "suffer no pain or sorrow save it were for the sins of the world" and that "Satan [can] have no power over them, that he [cannot] tempt them . . . and that the powers of the earth [cannot] hold them."[10] In the Book of Mormon, they escape from prisons, pits, and fiery furnaces without harm.[11]

The Three Nephites worked among the people of Nephi after Christ's ascension to heaven and after all the other apostles had died. By about AD 322, however, the writings of the prophet Mormon indicate that because of the wickedness of the people, the Lord "did take away his beloved disciples," the Three Nephites; consequently, "the work of miracles and of healing did cease."[12] Around AD 401, Moroni indicated that he and his father, Mormon, had been "ministered" to by the Three Nephites and that, aside from Moroni, the three disciples were the only righteous people remaining. The scripture makes it clear that they will be actively engaging with Earth's inhabitants:

> And behold they will be among the Gentiles, and the Gentiles shall know them not. They will also be among the Jews, and the Jews shall know them not. And it shall come to pass, when the Lord seeth fit in his wisdom that they shall minister unto all the scattered tribes of Israel, and unto all nations, kindreds, tongues and people, and shall bring out of them unto Jesus many souls, that their desire may be fulfilled, and also because of the convincing power of God which is in them.[13]

Thus, the seed for the emergence of the Three Nephites legend cycle was planted. This seed remained dormant until after Joseph Smith's martyrdom in

Nauvoo, Illinois, in the summer of 1844, and his successor, Brigham Young, had led the Latter-day Saints to their final refuge in the West.

Early church history records contain several accounts of unnamed eternal wanderers who seem to be one or more of the Three Nephites.[14] In an 1878 interview for the *Millennial Star* (an early Latter-day Saint newspaper), David Whitmer tells three stories that took place around 1829 that follow the Three Nephites story pattern. One involves the plowing of his field by an unseen hand.[15] Joseph Smith had requested that Whitmer take him and Oliver Cowdery (an early church leader) to the Whitmer farm. Smith needed a safe place to translate the gold plates he had discovered with divine assistance in the Hill Cumorah.[16] When Whitmer received the letter requesting that he leave his home in Fayette, New York; travel almost one hundred miles to Harmony, Pennsylvania; pick up the two men; and return as a company back to the Whitmer farm, he was hesitant to begin the journey. Whitmer explains:

> I did not know what to do, I was pressed with my work. I had some 20 acres to plow, so I concluded I would finish plowing and then go. I got up one morning to go to work as usual, and on going to the field, found between five and seven acres of my ground had been plowed during the night. I don't know who did it; but it was done just as I would have done it myself and the plow was left standing in the furrow. This enabled me to start sooner.[17]

In the same interview, Whitmer details an encounter with a mysterious stranger as the three men traveled from Pennsylvania to New York:

> When I was returning to Fayette, with Joseph and Oliver, all of us riding in the wagon, Oliver and I on an old fashioned wooden spring seat and Joseph behind us: while traveling along in a clear open space, a very pleasant and nice looking old man suddenly appeared by the side of our wagon and saluted us with, "good morning, it is very warm," at the same time wiping his face or forehead with his hand. We returned the salutation, and, by a sign from Joseph, I invited him to ride if he was going our way. But he said very pleasantly, "No, I am going to Cumorah." This name was something new to me, I did not know what Cumorah meant. We all gazed at him and at each other, and as I looked around enquiringly of Joseph, the old man instantly disappeared, so that I did not see him again.[18]

Whitmer remembers that the man they encountered was about five foot eight, had white hair and a white beard, and carried a knapsack with what looked like a book in it. He said that this "messenger" had taken the gold plates from Joseph before he left Harmony.

The Three Nephites are not mentioned in either of these stories. However, the sudden appearance/disappearance and the description of an older white-haired man inclines the LDS reader to consider the possibility that the visitor was one of the Three Nephites. Later retellings of the farming story feature someone who sees three efficient farmhands preparing the field at record speed. Versions of both of these stories appear in the collection. Modern Latter-day Saints often identify the stranger and the farmhands as the Three Nephites. Clearly, Nephites were on Whitmer's mind as well. In the paragraph beneath Whitmer's stories about the mysterious stranger, he mentions the Three Nephites, saying, "They are at work among the lost tribes and else where. John the revelator is at work."[19]

In 1852, Brigham Young gave a speech at the tabernacle about the "extensive character of the gospel."[20] In it, he tells the Saints that for "those who are faithful enough . . . there will be strangers in your midst, walking with you, talking with you: they will enter into your houses and eat and drink with you, go to meeting with you, and begin to open your minds, as the Saviour did the two disciples who walked out in the country in days of old."[21] These strangers would encourage temple and genealogy work. They would help the Saints understand the scriptures. They would make Saints feel as the ancient disciples felt walking on the road to Emmaus with Jesus. Young says, "You will begin to feel your hearts burn within you as they walk and talk with you."[22]

This reference inspires other important LDS Church leaders to mention the Three Nephites by name in the years to follow. Orson Pratt, in 1855, tells the Saints "how pleasing—how glorious it would be" to see one of the Three Nephites. He promises that this will happen but not without some difficult preparatory work on the part of the Saints. Pratt assures them that "just as soon as that [work] is accomplished [the Three Nephites] are on hand, and also many other good old worthy ancients."[23] By 1902, John W. Taylor indicates that the Three Nephites *are* currently "preparing the hearts of the children of men to receive the Gospel. They are administering to those who are heirs of salvation, and preparing their hearts to receive the truth, just as the farmer prepared the soil to receive the seed."[24] Whitmer's experiences and the comments by early church leaders set the stage for the possibility of Three Nephites appearances among church members and set the standard for the types of things they might be doing.

Three Nephites and Folklore Intersect

At this point in the nineteenth century, when Brigham Young, Orson Pratt, and David Whitmer were talking about Three Nephites encounters, folklore as an academic discipline was just a few decades old. The early folklorists were interested in preserving relics of the past, such as songs, handicrafts, and stories, particularly from those they perceived to be uneducated—think Grimms' fairy tales or Francis James Child's extensive collection of ballads. This may be why many people today hold "an almost intuitive, atmospheric sense of folklore as old, rural, mystical, and false," as folklorist Lynne McNeill puts it.[25] McNeill's 2013 definition of the word "folklore" makes it clear that current scholars have a different understanding of what constitutes folklore studies than their predecessors:

> Folklore is informal, traditional culture. It's all the cultural stuff—customs, stories, jokes, art—that we learn from each other, by word of mouth or observation, rather than through formal institutions like school or media. Just as literature majors study novels and poems or art historians study works of art, folklorists focus on the informal and traditional stuff, like urban legends and latrinalia.[26]

Although the definition of folklore has evolved since the early 1800s, both early and modern folklore scholars would agree that Three Nephites stories are ripe for collection and study: They are not part of official LDS Church policy or doctrine, yet they support policies and doctrines; they are generally shared in face-to-face communication within small groups; and they have recognizable consistencies while at the same time seemingly endless variations within the stable story lines.

Academics Notice the Three Nephites

By 1892, Three Nephites stories were pervasive enough within the Latter-day Saint community that outsiders began to take notice. Reverend David Utter, the first Unitarian minister in Salt Lake City, wrote a piece for *The Folk-Lorist* subtitled "Mormon Superstition." With more than a hint of disdain, he writes:

> Many of the saints now living tell that they have, at different times, seen one or more of these three immortal "Nephites." A daughter of Brigham Young, now a good Unitarian, has told me that her father told, with great and solemn pleasure, of an interview that he had with one of these remaining apostles in Liverpool, when he was on his mission. The apostle met him at the chapel door, an old man with a long gray beard, made himself known, and spoke many encouraging and helpful words.[27]

After this reference, Nephites didn't appear in academic journals again until Wayland Hand wrote an article about them published in the *Southern Folklore Quarterly* in 1938. Around that time, Austin Fife, who was raised in the Mountain West and learned folklore methodologies while at Stanford, traveled throughout Utah with his wife, Alta, gathering Three Nephites stories, which he used as the basis of several academic journal articles.[28] Austin and Alta Fife dedicated a chapter to the Nephites in *Saints of Sage and Saddle: Folklore among the Mormons*, published in 1956, a book Bert called "monumental."[29] Additionally, Hector Lee, who had written his dissertation on Three Nephites stories, published his findings in 1949 in the book titled *The Three Nephites: The Substance and Significance of the Legend in Folklore*.[30] Folklorist Richard M. Dorson, who eventually became Bert's thesis advisor, read these works and brought the Three Nephites legends to a broader consciousness through his popular books.[31]

Among scholars, these stories are often called supernatural legends or, as they are catalogued in the William A. Wilson Archives, "supernatural religious legends." A supernatural legend is a third-person narrative involving a supernatural experience that reports to be true but is ultimately unverifiable. When these narratives are told in the first person, they are typically referred to as "memorates." Among Latter-day Saints, these stories can be referred to as anything from a sacred experience to the somewhat pejorative "faith-promoting rumor." This spectrum of views is evidenced in modern church publications. In a November 2017 *Ensign* magazine, under a section titled "To the Point," the question is asked: "Are John the Beloved and the Three Nephites actually still on the earth? If so, what are they doing?" The response begins with a simple yes and then follows with "What they're doing is bringing souls unto the Lord until He comes again.[32] The same year, the Book of Mormon Seminary Teacher Manual outlined the story of the Three Nephites, suggesting an activity where students read 3 Nephi 28: 25–32 aloud "looking for people who have benefited and will yet benefit from the ministry of the Three Nephites."[33] The phrasing indicates an understanding that they are still ministering and blessing individuals today and will continue to do so in the future. A text box with the words "Avoid Speculation about the Three Nephites" in bold type reads, "Many have heard stories about supposed visits of the Three Nephites. Rather than share these stories, teach what is taught in the scriptures. Remember Mormon's statement that the Three Nephites would be among the Gentiles and Jews, who would 'know them not.'[34] Refrain from discussing stories or other information about the Three Nephites that is not found in Church-approved sources."[35]

A footnote to a chapter in *The Book of Mormon: 3 Nephi 9–30, This Is My Gospel*, titled "The Three Nephites and the Doctrine of Translation" (published by Desert Book, the official publishing company of the LDS Church), sums up the general feeling about these stories: "Thousands of stories abound concerning possible encounters with the Three Nephites. Although many of these accounts are true, a great many are not. We can safely assume that translated beings are not interested in making national headlines or in contributing to a collection of apocryphal faith-promoting stories."[36] Whether or not the Three Nephites are interested in having their stories collected is up for debate. But without question, intentionally or unintentionally, the Three Nephites are still contributing to stories in circulation today. Although church officials are sometimes uncomfortable with these stories, they do not question the Three Nephites' existence on earth.

In many ways, however, Three Nephites stories are more important to folklorists than to members of the Church of Jesus Christ of Latter-day Saints. The Three Nephites do not occupy a place of significance in the church, and stories about encounters with them aren't told as often as a collection of this size might suggest. The focus of the religion is on Jesus Christ and his atonement; the Book of Mormon (subtitled "Another Testament of Jesus Christ"); family, both those living and those who have died; and revelation, including that received from God personally and from a living prophet. Latter-day Saint children sing, "I'm trying to be like Jesus. I'm following in his ways."[37] Courageous figures from the Book of Mormon, such as Nephi, Ammon, and Captain Moroni, are mentioned frequently in church settings both large and small.[38] In contrast, the Three Nephites rarely feature in church and General Conference talks. If these stories did disappear from church culture, while surprising, it wouldn't change the daily religious practice of Latter-day Saints. That said, the stories are not inconsequential. They underscore the faith's belief in a loving God who is willing to intervene in the lives of Saints. Most importantly, the stories highlight the significance of the Book of Mormon in Latter-day Saint lives.

Modern Origins: Form and Function

Aside from personal narrative, stories circulating in any community are either borrowed or embellished versions of a story that resonates with group members. The legend of a hitchhiker vanishing from the backseat exists outside of LDS culture and, most likely, was adapted by LDS storytellers to better reflect the church culture. As stories are told and retold, they are socially constructed. Small details are changed. Perhaps the setting is moved to a landscape familiar to the storyteller and listener. Elements of the original story are deleted or altered to reflect the desires, concerns, and values of the group. These changes happen gradually with each subsequent retelling. Consequently, a story of a hitchhiker disappearing from someone's backseat told around a campfire in Wisconsin at a scout camp becomes a potentially faith-promoting story when told in a church setting in Utah when the hitch-hiker encourages obedience to church teachings before vanishing. The former is meant as a frightening cautionary tale; the latter promotes culturally appropriate behavior.

Something similar happens with embellishment. A friend tells a story about a rescue that seems similar to a story heard before. The person who hears it may unconsciously fill in details to make the story fit the expectations of the story type. A student in Eric's class experienced this phenomenon. The student was swimming in California and got pulled into the undertow. None of her family members noticed her perilous situation. She barely managed to make it ashore alive. As she was coughing and sputtering on the beach, a person walked by and asked her if she was okay. She was miffed that some stranger rather than her family had noticed her predicament. She related the story that way to several people in her community. A few weeks later, while at church, a woman approached her, expressing amazement that one of the Three Nephites had rescued her while swimming. Eric's student didn't want to burst her bubble or embarrass her. She also said, "In that moment I sort of realized, well, I don't know, I'm not one hundred percent sure it wasn't one of the Three Nephites who checked on me that day."[39]

And finally, many of these stories are firsthand experiences. The storytellers know what they experienced and believe they met one or more of the Three Nephites. Folklorist David Hufford points out that academics often automatically dismiss spiritual manifestations as imaginary events. And yet, near-death experiences, night terrors, visitations from deceased relatives, and encounters with something extraterrestrial occur among almost all cultures. They happen to people who previously had no belief system and among those who have deeply held faith traditions. Hufford rejects the notion that such experiences are always illusory, brought on by a mind saturated in a faith tradition.[40]

The Three Nephites stories have persisted within the LDS Church for over 170 years, suggesting that they continue to have a useful function within parts of the community. The most prominent functions are (1) to promote faith; (2) to underscore LDS ideas about the nature of Heavenly Father; (3) to highlight the importance of activities such as temple work,[41] genealogy work, missionary work, and service; and (4) to entertain listeners.

When the stories are told in earnest, promoting faith is generally one of the reasons for the telling. Kirk Hamilton related the following story to Brittany Koeler, who was doing research for a folklore class at BYU. He said the narrative has played an important role in his family for over four generations:

My great-great-grandfather was sent from Denmark to Norway on his mission. He was in jail, and the conditions were very bad, he wasn't very well fed, etc. A very nice man came to visit him in jail. He thought, "oh that's very wonderful," but he didn't know the man. The man gave him some bread, and the bread was hollowed out and filled with vegetables, which provided all the nutrients he was missing in his diet. When he turned to thank the person, he'd already left, like he didn't want the thanks. So he called for the jailer, saying, "could you please go stop that man so I can thank him?" The jailer said, "Nobody has come in, and nobody just left." Later, in some blessing, like when he was getting a calling, or something, . . . he was told that he had been ministered by one of the Three Nephites.

—Kirk Hamilton, 21. Freelancer and entrepreneur from Salem, Utah. Estimated time of event: 1857. Collected by Brittany Koeler in 2016. #1511

In contextual information included with this story, Kirk indicates that it is told in a private setting, just parent and child, from generation to generation. He says that "the story often serves to inspire" younger family members. It highlights with pride the ancestor's sacrifice of time spent in jail for his beliefs, a sacrifice comparable only to that of Joseph Smith, the founder of the LDS Church. Additionally, he says that it is told "as if it were absolute unembellished truth" because it was passed down directly from the person who experienced it in the 1850s.

Latter-day Saints refer to God as their Heavenly Father. They believe he knows each of his children personally and will occasionally intervene in their earthly trials. Three Nephites experiences confirm that God is aware of individuals and will send heavenly assistance. In 2019, a twenty-five-year-old recounted an experience from his childhood:

One year our family decided to go into the mountains and cut down our own Christmas tree. It was really snowy and we were driving deep into the mountains looking for the perfect tree. The road keeps getting narrower and narrower to the point where we could barely fit our van on the road. To the right of us was a sheer cliff. To the left, a ditch. We couldn't turn around and we were in serious danger of sliding off the cliff. At this moment, a jeep comes down the steep slope in front of us with three men in their 20s in it. They hop out of their car and ask if they can help. Of course, we said yes. They go behind the car and literally lift it off the ground. We were facing down the mountain. Everybody

> was crying. We told the men thank you and drove off. When we got to a fork in the road, we waited for the men to come down and thank them again. But they never came down. This was the only road they could have taken.[42]

The man who told this story said the family wouldn't speak of it often because it was special to them. But whenever they experience hardships, his mother would reference the experience, saying, "We are going to get through this because Heavenly Father cares about us specifically. He helped us out before."

Latter-day Saints believe in a loving God who is involved in their lives. As an expression of their devotion to God, they are encouraged to dedicate their lives to service not only within the communities where they live but also via missionary, genealogy, and temple work. Finding and baptizing people into the church community, whether in this life or vicariously for those who have died, is seen as the highest form of service because it brings people to Christ. Supernatural involvement in those activities confirms their significance to Latter-day Saint listeners. Bert identified the if/then structure inherent in these stories and describes it as follows: "If these events really happened, then missionary and temple work must be true principles; and if they are true principles, then we should diligently pursue them; and if we pursue them, then the Lord will help us become instruments in serving others. He will help us practice what we profess. These are the stories' most important messages."[43] The stories involving missionary, genealogy, and temple work demonstrate how stories revolving around such activities strengthen faith in the importance of these endeavors and motivate participation.[44]

Entertainment is another critical function of storytelling. An entertaining story is memorable, making it more likely that the purpose of relating the story will be retained: instilling faith, teaching about the nature of God, or encouraging some behaviors while discouraging others. Amusing stories, in particular, have social power. Sharing a laugh can create a bond or dissipate tension. The tall tale is a great example of a story that is told simply for its entertainment value. In 1969, Louie Black heard the following story from a man who claimed the situation took place "just as sure as I'm standing here today":

> It was a hot summer day of . . . I can't remember which year. I was in the kitchen baking some cookies when I noticed Lon Samson (his nickname) driving some of his sheep past the house. I felt sorry for the old cuss, in the heat and all, so I invited him in for some cookies and milk. That guy could really talk a streak and before I knew it, he had told me

everything from soup to nuts. After about thirty minutes, he decided he'd better get back to his sheep but before leaving he had to tell me one more story. I agreed, and he proceeded to talk. He told me how all of his life he had been troubled with constipation. In fact, he said that it was so bad lately that his health had been deteriorating. One night, after he had made camp and eaten a small dinner, he decided he was fed up with it. He said he got down on his knees and prayed that the Lord might help him out and make him well again. He then went to bed. Early that morning he swore he was awakened by the Three Nephites who picked his body up sixteen feet in the air and then dropped it back to earth. Evidently, they knocked the ____ right out of him. He told me that through all this he had suffered no broken bones and furthermore, had not been troubled with constipation since.

—Louie Elizabeth Black, 67. Housewife from Delta, Utah. Louie explicitly "*does not believe this particular story, even though it might be true. She has heard others which she does believe, however.*" Collected by Don Davis in 1969. #0312

The man's profession of sincerity followed by a highly unlikely event is a common tall tale story convention. Stories like these aren't believed but are fun to retell.

Sometimes the stories serve as a barometer for what those around them do and don't believe. In Jill's chapter, "Proclaiming-the-Gospel Stories," there is a story about a missionary who, after a severe crash in Argentina, underwent expert plastic surgery from a mystery surgeon (#1482). This story was told among missionaries at the Missionary Training Center in Provo, Utah. The person who submitted the story writes: "The missionary insisted that the history was true, since his friend had been in Argentina at the time. Nobody questioned its veracity. In fact, many of the listeners . . . were impressed and reassured at the spiritual power and protection." The telling of the surgery story inspired someone in the group to tell another Three Nephites story, a popular one about sister missionaries who are protected by three big men.[45] The person listening to this story didn't respond as he had with the previous anecdote. He explains: "After the first, the rest of the stories were simply regarded as swapped tales, and nobody really believed them" (#1482). Storytelling is a form of entertainment, and Three Nephites stories have entertained for generations. Sometimes they are swapped casually between friends for fun; sometimes they are passed from parent to child as a sacred transmission of faith.

Skepticism of the Supernatural

Scholars often denigrate supernatural experiences because they assume such things are products of the imagination. This is precisely the reason why religious individuals chafe at having their spiritual experiences called supernatural. Readers need to understand how folklorists define the term. Barbara Walker, former assistant director of the Fife Folklore Archives at Utah State University, writes:

> Referring to something as "supernatural" is not to call it unreal or untrue—on the contrary. The existence of the term itself is a linguistic and cultural acknowledgment that inexplicable things happen which we identify as being somehow beyond the natural or the ordinary, and that many of us hold beliefs which connect us to spheres beyond what we might typically see, hear, taste, touch, or smell.[46]

Latter-day Saints, however, would most likely call such events miraculous rather than supernatural. And they are cautious about the miraculous.

While the LDS Church is founded upon the miraculous story of God, the Father, and His Son, Jesus Christ, appearing to Joseph Smith in the sacred grove, modern practitioners would be skeptical if someone in their congregation claimed to have seen an angel. Members believe in the possibility of miracles and talk about miracles in their own lives; however, they tend to be subtler miracles, such as receiving spiritual guidance about what to do concerning a challenge or having someone show up at just the right time. They do not expect or ask for experiences like those in the scriptures or those experienced by Joseph Smith. Part of that is because they are warned against seeking signs or miracles. The LDS scripture called Doctrine and Covenants teaches: "Faith cometh not by signs, but signs follow those that believe."[47] Joseph Fielding Smith, the prophet from 1901 to 1918,[48] warned against seeking the miraculous: "Show me Latter-day Saints who have to feed upon miracles, signs and visions in order to keep them steadfast in the Church, and I will show you members . . . who are not in good standing before God, and who are walking in slippery paths. It is not by marvelous manifestations unto us that we shall be established in the truth, but it is by humility and faithful obedience to the commandments and laws of God."[49]

Additionally, Latter-day Saints are told that some spiritual experiences should be kept private. In a 2020 General Conference talk, Apostle Neil L. Anderson reminded church members that "some experiences are so sacred that we guard them in our spiritual memory and do not share them."[50] Knowing this about Latter-day Saint culture explains why some members would be hesitant to share extraordinary experiences. Tom Mould's excellent book, *Still, the Small Voice*, explores personal revelation stories in Latter-day Saint culture. Personal revelation is both miraculous and quotidian for members. They are encouraged to seek revelation from the Lord, and most feel they receive it from time to time. However, as Mould explains, they are still careful about when and how they talk about their experiences with others, often using coded language to describe them. He writes:

> To call one's own experiences revelation too closely echoes scripture and can suggest an authority one does not have, a decidedly immodest presentation of oneself to peers. Further, by not being explicit in terminology, one deflects possible ridicule incurred by forthright claims of powerful supernatural experiences. Instead, people employ words with wider usage outside of religion and with connotations that extend into secular matters, words such as "thought," "feeling," "impression," inspiration," and "prompting."[51]

Mould's observation about LDS language use surrounding supernatural experiences is insightful. If someone says, "I had a revelation," they clearly had a supernatural experience. On the other hand, saying "I felt prompted" veils the experience, allowing room for interpretation.

Those who have had either personal or family experiences with one or more of the Three Nephites tend to take a similar approach, often not naming the stranger specifically and allowing the listener to decide. During a recent church meeting I attended, a fellow congregant shared a family story about a stranger who asked for some money, and upon receiving it the mysterious stranger blessed the family with prosperity through the generations. Later, when I asked him whether or not his family had a sense of who the person might have been, he responded carefully, "I think . . . they think—they *think* it was one of the Three Nephites."[52] The triple emphasis on "think" makes it clear that although they have a belief about who it is, they are cautious about how they present that belief to others.

In 2016, Jody Hansen asked friends if anyone had had an experience with one of the Three Nephites. Mike Bateman said he had and agreed to be recorded. When Ms. Hansen recorded the conversation, she made the following observation: "As Mike arrived at the part of the story where he identified his visitor, he became self-conscious; however, the story was recited to me with the understanding that it was a Three Nephite Story" (#1505). That discomfort reflects what Mould describes. The storyteller is clearly trying to avoid "an immodest presentation of oneself to peers" by claiming a divine experience at the age of twelve. Note how he dances around identifying the visitor:

> I was twelve. Twelve years old. Pretty impressive, for a twelve-year-old. So I got to see one of the . . . somebody that wasn't there when we went looking for him. (laughs) . . . I have used [this experience] in my quorum, a few times, to tell some of the kids, you know, you'd better be good because you never know when you are gonna run into them or where you're gonna meet them at.
>
> —Mike Bateman, late 60s. Idaho resident. Collected by Jody Hansen in 2016. #1505

The added formality of being recorded heightened the storyteller's sensitivity to identifying the stranger, leading him to avoid naming who he felt the stranger was.

Another means of avoiding personally declaring an experience with the divine is to have an outside authority make that declaration. A parent, stake president, bishop, or a general authority of the LDS Church, upon hearing the story, sometimes identifies the unknown stranger as one of the Three Nephites. This removes pressure from the one telling the story because someone disconnected to the event has identified the stranger, as in the story below:

> Lena Butt saw one of the Nephites for the first time when she was walking to work across the fields in Notinghamshire [*sic*], England. For some weeks she had been considering the possibility of coming to America, but she hadn't discussed her plans with anyone. The man appeared before her and encouraged her to make the journey. He told her that if she worked hard she would be able to save enough money, and that she would have no trouble making the trip. He told her to pay her tithing and be good and [he] disappeared into the woods. She was aware that the man was quite small and dressed in a manner that was strange to her. She was not afraid of him and experienced little feeling or emotion beyond that. The girl decided not to tell her parents about the man, but told Mr. Orton, who later became her husband. She also told Heber C. Kimball, the missionary who had converted her. He told her that her visitor was most certainly one of the Three Nephites.
>
> —Mrs. Violet Clark, about 50. Parowan, Utah. Estimated time the story occurred: between 1846 and 1852. *Violet "believes this as a testimony of the gospel."* Collected by Marybelle Fenton in 1946. #1190

Heber C. Kimball was a member of the First Presidency of the church; as such, many would find his pronouncement irrefutable. Adding his statement at the end gives the story credibility and allows the stranger to be identified as one of the Three Nephites without making the declaration oneself.

Occasionally, the stranger identifies himself. This happens only twenty-two times in the Wilson collection. The following story is unique for many reasons. Not only is it a first-person experience without any variants in the collection, but it is also an example of self-identification. The following is an edited portion of Robert Mitchell's encounter with one of the Three Nephites:

> One day I was working a shift and this man started walking down the aisles. He would address each person in their native language. So I hopped over to him and said "Sprechen Sie Deutsch?" (which is the limit of my German) and without hesitation he spoke to me in fluent German. I asked him how he knew all these languages and he said "Go home and look up the word 'Nephite.' I'm one of those." I tried to remember the name but I didn't get it quite right. I wrote Nephemal and couldn't find anything online about it. A year or so later, my wife was meeting with the missionaries and I heard them say "I want you to open to the Book of Nephi." I stopped and said "hey, hey, hey . . . that's the word, 'Nephite'!" Then I told the astonished missionaries about my experience.[53]

Belief vs. Truth

Belief and truth pose interesting challenges for folklorists, particularly those who study supernatural or religious lore. Bert wanted to understand whether the story being told was believed by the teller. In stories collected by his students in the 1970s, there was a list of questions the storyteller had to answer, which included the following four questions: Does the teller believe this particular story? How does the teller feel about Nephite stories in general? Does the teller believe the Three Nephites exist? Does the teller believe one can be a member of the church in good standing and not believe stories about the Three Nephites?

Bert must have learned from experience that asking these questions directly wasn't always the best approach. They lead to yes and no answers and could potentially offend. In an essay titled "Documenting Folklore," published in 1986, Bert explained:

> I once listened to a tape-recorded story of a family supernatural legend in which the narrator became so emotionally involved in the story that she broke down in tears. When the narration ended, the collector, evidently remembering that she was supposed to record information about her con-

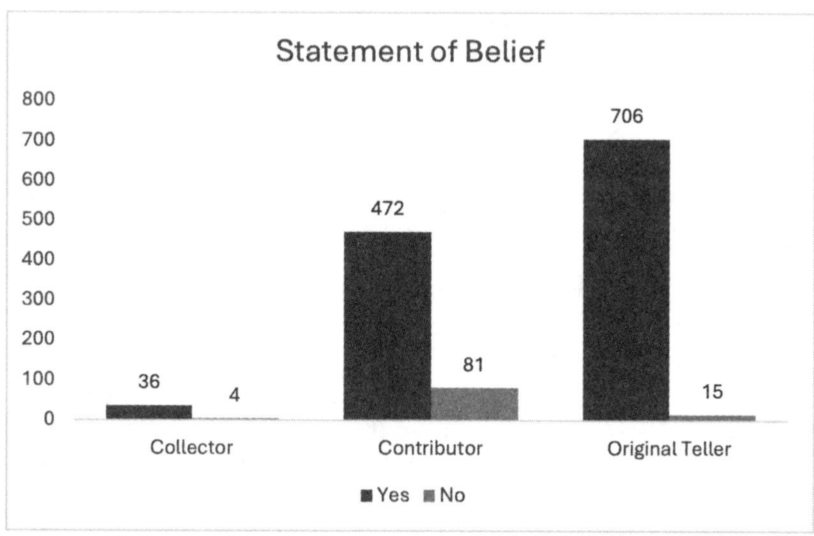

Figure 1. This bar graph illustrates the distribution of beliefs among three groups: "Collectors," "Contributors," and "Original Tellers." The dark gray bars represent those who believe, while the light gray bars represent those who do not.

> tributor's attitude toward her narratives, asked, "Now, do you believe the story?" The woman was highly offended, and rightly so. Of course, you will want to know what the tradition-bearers believe about their material, but if you will listen to and observe their performances carefully enough, and if you will get them to describe the social settings in which they have performed, or might perform the lore, then you won't have to ask boorish questions to get your information.[54]

Bert's later students spent more time asking tellers to reflect on the story: when it was told, why it was told, how the person who heard it responded. These questions usually led to a more nuanced understanding of how the person felt about the story and how it was used within that social group.

When entering belief or nonbelief into the spreadsheet, we were careful not to interpret. We indicated belief or disbelief only if the story contributor explicitly stated it one way or another. There were many instances where belief felt implied but was not marked as such. Figure 1 indicates that a large portion of original tellers believed the event took place.[55]

The more detailed the story, the more likely it is to be believed. Concrete details about place and time make stories feel less formulaic. The following story about an encounter with John the Beloved is a good example:

> These missionaries, they had an investigator who wasn't really progressing, and they were thinking that it was about time to wrap up teaching the discussions and move on to somebody else. They asked him if they could leave with a prayer and he agreed. One of the missionaries, while praying, felt prompted to promise the guy that, through his faith, if he prayed about it, his leg would be healed. And evidently, the guy had some sort of leg ailment that had been bothering him for a long time. And they asked, "can we make another appointment? One more appointment?" "Well, sure elders, but I don't know if this is gonna make much difference." A week or so later, when the Elders come back for what might be their last appointment, the man throws open the door and says, "I've got to tell you this wonderful story!" Apparently, the night before, the man decided to take the missionaries' advice and pray to know if the gospel is true, gets nothing, so he went to bed. In that time where he's not sure whether he's falling asleep or if he is awake, a man dressed in a white masseur outfit comes into his room and says, "I'm John, lie down, I'm going to fix your leg." And all night long, John massages the guy's leg and in the morning he wakes up and he's completely cured.[56]

Because this story has the unique element of a nightlong leg massage, and because the person who told the story was just one step removed from the event, it is more believable. The same holds true for stories throughout the Wilson collection. The stories with more detail and the stories where the person heard it from someone close to them or had the experience themselves are generally more likely to be believed.

Many of the people who tell these stories believe them. But as a Latter-day Saint folklorist, Bert was often asked if the stories were factually true. He typically responded by saying, "Just because something didn't happen, doesn't mean it's not true."[57] Sometimes he would quip, "These stories don't make themselves up," or "It depends on the truth you are looking for."[58] All of these responses indicate that truth is a larger and, in many ways, more complicated issue than belief. In his excellent lecture for the Leonard J. Arrington Lecture Series "What's True in Mormon History? The Contribution of Folklore to Mormon Studies," Bert outlines the several ways folklore might be true. First, stories thought of as folklore—legends, for example—often do correlate well with what took place historically. And even when the stories don't give an accurate picture of what happened, they indicate what people thought was happening and thus help explain the response to a historical event. Second, the stories reflect the culture of those who tell them. They indicate what is

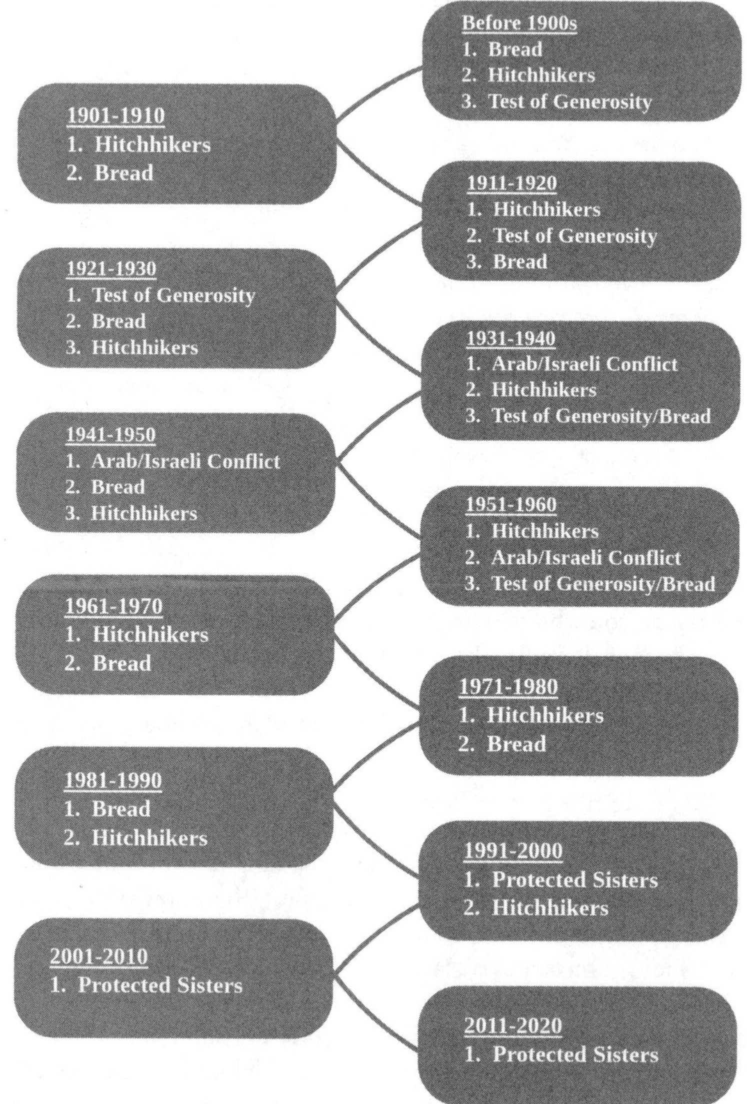

Figure 2. This timeline visualizes the recurring themes of "Bread," "Hitchhikers," and "Test of Generosity" throughout history, with the "Arab/Israeli Conflict" and "Protected Sisters" emerging as more recent focal points.

important to a culture and help define the group's "value center."[59] Third, the stories can be instructional, teaching what is right or wrong within that group. Fourth, the stories often serve as an affirmation of cultural instruction. Bert makes it clear that to "dismiss . . . narratives, as just idle tales with no historical significance would be folly. They are important cultural artifacts that reveal truth we cannot always get in other ways."[60] Finally, Bert always held out the possibility that a story is true because it represents what actually happened.

Figure 2 is a timeline of the most popular story cycles sorted by the decade when the story took place. Most stories in the collection take place between 1800 and the present. Motifs within popular stories do ring true in that they reflect what is occurring historically.

Stories about starving missionaries receiving bread or people being asked to share their meager portions with a stranger (something I have dubbed a "generosity test") are most popular before the 1950s. These stories reflect the economic hardships many in the United States experienced between 1797 and 1929. Hitchhiker stories spike between 1950 and 1970. Not surprisingly, this corresponds with the arrival of highways in the 1950s and postwar economic prosperity that fostered car ownership. Tales of three white-robed and white-bearded men convincing Arab generals to "surrender or face annihilation" became prevalent during times of conflict in the region, specifically 1948, 1956, 1967, and 1973.[61] Finally, more than sixty stories of sister missionaries protected from serial killers/rapists are set between 1991 and 2000. This corresponds with an increase in female participation in missionary work. Between 1980 and 2000, the number of women serving LDS missions went from 4,164 to 8,134.[62] Around the same time that more young women were leaving home for one and a half years to knock on strangers' doors, the famous serial killer Ted Bundy confessed to the rape, murder, or kidnapping of more than 30 women before being executed in 1989. Clearly, the Three Nephites stories "tell the truth" about the cultural concerns of the time.

Three Nephites by the Numbers

This section explores what the data from Bert's recreated worksheet reveal. While much of the information gleaned simply confirms what he already knew about the stories, I suspect some of it may have surprised him.

APPEARANCE

In several of his articles, Bert had pointed out that one consistency of Three Nephites stories is the inconsistency of the physical descriptions. They can be young or old or anywhere in between. They appear casually in jeans and a T-shirt or nicely groomed. They can be dressed as farmers, doctors, mechanics, ancient warriors, or missionaries. They can have hands "unused to physical labor" or have "leathery" skin. Race varies as well. Sometimes they are described as having "Jewish" features, probably a remnant of "Wandering Jew" stories, of which LDS migrants from Europe were familiar. They are also frequently described as Native American, Polynesian, Middle Eastern, and Caucasian. Once, one of the Three Nephites looked like Santa Claus. Once, like a vampire.

The spreadsheet data makes it clear that even when there isn't consistency about appearance, a collection of this size and scope reflects changes in culture. In 1940, Austin E. Fife drew the following conclusion from his collection: "They wear poor, simple, and often tattered clothing, and almost universally have white hair and long white beards."[63] But, surprisingly, beards aren't mentioned often in the Three Nephites collection; only 103 out of over 2,600 stories feature a beard. Dr. Fife was collecting and writing at a time when the popular stories dealt with men who are looking for charity. If researchers looked at Three Nephites stories from only the 1980s, they would assume that Latter-day Saints visualize them as stereotypical Native American warriors. While there can be visual consistency within a story cycle, the Three Nephites' appearance is fundamentally dynamic. What follows are two particularly interesting examples. In the first, the Nephite can shape-shift, something that happens in a few of the stories collected. In the second, the Nephite is a woman. What is particularly interesting in this story is that her gender isn't remarkable to the person telling the story. It's just a statement of fact.

Shape-Shifting Police Escort

It was just past midnight when a woman who was working a late shift found it necessary to walk home, as the last bus had already left. Often she had walked alone in the dark but this night she was frightened. As she approached the viaduct, a huge German police dog came toward her. She found the sight of the dog reassuring and wished it would walk home with her. When the dog was beside her, it turned and began trotting in the direction she was going. While they walked on the viaduct a car drove up, stopped beside her, and a man leaped out. The dog, which was walking a little ahead of the woman, turned and dashed toward the man, who jumped back into the car and drove away. When the woman reached her home, she called to her protector to come close so she could pet it, but it stood quietly a short distance away looking at her. She called through the door to her mother to come and see the beautiful creature, but as her mother opened the door, the dog vanished. She believed that a Nephite had taken the form of a dog to protect her.

—Miss Monza Higgs. Collected by the Archives of the Utah Humanities Research Division. #1205

Stranded

In the winter of 1991, we were returning to California after celebrating a family wedding in Salt Lake City. By the time we reached Nevada, it was snowing hard and the van started making weird noises. Lots of cars were stranded. We pulled over and my dad walked to the nearest town for help. He returned shortly after in a huge camper van driven by a nice lady. She arranged to have our car fixed by morning and took us to a hotel. The same lady showed up in the morning and took us to a breakfast place where we had breakfast. She then dropped us off at the mechanic shop where we got back into our van and started our journey back home. While driving my mom turns to my dad and said that it was so nice to have that lady help us and we needed to say a prayer of thanks to the Lord for sending her our way. After our prayer, I remember my dad saying that the Lord was mindful of us and sent one of the Three Nephites to help us. It was not until I was older that I thought back to that winter and remembered seeing several people on the road that night who needed help on the road. Yet within a day we were taken good care of by this nice lady and were sent back on the road with a full stomach.

—Hefolau Lavaka. Senior accountant from Lehi, Utah. Collected by Lipina Lolohea in 2018. #1667

FEATURES

Many of the items Bert identified as features, while interesting, actually didn't appear very often in the stories. Figure 3 highlights the features he was looking for and how often they appeared. Although the numbers for many of the features aren't substantial, they represent some of the features that might be associated with one of the Three Nephites. Consequently, they are worth exploring.

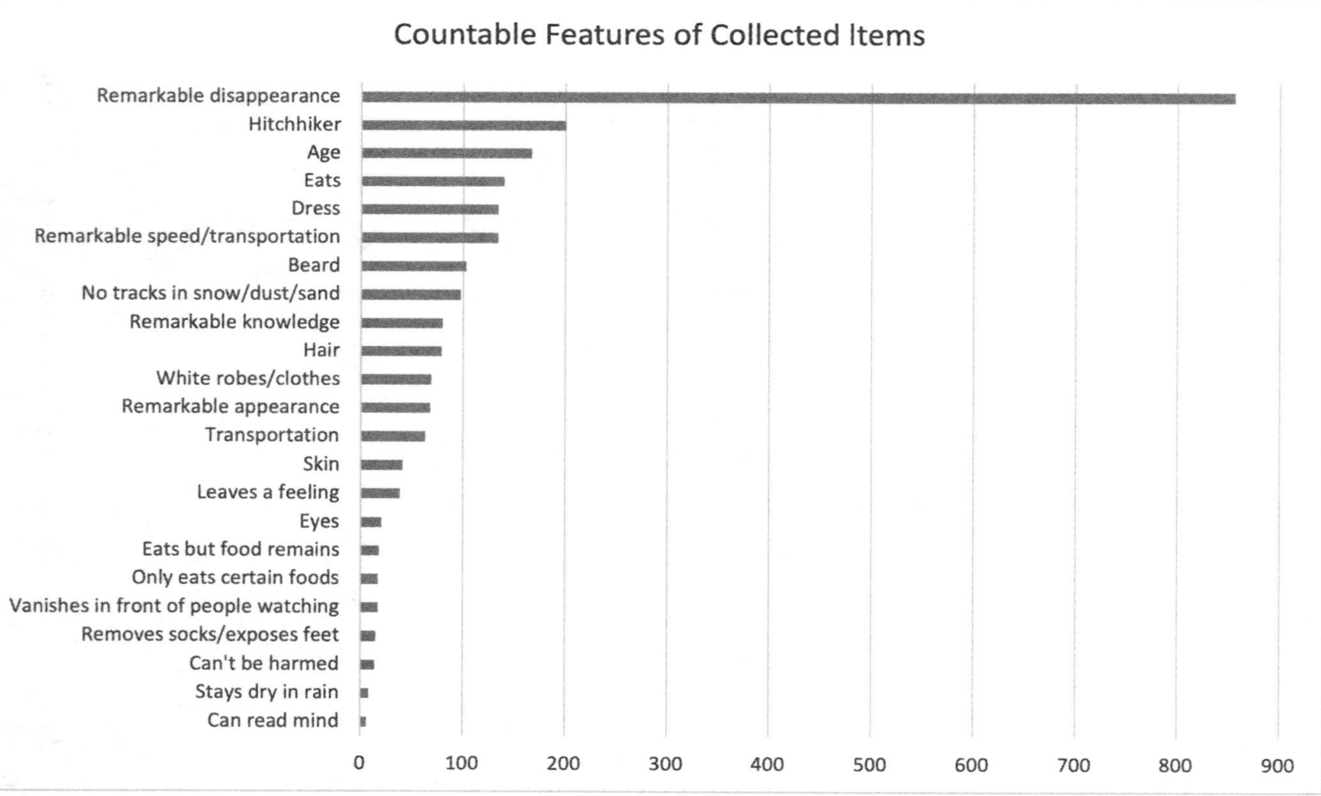

Figure 3. This bar graph depicts the frequency of various countable features found in a collection of story items. The features range from physical attributes like "Age," "Dress," and "Hair" to more intangible qualities like "Leaves a feeling" and "Can read mind." The *x* axis represents the count of items exhibiting each feature, while the *y* axis lists the different features.

LEAVES A FEELING

Appearances by the Three Nephites vary widely, but the feeling of being in their presence is reasonably consistent. A few people mention feeling scared (as the boy above), but, overwhelmingly, the feeling is positive. The Nephite's voice is often described as "soft" and "gentle." He is "cordial" and "caring." People describe feeling "joy," "calm," "blessed," "confident," "relaxed," and "holy" when he is near. His "saintly personality" inspires trust. One person describes him as having a "dynamic influential personality." The next storyteller explains that the stranger's charisma allowed her to put total faith in him:

> It was in 1988. I had a 13-month-old baby and had to fly to meet my husband, who was in the Airforce, in Berlin. I was really nervous because I hadn't had much experience flying. The man next to me on the plane just started talking to me. And normally, I wouldn't talk to strange men. He was from another country. It was very evident that he was either Arabic or mid-eastern descent, but I felt completely calm around him. Other passengers were kinda staring at us, wondering, "Why is this young white woman with a baby talking with a stranger?" But we got talking and he asked me questions and he talked to me as though he knew my life. I just felt completely at ease with him. Even when I tried to make myself alarmed, I wasn't. I was completely calm. Something in my spirit said that there was something about this person. . . . I felt the Spirit say, "Trust him. Follow him. He will help you." And so we did. . . . I just had this funny feeling. It's like he knew me. I knew he knew me because of certain things he said, and I honestly don't remember our conversation, but I was dumbfounded on the plane. He just seemed to know me and my circumstances. Everything. And so I honestly, with all my heart, believe that he was one of the Three Nephites. And nobody can persuade me otherwise. It was the feelings I had, and just the total trust that I had. I knew that God sent him there to help me and Alicia get safely to Berlin, Germany. And I know that. I have no doubt.
>
> —Nancy Weber, 53. Relief Society compassionate service coordinator from Idaho Falls, Idaho. In the unabridged recounting of the story, Nancy claims, "*I honestly, with all my heart, believe that he and his companion were two of the Three Nephites. And nobody can persuade me otherwise.*" Collected by Christine Wilkins in 2016. #1504

SUPERNATURAL FEATURES

Many of the supernatural features identified relate to the scriptural information we have about Nephites found in 3 Nephi 28:19–22:

> And the prisons could not hold them, for they were rent in twain. And they were cast down into the earth; but they did smite the earth with the word of God, insomuch that by his power they were delivered out of the depths of the earth; and therefore they could not dig pits sufficient to hold them. And thrice they were cast into a furnace and received no harm. And twice were they cast into a den of wild beasts; and behold they did play with the beasts as a child with a suckling lamb, and received no harm.

However, not all of the features found in the collection are simple reflections of the scriptural description. Some just indicate that the person in question is not mortal.

HOW AND WHAT NEPHITES EAT

How the Three Nephites engage with food signals that there is something unusual about them. Many times, they ask for a meal; however, they are sometimes picky about what they will and won't eat. In some stories, the Nephite refuses pork specifically or meat generally. Often, when offered a meal, they request simply bread and water, reminiscent of what is eaten at the sacrament during LDS Sunday worship services. Even more evocative of the sacrament is when the Nephite specifically asks that the bread be broken. Occasionally the Nephite eats a meal but, miraculously, the food remains behind. This story is representative of that pattern:

> My mother and her sisters were converts to the church. My grandmother left her father, brother, and two sisters in Alabama and came west with the church. When they came to Utah, they had little money, but they were saving to buy a house. As a result of their saving or trying to save, they had barely enough to eat. They kept themselves on a very strict budget. One evening Georgia, who was in her twenties, and Mother were there alone. They were ready to eat, and because of their budget, they had distributed things proportionally. They were just ready to eat when an older fellow knocked on the door. Mother knew that they didn't have enough food for all three, so they let the stranger have his wish and eat first. They watched him eat. Then, after the stranger ate,

he thanked them profusely and left. They ran to the door and looked out, and he disappeared. They saw him eat and use the silverware but it wasn't dirty and no food was taken.

—Anonymous 28-year-old woman. *The informant believes this story, but has been laughed at for it, and so requested anonymity.* Collected by Harold Trussel in 1967. #1007

IMPERVIOUS TO WEATHER

Many of the stories suggest the Three Nephites are not affected by the weather. They don't get, thirsty, wet, hot, or cold. The following story touches on many of those features in addition to the food particularities mentioned above:

In 1916 I was in the Teton Basin area of Idaho herding sheep for ________. I was in this area when I had a most unusual and fascinating experience. This experience occurred just after dusk in the midst of a violent storm. I had retired to my tent where I listened to the sounds of the storm. In the midst of the storm I was surprised to hear a rapping on the tent and a voice say, "May I come in out of the storm?" I arose and invited the man in. I was surprised to see that the man was carrying his coat over his arm and appeared to be dry. I asked the man where he had come from, what he was doing up there, and where he was going. He never answered these questions, but immediately changed the subject. . . . The next morning I prepared breakfast for the two of us. My visitor did not eat any of the meat. He informed me that there were only certain foods that he could eat. After breakfast he asked me if I had any water that he could wash his shirt in. I told him to use what I had in camp and that I would get some more from a spring nearby. I went to the spring and from there observed the man wash his already clean appearing shirt. He removed it from the water, shook it a few times, and put it back on. Upon arriving back with the water, I was surprised to see that his shirt was actually dry. The stranger then thanked me for my hospitality and said that he must be going. He then went down the hill and entered into a small grove of trees. I watched for him to come out of the grove, but he didn't come out. This, naturally, struck me as very strange, for I could see completely around the grove from where I was. I finally went down and searched the grove for him, but he was not there. Because a natural man could not have left without my seeing him, I have concluded that this man must have been one of the Three Nephites.

—Brother George C. of Blackfoot, Idaho. *Brother C requested to remain anonymous because the story is sacred to him.* Collected by Verl L. Giles in 1964. #0634

ABILITY TO APPEAR TO WHOM THEY CHOOSE

A feature not on the original worksheet and not included in the spreadsheet is the ability to appear to whom they choose. This ability relates directly to the scripture in 3 Nephi 28:30: "And they are as the angels of God, and if they shall pray unto the Father in the name of Jesus they can show themselves unto whatsoever man it seemeth them good." Stories in the story cycle of sister missionary protection often mention that only the "evildoer" saw the large men protecting the women. Here is a different example:

I had been left in charge of my two younger sisters while my parents were attending to chores that took them away from home. We had always been strictly cautioned about letting strangers into the house and knew that this was something that we would just never do. This particular afternoon, I heard a knock at the door and went to answer it remembering that I was the oldest and therefore in charge and responsible for my safety and that of my younger siblings. Imagine my consternation when upon opening the door, a man asked if I might provide him with a meal. I felt completely at ease looking at him, however, he had a full head of white hair and was dressed in grey trousers with a white shirt and suspenders—very much the common dress of the day. Remembering the admonitions of my parents, I told him I would be glad to give him some food but wondered if he would mind sitting on the porch to eat it. He responded that this arrangement would be fine and I proceeded to fix him a plate. While he was eating, I was rather nervous about the whole situation so I decided to calm my nerves by playing the piano for a few minutes. Imagine my surprise when the white-haired man knocked on the door after having finished his meal, thanked me and handed me his plate. Then he brushed by me entering the house going directly to the room where the piano was located. He sat down at the piano and proceeded to play the most heavenly music I had ever heard. After playing he told me to develop my gift for music. Then he smiled benevolently at me and stood up and left the house. I peeked out the front window to watch his departure thankful that he was gone yet deeply moved by the spiritual nature of this man. As I looked, I saw my father coming down the lane and I immediately shivered knowing I was in big trouble. I asked Dad if he hadn't passed the man as he approached the house but he said he had seen no one; they would have had to pass one another as there was only one lane. This immediately caused us all great consternation and Dad went outside and walked along the lane where the visitor would have had to be. As he was doing so, his [f]ather came along and together they searched every possible avenue of departure. They even searched around the trees thinking he might be hiding. No one was visible, least of all our glowing, white-haired visitor. Dad and Grandpa concluded that we had indeed been visited by one of the Three Nephites. I might add that what he had eaten was not missed from the evening meal. There was more than enough for everyone.

—(FIFE Archive) Lucille Hall, 78. Logan, Utah. Estimated time the story occurred: 1925. *Lucille believes she met one of the Three Nephites.* Collected by Delores Mangum in 1991. #1372

ANIMAL CHARMER

While not in the features Bert identified, the Three Nephites' ability to calm animals appeared a few times in the collection and is another feature that correlates directly with scriptural information about them. In the Book of Mormon, when the people became wicked and refused to listen to the Three Nephites, they made many attempts to kill them. In 4 Nephi 1:33, it reads: "And they did cast them into dens of wild beasts, and they did play with the wild beasts even as a child with a lamb; and they did come forth from among them, receiving no harm."[64] Here Brigham Young's daughter is said to have encountered a Nephite:

During the winter of the early 1870s, Clarissa Young, daughter of Brigham Young, was visiting her aunt in Provo. One afternoon a stranger knocked at the door and asked for something to eat. He was a tall man, very pale, and wore a straw hat, a blue jacket and blue overalls. Their watchdog, usually unfriendly to strangers, merely raised his head and looked peacefully at him. Clarissa and her aunt prepared a meal for the stranger and went on with their work. After a while the man, thanking them for the meal, left quietly. They then discovered that the food was still on the table uneaten; only a piece of bread had been broken. They opened the door, but the man was nowhere in sight. No footprints could be found in the newly fallen snow on the porch or walk. He had completely disappeared. On hearing the story later, Brigham Young said, "I believe this house has been visited by one of the Three Nephites."

—Clarissa Young Spencer. Published in *The Improvement Era* in 1931.[65] #1250

SPEED OF TRAVEL

One contributor said that the Three Nephites could travel as "fast as electricity." Several story cycles that will be discussed later in the book highlight this ability (see chapters 2 and 3). There is a small cycle of stories that feature one of the Three Nephites speaking in buildings that are geographically very far apart on the same day. The following is a representative example:

> In a certain community in Central Utah a strange personage appeared in a fast meeting, gave a moving sermon, and bore his testimony to the divinity of the Gospel of Jesus Christ as restored in these latter days by Joseph Smith.[66] At the close of his remarks, he took his watch from his pocket and told the audience that he was due to speak at that very instant in a certain ward in North Ogden, about one hundred miles away. He then immediately left the meeting, and a member of the congregation, wishing to verify the truth of this singular statement, stepped immediately to a telephone and called the bishop of the North Ogden ward, asking if this certain individual was there. The bishop replied that he was there and that he was speaking to the audience at that very moment.
>
> —M. W. Paulson. Provo, Utah. Collected by Hector Lee in 1942. #1086

LEAVES NO TRACE

Even though this feature appears only ninety-eight times in the Wilson collection, it still seems to be part of the collective consciousness about Three Nephites stories. The following is a representative example:

> When I was a little girl, about five or six, my brother and I went to a one-room school on the outskirts of town. One day, while we were in school, it started to snow really hard and a strong wind with it. Soon it was a blizzard and the teacher sent us all home early and in a hurry. My brother and I lived the furthest from the school and it wasn't long before we could only find our way by the tops of the fence posts. I was really

tiny and the snow was blowing drifts over my head. We were holding hands and both of us were starting to get really scared, though my brother was trying to be brave. Just then we saw a man come out of the swirling snow. He had on a long cape, not a coat like the men wore then, and a slouch hat. We were afraid of him until we looked at his face, and it seemed to have a special glow. He picked us both up and took us home to our front door. Mother was so glad to see us and asked us how in the world we got home. We told her this man had brought us, but when we turned around . . . he was gone, and there were no footprints in the new snow, not on the walk or in the road.

—JoAnn Autry, 42. Coordinator of the Drug and Alcohol Prevention Department at Utah State University, from Hyrum, Utah. Collected by Jane Bunker in 1991. #1376

APPEARANCE AND DISAPPEARANCE

Remarkable disappearance—and to a lesser degree remarkable appearance—is often thought to be the defining feature of Three Nephites stories. Bert described the basic structure of the stories in a 1976 article titled "The Paradox of Mormon Folklore": "Someone has a problem; a stranger appears; the stranger solves the problem; the stranger miraculously disappears." Bert stated emphatically that any Three Nephites story "*must* have these features."[67] If the story is missing one or more of those elements, it will be molded by the storyteller to fit the structure; most likely, that story shaping takes place unconsciously. Bert found remarkable disappearance a particularly intriguing story detail. He wrote:

> I see no compelling reasons why the Nephites must disappear. In Book of Mormon times, they were thrown into prisons, dens of wild beasts, and into furnaces, and in none of these instances did they solve their problems by disappearing. But in modern stories, they vanish from the back seats of speeding cars; they vaporize before one's eyes; or they walk away and someone later tracing their footsteps in the snow finds that they abruptly end. The Nephites disappear, I believe, because the story *requires* it. The disappearance is the climax toward which the narrative builds, overshadowing in many instances the kindly deeds the Nephites came to perform in the first place.[68]

However, our data suggests that remarkable disappearance isn't as prevalent as Bert believed. One explanation has to do with the way it was counted. We didn't break "remarkable disappearance" down: differentiating between when someone simply says "we never saw him again" versus "he vanished before my very eyes." Notice the challenge in determining whether or not the following story counts as a "remarkable disappearance":

> When two years of age, I became very ill with acute meningitis. My body was so badly drawn that the back of my head and my feet were touching. My family had called in five of the leading physicians in New Orleans, and all pronounced the case hopeless. One day my father was standing on the lawn in front of the hotel talking with some of the boarders when a well-dressed man with skin so fair it was almost transparent appeared before him and asked if he had any work he could do. Then he said, "I understand that you have a very sick child." . . . Mr. Kayne came into the room and said, "Don't grieve. Your baby is not going to die. I have communed with the other world and she cannot go. She has a work here on earth. She will pass the crisis tonight, and you will see a marked improvement." The next day, the stranger vanished. I had no after-effects at all from my illness. I recovered quite rapidly from my illness after that evening, and I haven't been ill to speak of from that day.
>
> —Helena Woody. Chilhowie, Tennessee. Estimated time the story occurred: 1900. Collected by Marcia Gunter in 1973. #0731

The word "vanished" is used to describe his disappearance, but it happened the next day, leaving open the possibility that the person simply left town in the night. We didn't count anything unless it was very clearly remarkable. If the storyteller said, "I didn't see him anywhere," that was too vague to be counted.

Taking our approach to counting remarkable disappearance into consideration, however, the numbers seem very low for a feature Bert called a "must." As his career progressed, Bert's language about the story structure and the role of remarkable appearance softened a bit. In his 2007 lecture "What's True in Mormon History? The Contribution of Folklore to Mormon Studies," he states that Three Nephites stories "almost always have the same narrative structure: someone has a spiritual or physical problem, a stranger appears from nowhere, the stranger solves the problem, the stranger disappears, *usually miraculously*."[69] Yet, remarkable disappearance occurs in only half of the stories in our collection. Remarkable appearance appears even less frequently. For example, the family who was taken care of by a kind stranger when their van had mechanical issues in Nevada (see story #1667 in the "Appearance" section) doesn't even mention the disappearance of the stranger at all:

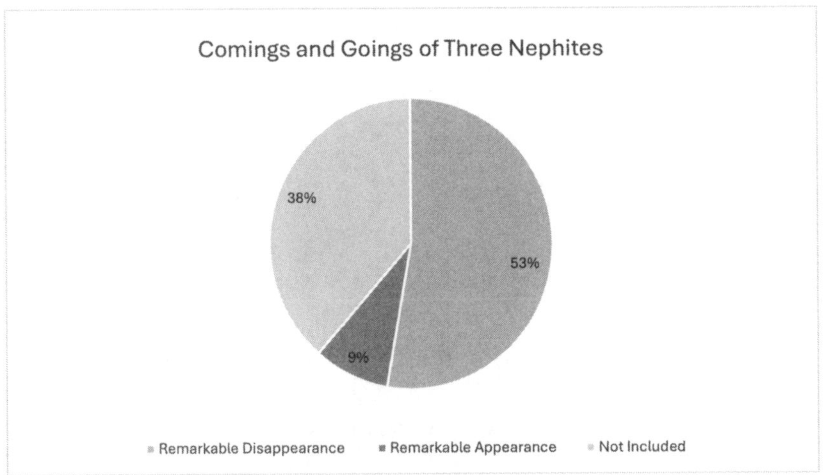

Figure 4. This pie chart illustrates the distribution of appearances and disappearances of the Three Nephites. Fifty-three percent of their appearances are categorized as "Remarkable Disappearances," 38 percent are not explicitly included in the narrative, and 9 percent are described as "Remarkable Appearances."

> The same lady showed up in the morning and took us to a breakfast place where we had breakfast. She then dropped us off at the mechanic shop where we got back into our van and started our journey back home.

Perhaps with Three Nephites stories there is another, more ephemeral aspect to the form that marks it as belonging to the cycle: the feeling people have in the presence of the stranger. People describe feeling "peace and light" (#1683) or a "kind of spiritual radiance" (#1133) when they are with the stranger, which leads them to conclude they experienced a visitation from one of the Three Nephites. Or perhaps it is the combination of elements. As one story collector explained, "She firmly believes that this was one of the Three Nephites or John the Beloved because of his dress, entrance, departure, *and* the feeling of calm he gave her" (#386; emphasis added).

NEPHITES—PARTY OF ONE

Because they are often referred to as a collective, it would be natural to assume that the Three Nephites travel together. However, they most commonly appear solo. Sometimes they come in threes; rarely do they appear as a set

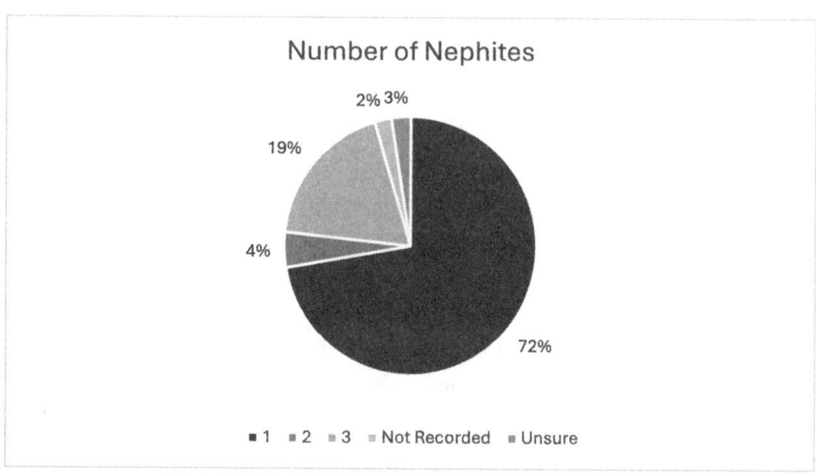

Figure 5. This pie chart illustrates the distribution of the number of Nephites involved in various events. The largest segment represents events where only a single Nephite appears (72%). They appear as a threesome 19% of the time, and in groups of two only 4% of the time. The smaller segments represent stories that don't mention how many individuals were involved or where the person was uncertain. For example, a semi-conscious person being pulled from a car wreck feels "hands" helping them out but couldn't say how many people were there.

of two. That's what makes a particular conversation between a missionary and his companion particularly intriguing. They were talking about Nephite experiences and concluded the following:

> In the scriptures, the only individuals who had been given the gift of serving on the earth until the Second Coming were the Three Nephites and John the Beloved. As we were talking, we realized that that meant there were two companionships of eternal missionaries. We both said we'd never heard a Nephite story that only had one Nephite, so we, excitedly, saw the same companionship patterns we were assigned to. Even the stories that have three extraordinary missionaries/individuals are accounted for since some missionaries are assigned to trios for a time.
>
> —Stirling Miller. Librarian and freelancer from West Haven, Utah. Collected by Stirling Miller in 2019. #1676

It's an interesting idea, but the numbers suggest otherwise. As mentioned above, the stories in our collection indicate that the Three Nephites typically travel alone and only occasionally show up as a trio.

Conclusion

In 2017, I received a copy of *LDS Living* magazine in the mail. I had no idea why it came it me; I hadn't subscribed. Flipping through it, I paused on the publisher's note, "What I (Don't) Know." The subtitle read: "There are plenty of things I don't know. Who will take care of me in my old age? Why does cilantro exist? Where are the Three Nephites right now? (No, really, I would like to know)."[70] Although this book makes no attempt to locate their specific whereabouts, it does give good insight into their location within the collective LDS consciousness and indicates that we can expect to hear more of them.

A story I heard recently from Dan Davis might clarify why Three Nephites stories show no signs of dwindling within Latter-day Saint culture:

> Around 2004, we were driving in a little two-car convoy heading back to Salt Lake City from Idaho Falls. The car behind me, with my daughter and son-in-law in it, started flashing their lights on and off. So I immediately pulled over and got out and said, "What's wrong?" He says, "The engine's running but the car's not going. It just quit going." So I said, "Let's check your transmission fluid." Sure enough, there was no fluid on the dipstick. It's late Sunday afternoon. We're in a rural area. I don't think we're going to find any automatic transmission fluid anytime soon. It was hot. I'm tired and we were basically in a no man's land.
>
> So . . . as I was standing there thinking, "Today would be a really nice day to have a miracle," a car pulled up behind my son-in-law's car and a guy got out. And there was something different about this guy. I can't tell you what that is. Because he had a pair of jeans and a white shirt. And he was tall and slender. And he seemed to be like a really, really nice person. And he said, "You guys having some trouble? Can I help you with anything?" I said, "Well, not unless you have a quart or two of automatic transmission fluid."
>
> "Sure, I've got some right here. I'll just go get that."
>
> And he goes and he pops his trunk and he comes back with a couple of quarts of automatic transmission fluid. He said, "Will this do?" And so I poured it in. And it brought the fluid level up. I told my son-in-law to see if the car could go now. And it did. I was so, so grateful. This young man had saved my day. And he says, "Is there anything else I can do to help you today?" And I felt somewhat dumbfounded. What??? And I thought about saying something amusing and lighthearted. but all I could think to say was "Thank you so much for your help." And he said,

> "Oh, anytime." And he got back in his car. And he started to drive off. I turned around, looked down the road to see where he was. And he wasn't there. I don't think anybody else noticed that. I thought as I got in the car, "If I had found my words, I would have said 'Are you one of the three Nephites?'" That's exactly what I would have said.[71]

Everyone finds themselves in predicaments occasionally, situations in which it seems that nothing short of a miracle can solve the problem. When someone unexpectedly appears and solves the problem, some might call it luck. But for Latter-day Saints, there will always be another possibility that raises the question, Was that one of the Three Nephites?

1

Vanishing Hitchhiker Nephites

ERIC A. ELIASON

So let us rather not be sure of anything,
Beside ourselves, and only that, so
Miraculous beings come running to help
—Jalāl al-Dīn Muḥammad Rūmī, thirteenth-century
Persian Sufi poet, as translated by Colman Banks

Ask any professional folklorist or North American Latter-day Saint what the most significant genre of Mormon folklore is, of any variety, whether oral narrative, customary, or material culture, and the answer might likely be "Three Nephites stories." Ask for a typical example story from the genre, and you could well hear a variant of one of this chapter's collected narratives. In William A. Wilson's original collection of Three Nephites stories, "vanishing hitchhiker" stories show up more often than any other variety. Hence, these are not only the best-known kind of Three Nephites story; they may also, to insiders and outsiders alike, be *the* quintessential creations of Mormon folklore.

A Tale of Two Folklorists and Two Tale Types

This prevalence flows in concert with the considerable impact of one of the best-selling books of American folklore scholarship ever—a 1981 collection and analysis of "urban legends." The book's popularity turned an obscure folklore studies technical term into a common part of English speakers' everyday vocabulary. Yet, the book was not called "Urban Legends," as it might have been. Instead it was named after one of the more memorable story types it featured: *The Vanishing Hitchhiker*. This book's popularity made its author, Jan Harold Brunvand, the most famous folklorist in America. He appeared several times on late-night TV talk shows and—prodded by his big New York publisher, W. W. Norton—produced several *Hitchhiker* sequels, also named after common urban legend types, such as *The Choking Doberman* and *The Baby Train*.[1]

Notably, Professor Brunvand spent most of his career in Utah teaching predominantly Mormon students.[2] Jan Brunvand (at the University of Utah) and William A. "Bert" Wilson (at Brigham Young University) were friends who followed similar methods. Both trained at Indiana University under the most prominent academic folklorist of their day, Richard Dorson. Both assigned their own students to collect and transcribe stories they heard around them in the contexts of their everyday lives. Both scholars also then featured these student-collected stories in their publications. Perhaps it should not be surprising that many of the stories in Brunvand's books have a local Utah/ Latter-day Saint flavor; the Three Nephites even show up a few times. In comparing Brunvand's and Wilson's work, the overlapping nature of each scholar's favored oral narrative genre becomes apparent. These are, respectively, *urban legends* and *supernatural religious legends* (to use yet another specialized folklore technical term).

Even without these two Utah folklorists' proximal and parallel work histories, looking at the broader overarching category of "vanishing hitchhiker" urban legends would be particularly relevant to understanding Three Nephites stories. The latter might even seem an *oikotype*, or localized culturally specific variant, of the former.[3] A common sequential string of motifs, or story elements, in both narrative types includes (1) an unsuspecting motorist giving a ride to a stranger, initially presumed to be a regular person in a normal mortal state; (2) the passenger saying or doing a number of auspicious things, but; (3) in the end, the stranger uncannily vanishes. This final defining motif highly suggests that the hitchhiking stranger was anything but a regular person in a normal mortal state.

In the "vanishing hitchhiker" urban legend cycle (referring to all the stories circulating about a particular person or topic), the passenger is often revealed at the end to have been the ghostly apparition of someone tragically deceased. But they now haunt the roadways, perpetually looking for a ride home. In one such story, a motorist discovers that his hitchhiking passenger is suddenly no longer in the backseat when arriving at the house address to which the passenger had asked to be taken but that she has left her purse in the car. The motorist takes the purse to the doorstep and rings the doorbell. An older couple answers and explains that their teenage daughter died years ago, on this very day, at the very spot the motorist found her hitchhiking. The parents further explain that over the years the motorist is not the first to have driven home her ghost and to have returned her purse.

In comparison, a common type of Three Nephites story also features an automotive theme. A road-tripping couple picks up a hitchhiker who echoes LDS Church teaching in admonishing the couple to get their food storage in order. The hitchhiker warns, "Prepare! For the end is nigh." The wife pivots in the shotgun seat of the speeding vehicle to ask the hitchhiker how he knows any such thing. She discovers that the traveler, who had spoken only seconds before, is no longer in the backseat. The car's doors are still shut and locked, and no one is to be seen on the bleak desert landscape for miles in any direction. Several elements of this story, especially the uncanny vanishing, would strongly suggest to Latter-day Saints that the narrator intended the disappearing passenger to be understood as no mere mortal, but perhaps one of Mormondom's angelic Three Nephites.

It is easy to regard these two stories as similar when comparing their distinctive motifs, as well as the particular order in which they occur. In many vanishing hitchhiker stories, a grieving parent or a spooked policeman makes clear that strange things are afoot by saying something like "You are the fourth person tonight to tell me you picked up that hitchhiker." This "spooked policeman" motif appears in this chapter's stories "'No. Can I Help You?'" and "A Shabby Old Man." The latter also features the "scary following vehicle flashing its lights" element found in Brunvand's classic "Killer in the Backseat" urban legend.[4] But in this chapter's Three Nephites story, this element thankfully augurs something else, even while its presence further underscores the many elements these seemingly sibling cycles share.

Oikotypes? Maybe Not . . .

Three Nephites and hitchhiker story cycles do display remarkable similarity in their shared themes of uncanny personal encounters. Especially, their shared "vanishing" motif at (or close to) the story's ending serves as a near-essential defining marker for both genres. However, when one also considers the two cycles' distinct differences in their most common tones and settings, they not only begin to appear less alike but may even come to seem like quite different kinds of story altogether.

Folklore student Ethan Dunn discovered significant differences in a comparison he undertook of stories from both cycles.[5] The primary natural habitats for "Brunvand-esque" vanishing hitchhiker stories are "scary story times" around campfires or at young teenagers' sleepovers or "late-nighters." The mood they evoke is typically one of supernatural spookiness, neither religious nor spiritual. Conversely, this chapter's Three Nephites story collectors often describe their storytellers' tone and audience reactions as awed reverential wonder at the possibility that the events recounted might be genuinely miraculous. The stories' settings are more likely familial or informal among close friends after church, and they interweave with aspects of tellers' and hearers' lived religion.

To Latter-day Saints who share Three Nephites stories, one of their functions is William Bascom's classic role of maintaining community worldviews and institutions.[6] Plotlines can seem tailored to bolster underlying spiritual and metaphysical tenets of the restored gospel worldview—namely, a world in which the events and people of the Book of Mormon are real and where resurrected persons have been, and still might be, appearing to people as angelic beings.

For Latter-day Saints, this way of understanding reports of subjective visitation experiences begins with, and is typified by, Joseph Smith's famous formative visionary experiences. In The Prophet's own telling, God the Father and Jesus Christ appeared to him in the spring of 1820 in what has come to be called "The First Vision." Later, the angel Moroni appeared to Joseph to commission him to translate the golden plates into the Book of Mormon, named after its primary compiler, Mormon, who was Moroni's father and the source of the Latter-day Saints' "Mormon" nickname. Smith understood Moroni to have once been a mortal prophet in the ancient Americas who buried the gold plates for Joseph Smith to find hundreds of years later at the resurrected Moroni's direction.

Within the big tent of Abrahamic religions, acceptance of the New Testament as scripture alongside the Old Testament (or Tanakh) is a primary distinguisher between Christians and Jews. Likewise, acceptance of the Book of Mormon as scripture alongside the Bible is a primary distinguisher between communities that accept Joseph Smith's restoration as being from God and the beliefs of other Christian faiths. The First Vision and Moroni's appearance are central founding stories of Mormonism. They also serve as models for a hermeneutic tradition that can help make sense of church members' own experiences or others' reports of potentially angelic encounters. These interpretive tools persist with regular everyday Latter-day Saints and emerge as needed, perhaps especially when picking up hitchhikers.

This is a different kind of work for a narrative to do than contributing to an evening's chilling entertainment while making s'mores. As experienced by tellers and hearers, Three Nephites stories can be quite distinct from vanishing hitchhiker urban legends. Perhaps a better understanding of the relationship between the Three Nephites and vanishing hitchhiker story types would be that they are sister genres with different personalities, often sharing some significant defining tropes but not really oikotypes of the same narrative variety. Formerly, following methods typified by Vladimir Propp, folklorists might have identified an example of a specific genre by comparing the motifs and plot structure of any transcribed speech act to a folklorist-constructed checklist of internal textual elements appearing in a certain order.[7] If any given utterance's features matched a particular genre template well enough, it could be categorized as an example of that genre. The sense that Three Nephites angel stories and vanishing hitchhiker ghost stories are very different beasts, despite many shared elements and structural similarities, underscores the limitations of Propp's method.

Since American folkloristics' performance-centered revolution of the 1970s,[8] contextual factors must be considered as well in genre classification. The physical setting, the social occasion, the performer's reputation and tone, and who the audiences are all contribute to how the various participants in a narrative event may understand a story's genre. Or as Ian Brodie explains, "It is not internal motifs or elements and their order but, more importantly, expectations and how they are set, met, and/or surprisingly upended, by which genres emerge and are defined."[9] This understanding helps explain why comparing two narratives, markedly alike by internal textual comparison, could seem ridiculous—maybe even sacrilegious—according to the same Latter-day Saint teen who heard one story at a campout and the other from a devout grandmother sharing a revered family history pioneer story during the Latter-day Saint devotional practice of family home evening.

Memorates and the Failure of Genre to Contain Uncanny Events

Yet again, on the other hand, perhaps we should not move too quickly toward a difference-focused characterization of these two genres' relationship just yet. In this volume, Julie Swallow's introduction draws on Jill Rudy's chapter to point out that performance contexts may not always be so neatly and starkly contrasted. Along a sliding spectrum rather than across a clearly delineated boundary, a sacred Three Nephites story may nonetheless be recognizable to an audience of church members as being similar to vanishing hitchhiker stories. So the storytelling may veer toward the sensational in the right situations.

There may be an even deeper original connection between the two genres as well. It is a potential connection inherent in all "friend of a friend" (FOAF) stories, from urban legend ghost stories to religious/supernatural being encounter legends. This is the plausibility, or at the very least the notional framing device, that presumes FOAF chains do indeed trace back, person-to-person, to an originating event or encounter that launches a narrative cycle of which any given telling is an example. It turns out that some precipitating uncanny events can very quickly spawn multiple competing narrative cycles, in wildly different genres, as word of an unusual happening spreads to various groups of people who try to make sense of it.

Folklorist Bill Ellis investigated the many interrelated vanishing hitchhiker–like stories that began circulating in response to a set of reported uncanny experiences in eastern Pennsylvania in 1993. Ellis noted that storytellers reporting on the "hitchhiker" they encountered considered several main possibilities. Were encounters with the being parts of an elaborate hoax, anomalous Fortean phenomena, a divine being, a ghost, a demon, or a cosmic trickster? These differing possibilities occurred not only between stories he collected but also within stories from the same storyteller.[10] Ellis's work suggests that a single set of anomalously ambiguous encounters can solidify into several possible distinct interpretations along the various chains of custody through which narratives may pass. How often might tracing back a particular scary story (about a ghost) told around a campfire, as well as a different supernatural religious legend (about an angel), lead to a single eyewitness's memorate narrations of one occurrence about which the teller was deeply unsure as to the identity of whom or what they encountered?[11]

The Ancient World of the Bible as Source for Today's Ghosts and Angels

Ellis seems to have identified an instance of a type of encounter phenomenon that Jacques Vallee has discovered all over the world and all throughout world history.[12] But perhaps most relevant to making sense of the Three Nephites cycle are the numerous examples found in the Bible. Quite a few familiar (and some not so familiar) Bible stories share many elements of both vanishing hitchhiker urban legends and Three Nephites supernatural religious legends—so much so that these ancient accounts might surely seem examples of a significant shared common ancestor genre of both the current hitchhiker and Three Nephites narrative genres. These Bible stories' anomalous elements are often not highlighted, hence easy to miss, in their tamed and paraphrased versions commonly told in children's Sunday school. But a close reading of the relevant texts reveals several stories of a similar type, where ancient authors seem intent on carefully presenting narrative accounts of unusual episodes of meeting auspicious persons, relating their stories with a considerable degree of purposeful ambiguity.[13] These Bible encounter stories are characterized by the following elements: (1) Even though the strangers are in human form, there is considerable uncertainty, and often one or more massive shifts in perception, about who or what was actually encountered. (2) Perhaps surprisingly for a book to which believers have traditionally turned for clear and unambiguous answers, these Bible stories are slow to confidently identify anomalous strangers, and sometimes never do, and sometimes even seem intent on purposefully exacerbating rather than resolving identity ambiguities. (3) One identity possibility, often the initial presumption, is that the stranger described in the story is an unfamiliar but normal, mortal living human. (4) The story's narration relates a number of seemingly impossible occurrences that make it extraordinarily difficult to identify the stranger as a "regular mortal human." (5) Witnesses in the story experience awe, surprise, bafflement, and even terror in the presence of the auspicious stranger(s). (And how different is all this from campfire "chills" really?) (6) And the main identity options range dramatically but are still constrained within a limited set of possibilities, from a previously unknown mortal human divine messenger (a living prophet); to the spirit of a deceased person making an appearance from the world of the dead (a ghost) or a malevolent or evil spirit; or to a divine messenger from realms of glory (an angel) or even "a" god or the Lord God himself.

The Bible is composed of material from many oral and literate genres, including transcribed folk-song lyrics, parables, instructions for religious rituals, royal dynastic histories, transcriptions of ancient prophets' oracles, and collected story cycles about ancient heroes such as the heroes in Judges, the prophets Elijah and Elisha in the book of Kings, and Daniel in his eponymous book.[14] Bible scholars and folklorists alike see many instances of the scripture's text as transcriptions of firsthand or passed-on accounts that first circulated orally in mostly illiterate societies but have now long been made permanent in the received text of the written Bible. Understanding the importance of genre, cultural context, and how stories are both preserved and developed through oral transmission has long been important to both disciplines.[15]

For the purpose of this chapter introduction, the most relevant parts of the Bible are those where authors seem to be transcribing and editing for reading firsthand or orally transmitted accounts of uncanny encounters. Such narratives, as found in the Bible, have both created and reinforced a worldview about the nature of supernatural entities. Their patterns delineate some parameters for a set of narrative elements that continue in both vanishing hitchhiker and Three Nephites stories. This makes both cycles examples of the Bible's vast and multifaceted reception history and shows such encounters to still be a significant influence on Abrahamic religious—and post-religious—societies such as our own.

In the Restoration tradition, a living person, a ghost or deceased spirit, an angel, and (at least in the case of Joseph Smith's first vision) "God himself" have all been possible answers to the question "Who was that?" However, since the early nineteenth-century waning of the notion that the church's apostles should experience a personal visitation of Jesus Christ in order to qualify for the office, seeing God himself might more likely be seen these days as a sign of kooky overzealousness rather than extraordinary faithfulness.[16] Today's interpretations of vanishing hitchhiker urban legends mostly dispense with God(s) and angels as live options and consider only "normal mortal person" and "ghost" as possibilities. But make no mistake, while entertaining the Western idea of a ghost no longer implies any particular religious belief, the origins of ghosts as a possible interpretation in our culture is, at least in part, a lingering legacy of Christian civilization into a post-Christian era, a survival from a less disenchanted time.

"God himself" as an option has, for at least eighteen hundred years or so, seemed alien to educated theological arbiters of orthodox post–Apostolic era credal Christianity for another reason as well. In traditional Protestant formulations of Christian belief, but not for Latter-day Saints, God has no physical form, let alone a human-appearing one. He does not even feel emotion like we do. He is, as the Westminster Confession succinctly states, "without body, parts, or passions."[17] However, scholars of the Bible and Ancient Near East, as well as Latter-day Saints, understand many parts of the Bible as portraying God as having human form and emotions. For example, James Kugel's *The God of Old* makes the case that over the years that the Bible text took shape, later contributors began to prefer a more abstract God and not entirely successfully tried to remove anthropomorphic references to God in the literature that came to be the Bible. According to Kugel, it may be that some ancient stories were so well known and respected for so many years that it was difficult for later redactors to remove such depictions of God altogether.[18]

Following are a few examples of the Bible's person/angel/evil spirit/ghost/god/God ambiguity stories, all of which are relevant to understanding the later-emerging genres of vanishing hitchhiker and Three Nephites stories. While reading, it may be useful to keep in mind that though much theological vocabulary is shared, in most traditional Abrahamic faiths, God, angels, and humans are three very distinct classes of being—the first being uncreated and the latter two each being separate types of creation made by the first.

Conversely, Latter-day Saints' underlying theological assumptions see God(s), pre-mortal spirits, mortal humans, disembodied spirits of the deceased, and resurrected beings like Moroni and the Three Nephites as all of the same class of being along different stages of eternal progression. Angels are people like us who may be spirits yet to be born, or who have died, or who are awaiting resurrection, or who have already been resurrected.[19]

For the purposes of this volume, the Bible stories and exegeses recounted here are not primarily intended as evidence of what actually happened, nor are they necessarily presented to suggest that the nonmortal extraordinary beings they describe really exist and appeared anciently to mortals. However, these stories and others like them in the Bible do show that biblical authors seemed to want their readers to believe in the possibility that human prophetic messengers (both living and from the world of the dead), angelic divine beings, and the Lord himself are all real and may appear to mortals from time to time in ways that astound and perplex.

Examples of Ambiguous Identity Biblical Being Stories

Genesis 18 says, "The Lord appeared to Abraham at the Oaks of Mamre . . . during the heat of the day. He looked up and saw three men standing near him." Abraham bows, face to the ground, before the visitors, showing them extreme deference and hospitality, perhaps serving as an early model for, or participating in an already venerable tradition of, hospitality in case of holiness. In some Christian reception and artistic traditions, the seeming contradiction between a monotheistically single "The Lord" and "three men" is ameliorated by understanding "God" in triune terms as Father, Son, and Holy Ghost. The most famous of all Russian Orthodox icons, Andrei Rublev's *The Trinity* (aka *The Hospitality of Abraham*), depicts God in Abraham's theophany as three human figures sitting at a table for Abraham's prepared meal.[20] Later in the narrative, Abraham's cousin Lot displays a similar reverence for these auspicious visitors, whose number has, without explanation, been reduced to two. But this time they are called neither "The Lord" nor "men" but are explicitly identified as "angels" (Genesis 19:1).

Genesis 32:22–32 has traditionally been known as "Jacob wrestling with the angel," despite the Hebrew word for "angel" never actually appearing in the text. In one passage, Jacob's opponent is called "a man" by the narrative voice (24–25). In another passage referring to the encounter, Jacob says, "I have seen God face to face" (30). Never is an "angel" mentioned. Is this extra-biblical appellation an ancient traditional extrapolation that attempts to bridge these two other appellations, made possible only by Hebrews' earlier, more anthropomorphic conceptions of God? Perhaps this identification comes to us from an oral tradition long passed on along with the written text's transmission. The episode is no anodyne tale about friendly roughhousing, nor merely an internal spiritual conflict where Jacob metaphorically "wrestles" with his conscience or God's commands. Rather, the story recounts a harrowing up-close and personal all-night combat ending in the body horror of Jacob's powerful opponent wrenching the poor patriarch's hip out of its socket so that he limps painfully home (31). This story is presented as an etiological narrative explaining why eating meat or tendon attached to hip sockets is unkosher (32). All of these details seem designed to mitigate against any possible nonphysical "spiritualized" interpretations of the event.

Then there is Joshua's supremely ambiguous encounter, before the battle of Jericho, with someone that the narrative voice of the text variously calls "the Lord" and "a man." Adding even further to the reader's bafflement are the interloping stranger's own words to Joshua. The Hebrew general, wisely wanting full situational awareness as to who is on his battlefield and why, asks the enigmatic person whose side he is on, the Israelites' or the Jerichoans'? The mysterious being answers obliquely, referring to himself neither as man nor God, as the narrative voice does elsewhere in the story, but as the "captain of the Lord's host" (Joshua 5:13–15, KJV). "Host" means a military unit of angels or divine beings. The stranger then tells Joshua to remove his shoes, which is what the Lord told Joshua's predecessor Moses when he was on holy ground during his famous burning bush theophany (Exodus 3:5). As Sunday school alumni know, the Bible depicts Jericho's walls miraculously falling down after Joshua and his army marched around it blowing trumpets. What the Lord's angelic armies and their captain were doing during this unusual siege is not mentioned in the text because they have disappeared from the narrative. Were they there "in spirit" causing the walls to fall? Or were they aloof, not taking sides?

Judges 13 recounts considerable ambiguity over the identity of the being who announces Samson's imminent birth to his future parents. The famous long-haired, ass jawbone–wielding hero's perplexed mother-to-be refrains from confident identification but tells her husband, "A man of God came to me, and his appearance was like the appearance of the angel of God" (Judges 13:6, ESV). Later, when Samson's father-to-be also encounters the same being, the narration claims it was indeed the angel of the Lord (16), but the awestruck man fearfully tells his wife, "We shall surely die, for we have seen God" (22). But they do not die.

In a rare occurrence of identity ambiguity being fairly clearly resolved, the young temple servant Samuel, with his master's help, eventually realizes that the voice calling his name is not the priest Eli's but the voice of the Lord calling him to be a prophet (1 Samuel 3:1–14).

After his lifelong ministry and eventual passing, Samuel himself becomes the subject of a case of uncertain identity. In an episode traditionally referred to as "The Witch of Endor," 1 Samuel 28 tells of a nervous necromancer calling up Samuel from the grave at the behest of the ever-mercurial King Saul, who had just recently banished this sort of practice from the land (1 Samuel 28:3). The necromancer first describes what she sees with the wildly polysemous Hebrew word *elohim*. This word is central to this story's continuing crazy level of ambiguity for Bible readers. So it needs an explanatory aside.

The Hebrew word "el" is a generic term that can variously refer to any "god" or "divine being" of any pantheon or to the Israelites' own "God." "El" is also the name for the supreme father god of the Canaanites, whose gods the Bible is most adamant that ancient Hebrews not worship. Unfortunately, unlike English, Hebrew orthography makes no capital/lowercase distinction that might help resolve any ambiguity. In some cases, el seems to mean "angel," or "spirit," or even something like "demon" or "evil spirit." The-im suffix usually pluralizes Hebrew nouns, making multiple gods/divine beings/spirits all possible meanings of elohim. Or-im might instead indicate a grammatical "majestic plural" with a single referent, as in the United Kingdom's "royal we" that the monarch uses on some formal occasions, as in "We the King hereby decree. . . ." This understanding, if correct, would suggest something like "great or majestic god" as a meaning for elohim. In this sense, the word was used even to refer to the Moabite god Chemosh or the Sidonian goddess Astarte by their devotees. Or elohim could mean "Elohim," one of Hebrew scripture's many proper names for its authors' own god, whom they believed was *the* "God" rather than a "god." Following Joseph Smith's lead, Latter-day Saints often use "Elohim" as a name/title to distinguish God the Father as a person from "God the Son," Jesus. This parallels the similar-sounding term "El Elyon," meaning "Most High God," a common description/title for Israel's God. However, El Elyon is also an honorific by which the Canaanite god El is commonly styled. This is particularly problematic in biblical interpretation when worshiping the correct god, and him only, is one of the overriding concerns of Bible authors. The Canaanite El Elyon had a son named Baal. Some textual, and much archeological, evidence points to the Israelites having a similar familial conception of their high God, who had both a wife and a son in the minds of many ancient Israelites.[21] This persisted even after King Josiah's reforms began in earnest to try to stamp out these ideas in favor of strict monolatry (2 Kings 23–25; 2 Chronicles 34). If all of this were not indeterminate enough already, elohim can also be a respectful title for a mortal earthly ruler or judge, or akin to the term "elder" or "lord." Again, without a capital/lowercase distinction, whether a biblical instance of elohim means something more like "The Lord" (of the Universe), or "the lord" (of the manor) can be difficult to determine. In numerous passages, Bible translators have faced exactly this dilemma.[22]

Semantic and grammatical context can sometimes give Bible translators clues as to which of the many above meanings might appertain to any passage of text. Yet, throughout the Bible, and especially with the Endor episode, frustrating uncertainty remains. The whole meaning of the story hinges on which possible elohim referent one chooses. Curiously, all of el/elohim's possible meanings occur within a semantic probability field whose scope overlaps rather nicely with the awe-inspiring frightening/comforting God/angel/person uncertainty that characterizes the Bible's uncanny encounter narratives themselves, as well as with the fairly similar particular set of identity ambiguities that characterize Three Nephites stories. But does el/elohim's specific semantic range of possibilities help to cause this uncertainty? Or do elohim's particular set of possible meanings starkly and accurately capture an essential type of metaphysical reality that is quantum science–like in its indeterminate nature? A metaphysical reality occasionally made manifest in the usual range of possibilities that come to mind after a particular kind of powerful phenomenological encounter that might happen in ancient Israel, modern Mormon country, or anywhere?[23]

But back to the Witch of Endor story . . .

After the women speaks of elohim, Saul, who wanted her to bring up Samuel, then asks, "'What is his appearance?' and she said, 'An old man is coming up, and he is wrapped in a robe'" (1 Samuel 28:13–14). The traditional appellation for this woman as a "witch" is not actually in the text and poisons the well as to how to interpret the legitimacy of her practice and who it is, in fact, that appears to her. She accurately prophecies King Saul's death, which comes to pass later in the narrative (2 Samuel 1:4). Bible readers have wondered at the story author's intention for centuries. Was the woman a tricky ventriloquist? Does the text intend to imply that Samuel's true spirit self appeared, or merely an apparition resembling him, or maybe an imposter evil spirit seeking to deceive? Did "elohim" refer to Samuel or something seen before his appearance?

In pioneer Utah, some Latter-day Saints recast the "witch" as a legitimate prophetess rather than a divinely unsanctioned medium. They pointed to this story as biblical precedent for long-deceased prophets returning from the other side to deliver important messages.[24] If Samuel can appear, then why not Moroni, or the Three Nephites? After a nineteenth-century spiritualistic schism led by the séance-holding Salt Lake City businessman Francis Godbe, and again after the 1970s blockbuster film *The Exorcist* and the ensuing Satanic Panic of the 1980s and 1990s, pioneer-era Latter-day Saints' descendants have become more likely to invert their interpretation entirely and regard the story as a warning not to fool around with Ouija boards or any such divinatory paraphernalia.[25]

Encounters like these are not unique to Hebrew scripture. In the New Testament, Jesus takes his apostles Peter, James, and John onto a mountain, where the long-dead Moses and Elijah appear to them and the voice of God speaks from a cloud. This all terrifies and stuns the apostles. The story abruptly ends with a Three Nephites cycle–esque "suddenly they looked around and saw no one with them anymore except Jesus alone" (Matthew 17:1–8; Mark 9:2–8; Luke 9:28–36).

According to the Gospel of John, Mary Magdalene was the first to see the resurrected Jesus. But she at first thought he was the gardener (John 20:15). Later, all four Gospels recount the story of a group of grieving disciples journeying on the road to Emmaus. With a stranger who had joined them in traveling, the travelers lament and wonder aloud at the meaning of Jesus's recent execution. Only later do they realize their peripatetic companion had been the resurrected Jesus himself (Luke 24:13–35; Mark 16:12–18; John 20:19–25; Matthew 28:16–20).

In John 21:20–23's wording, Jesus neither promises nor closes off the possibility of his "beloved" apostle John continuing to live on earth until his Second Coming. But Jesus's words evidently caused a rumor to spread that is addressed, but not resolved, in the narrative. Like a careful folklore scholar, the writer records, "Then went this saying abroad among the brethren, that that disciple should not die. Yet Jesus said not unto him, 'He shall not die'; but, 'If I will that he tarry till I come, what is that to thee?'" (23). For centuries in Christian folklore, this open-ended passage has led to a variety of understandings of what happened to John the Beloved, including that he died and was buried or that he was buried but is somehow in occultation (or living stasis) in his grave, ready to emerge in the future. Or, as Latter-day Saints believe, that like the Three Nephites, John the Beloved yet wanders the world and will continue to do so until Jesus's Second Coming. The Book of Mormon's depiction of Jesus promising three of his analogous New World apostles that they too would live and serve past their normal lifespan until Jesus comes again is certainly resonant with this New Testament pericope.

Joseph Smith presented a revelation, now canonized as Doctrine and Covenants section 7, that resolves at least this last biblical example of narrative ambiguity in favor of John indeed roaming the earth like one of the Three Nephites.[26] But no such revelation has even bolstered, let alone given imprimatur to, any particular orally circulating story from either John the Beloved's or the Three Nephites' folk-narrative cycles. As with similar stories in the Bible, the Three Nephites cycle's narratives are often only obliquely hinting and suggesting, rather than confidently proclaiming, that their depicted uncanny encounters were with the ever-living Three Nephites. This uncertain tone, apparent in the text of both stories, as well as their contextual cues observed by story collectors, is so common it could be considered a distinctive feature of the genre.

Secular Angels? Religious Ghosts?

Not only do the preceding Bible stories show elements familiar to Three Nephites story connoisseurs, but the sudden changes in perception of who, or what, a stranger really is are also common in vanishing hitchhiker ghost stories. As with today's ghost stories, the Witch of Endor and the Mount of Transfiguration narratives even portray active engagement with ancient prophets who could not possibly still be alive by any normal reckoning. The idea that vanishing hitchhikers are "secular" and Three Nephites are "religious" is a distinction much more recent in world history than the ancient, and likely prehistoric, emergence of the shared ancestral antecedent stories of narrative genres featuring the motif of an uncannily disappearing stranger who might not have been a normal mortal human. Even the binary presumption that ghosts are scary and spooky while angels or deceased relative visitations are necessarily only warm and comforting is a dichotomy that often collapses when listening closely to the details in the wide variety of narratives that emerge from reports of these sorts of experiences. As with Bible accounts, personal encounters with one of the Three Nephites can leave the witness awestruck or even petrified, as in "A Shabby Old Man" in this chapter.

Yet, in both our secular and religious cultures of today, ghosts are often associated with the occult and evil spirits, while angels are holy. Although they may seem like opposites, much of our popular understandings of both ghosts and angels seem to emerge from biblical incidents, where there is much more precedent for uncanniness and ambiguity than people often realize. Any relatively recent supposed distinction between "secular" ghost stories and "religious" angel encounter stories, however significant they might seem to us, might have seemed strange and irrelevant to the ancients.

Once, after I shared a vanishing hitchhiker story in class, a student responded, "No way that really happened. Mormons don't believe in ghosts!" Then I asked her if she believed that the angel Moroni, as a resurrected former inhabitant of the Americas, appeared to Joseph Smith, or in the personal experience narratives Latter-day Saints sometimes share about the spirits of deceased relatives appearing to them.[27] "Sure!" she said, and even shared an experience of the spirit of a deceased grandfather comforting one of her family members. The student concluded, "But that's different!" without really being able to articulate why, though I could see on her face that she was trying to figure out exactly how to do so.

That such apparitions can be seen as separate types of phenomena is a testament to the importance of setting, cultural context, and tone in making what seems similar on paper quite different in experience. There can be great variety in how this all works out in the minds of individuals, even those belonging to the same faith community. This can be seen in what another student said in response to the first: "What are you talking about? It is precisely because of our theology that we know ghost stories might be real! Don't you believe in the Holy Ghost?"

So there are many layers to peel back in order to reveal the full richness of the multivalent relationship between the Three Nephites and vanishing hitchhiker legend cycles. At first glance they seem quite similar, oikotypes even. On closer inspection, however, considering their differing common tones and settings, they seem to diverge. After even fuller examination of their biblical underpinnings, they start to seem similar again.

All of this is important for understanding Three Nephites narratives for several reasons: (1) Even in our increasingly post-Christian and much-secularized Western civilization, the Bible, and its worldview, still deeply and significantly shapes how Westerners understand and talk about narratives concerning ambiguous perceived encounters with spiritual or uncanny individuals,[28] and (2) among the remaining religious folk groups for whom the Bible is still important, Latter-day Saints are among the most biblically literate, making Bible stories and their underlying worldview even more important in shaping how Latter-day Saints might receive both vanishing hitchhiker and Three Nephites stories.[29]

A Cultural Inheritance or a Pre-Cultural Experiential Phenomenon?

As is perhaps appropriate in analyzing similarities between distinct narrative cycles characterized by inference, allusion, and uncertain sudden bouncing between multiple being–identification possibilities, there is yet again an "on the other hand" possible explanation to consider here. While similar features certainly abound between the vanishing hitchhiker, Three Nephites, and biblical narratives considered above, it may not be that the Bible's ostensibly continuing cultural influence is required at all to explain these resonances. Rather, they may stem more from underlying neurological and perceptual phenomena prevalent among humans throughout all times, and across all cultures, that manifest in all three narrative sets.

In the human condition, the possibility seems to exist for experiencing a particular type of pre-cultural anomalous personal encounter involving awe-inspiring anomalous beings and other effects that break with our everyday experience of the world around us. Memorates that are related about such experiences, as they begin to spread, can begin to conform so much to various cultural, religious, and oral narrative genre expectations, and they can solidify so comfortably into a number of different legend cycles so different in tone and meaning, that they come to be seen as totally unrelated. The sensationalistic nature of this topic and the goofy way popular culture usually treats "the paranormal" have made the humanities, social sciences, and natural sciences slow to dive into investigating such phenomena. But this is beginning to change.[30]

The study of folklore has frequently shown how traditional societies can pass on sophisticated knowledge about the workings of nature that scientific disciplines may have missed, which they only come to embrace later. Several folklore-adjacent disciplines have emerged and thrived due to this fact. Ethnobotanists have developed hundreds of modern pharmaceuticals from tribal groups' medicinal plant use around the world. Ethnomusicologists have shown that the world's traditional types of music can be as sophisticated and profound as the music of elites. Oral historians have discovered time and again that preliterate societies' rigorous oral traditions can pass on accurate information later verified by genetic testing or archeological finds.[31]

Unfortunately, scholars have been less engaged with the question of what insights narratives of encounters with uncanny beings may reveal about the nature and workings of psychological and spiritual matters. One reason for this is the presumption that theology and cultural expectation are the main shapers of memorates' content and texture, leading them to presumably vary widely across time, place, and between cultural communities. According to this view, memorates would be expected to reveal little about the fundamental truths of human perceptual psychology, let alone accurate information about any spiritual world beyond our mundane one.

Attempting to remedy this research paucity and these dismissive assumptions, folklorist David Hufford's work concedes that the "cultural source hypothesis" is real and can shape narratives to a great extent.[32] But he has also found that much of the content of some common specific kinds of memorates seem to be pre-cultural and show similar features across time and society. Hufford regards reports of encounters with children not yet born, deceased relatives, and human-shaped beings (perceived as either divine or diabolical) as a specific and common type of subjective experience that is akin to other kinds of firsthand empirical evidence about the nature of ourselves and the world around us. In his "experience-centered approach," memorates are not anomalies to be ignored, fatuous fantasies to be explained away, or delusions to be cured. They are instead potential means by which to begin to uncover the nature of some common psychological, and perhaps even metaphysical, realities.

Hufford found that such experiences happen to around 20 percent of people. This rate does not correlate with any psychiatric diagnoses or cultural, educational, or religious background. They seem to occur broadly across populations. In such memorates, the teller describes encountering a being in human-like form that can often seem unremarkable at first but can suddenly appear to be more than they first seemed. The being does not appear as an animal or mystical creature of some kind; human appearance is the norm. Individual perception of having an encounter with an uncanny being happens more frequently than the more academically respectable mystic or transcendent states of notable people in various religious traditions. In fact, rather than sensationalizing a mystic experience by presenting as it as tangible, Hufford has found that people are more likely to obfuscate or "mystify" what were originally straightforward meetings with person-like beings.[33]

Hufford suggests that some cultural and religious traditions may be more robustly equipped to make sense of memorates and provide social and conceptual coping resources for those who experience their power. He has noted that Latter-day Saint theology and lived folk-religion have a particularly good handle on the several dimensions of the most common types of memorate encounters.[34] And just as living among a folk group that understands the medicinal uses of a certain plant, which has not yet been discovered by ethnobotanists, might provide certain physical health advantages, so too living among folk for whom Three Nephites stories are valued and normalized, rather than seen as pathological, might impart mental health advantages for those who personally have had such experiences.

In a society whose members may mock the credulity of those who report seeing angels, where health care professionals may well misdiagnose a patient with schizophrenia and prescribe inappropriate antipsychotic drugs with adverse side effects, people learn to be hesitant in sharing their stories about visitation experiences. That the United States has been such a society, and that most of the stories in this volume were collected from Americans, may also partly explain some of the hesitant tone prevalent throughout the cycle. Hufford spent the last years of his career at Penn State College of Medicine training health care professionals to realize that not all reports of such encounters indicate a debilitating mental illness, no matter how unsettling they may be to those who experience them. The best clinical outcomes for patients are achieved when they feel like they can share their experiences in a friendly, open, and listening environment where they occasionally might be able to escape some of the isolating effects such an experience can have for modern people. Perhaps by conversing with someone who feels comfortable enough saying, "I too had such an experience. It happened like this. . . ."

Motif Survivals: Teleportation and Food Storage

Leaving the experience-centered approach behind and turning to the content of this chapter's stories on their own terms, enmeshed as they are in the multi-threaded fabric of Latter-day Saint history and culture, several significant patterns emerge. Perhaps the most common motif in the whole cycle, and especially prevalent in this chapter, is the Three Nephites' instantaneous vanishing near the end of the story. For cultural insiders, a storyteller may not even need to offer a post-telling analysis of "So maybe it was one of the Three Nephites," because this is the strong implication of the vanishing, making it not only a common genre motif but a defining one as well. The vanishing motif's genre-establishing function is another fundamental similarity with vanishing hitchhiker urban legends, whose very name comes from this end-of-story element.[35]

As with vanishing hitchhiker stories, the Three Nephites very rarely disappear in a *Star Trek*–style dematerialization in front of attentive onlookers, but rather the disappearance is most often reported as "just not being there anymore" when all available potential witnesses were momentarily distracted, looked away, or took their eye off the situation for a second, as in the story "No. I Can Help You!" in this chapter. They are not as dramatic or vivid as a “special effects” disappearance but nevertheless display features hard to square with disenchanted world views. Footprints go some yards out into the snow and then just stop, as in “Footprints in the Snow.” Or the backseat of a car traveling seventy-five miles an hour on the interstate is now suddenly empty of any interlocutor. Or from a locked bathroom “even though there was not another possible way out of the room,” as in “Such a Strong Feeling” in this chapter.

What begs to be explained about this is that the ability to miraculously disappear and travel virtually instantly from one place to another does not show up anywhere in the Book of Mormon, the text-source wellspring of all Three Nephites lore. The legend cycle (see “Shoveling Snow” in this chapter), as well as the Book of Mormon text, describes some superhuman abilities of the Three Nephites, but the written and oral narrative sources show some marked differences in emphasis. In scripture, their longevity is central, and they are described as being able to withstand attempts to kill them or cause them pain (3 Nephi 28:7–9). Oddly, invulnerability is rarely referenced in the oral narrative cycle. But even more oddly, teleportation is not mentioned at all in the Book of Mormon. So how did this disappearance motif get into in the legend cycle and come to be a central defining element?

One possible explanation is that the Three Nephites narrative cycle preserves an earlier Latter-day Saint folk belief that was much more commonly known in the nineteenth century. This belief rarely comes up today outside of Three Nephites stories and theological discussions about “translated beings” that rely more on other sources than on the Book of Mormon. In the early days of the church, an institution emerged called “patriarchal blessings.” These are still part of the Latter-day Saint religion today but typically far less spectacular than they used to be. After the manner of Jacob’s blessing of his sons as recorded in Genesis 50, designated patriarchs will lay hands upon a church member’s head and, by inspiration, pronounce blessings and prophesy on their behalf. Today a young Latter-day Saint might be promised blessings of happiness and marriage should they follow the Lord’s commandments. In the 1830s, they might also have been told that they would live until they saw Jesus’s Second Coming in the flesh, or perhaps that they would be able to travel instantaneously about the world like a translated being and hence presumably also disappear in an instant.[36]

Of course, folklore would not continue to be shared if it did not have relevant resonance with people’s current concerns, but it is also capable of preserving legacies from the past that have disappeared elsewhere. Consider, for example, how very few in Louisiana’s Cajun country could begin to carry on a conversation in Cajun French at all anymore. But when the accordions and fiddles come out, and the old traditional songs are performed, with their deep centuries-old patterns that tend to hold things in place through time, most of the lyrics are quite expertly sung in the local creole tongue. Do Three Nephites stories exert a similar influence in Mormon country, preserving and perpetuating a set of ideas about translated beings that were more common in the past but have been virtually forgotten today?

Another slippage occurring between Three Nephites narratives and current LDS Church policy and practice is in their portrayal of the church's preparedness teachings. In the past, the church officially promoted keeping a supply of food enough for two years and then, later, for just one.[37] This guidance stemmed both from apocalyptic expectations of end-times chaos, and from a heritage of "lessons learned" by hardscrabble pioneer ancestors who eked out a precarious living in the arid and difficult-to-farm Great Basin. Still today, Utahns and Latter-day Saints are disproportionately influential in the more widespread American "prepper" movement and its associated industries.[38] Comparing the collection dates of the Three Nephites stories in this volume with evolving church guidance shows a lag time between changes and the details that appear in the stories. Many members still talk as if a one- or two-year supply is current church teaching, but these actual year numbers do not show up in the church's current official literature.

Helping people prepare to weather the apocalypse shows the Three Nephites acting in one of their most common roles as depicted in their narrative cycle: that of kindly preservers of life and providers of protective assistance to people, as in "The Color of His Eyes," where one of the Three Nephites cures a drowsy driver's sleepiness, and in "Coming Back to the Faith," where a mortal is given ample warning, but only just enough time, to repent to avoid calamity. This life-preserving role is most dramatically displayed in "Suicide by Serial Killer" and "Elmer's Wife Prophesied," where troubled souls decide to reconsider plans to kill themselves because of an encounter with one of more of the Three Nephites.

Nonetheless, Latter-day Saints do perpetuate other robust narrative cycles where divine retribution is violently meted out to evildoers. Notably, the Three Nephites are usually absent from such narratives, leaving the destroying angel role to others.[39] When they occasionally do herald unavoidable punishment, as does "Too Late!" this might be surprising to most Latter-day Saints who are familiar with the Three Nephites genre.

The Vanishing of Hitchhikers and Hitchhiking Culture

Another example of the sometimes conservative nature of oral narrative traditions is the persistence of "vanishing hitchhiker" Three Nephites stories in a society where hitchhiking's prevalence has dropped off considerably from its apogee in the mid-twentieth century.[40] Skepticism toward hitchhiking (and, even more implausibly, giving hitchhikers rides) as believable contemporary occurrences is sometimes addressed within the narrative with validating details to make this choice seem more credible. In one story, the protagonist is actually hoping to commit "Suicide by Serial Killer" by getting picked up by a murderous motorist. More commonly, the storyteller acknowledges the protagonists' danger but depicts them as picking up a hitchhiker only because of a spiritual impression, or "prompting" in Latter-day Saint parlance, to pick him up.[41] This happens in "Such a Strong Feeling" and in "Shabby Old Man," related hereafter. When the narrative depicts a lone female driver picking up a hitchhiker, the presence of strong validating formula explanations for this indicates that tellers believe this situation might especially require even more special explanation to be credible.

Subtly Guiding the Discernment of Divine Intervention

Another notable feature of these famously supernatural stories is that they can actually often be quite subtle and reserved in how they make their point or about whether they even are providing evidence for making a point. As mentioned, Three Nephites stories are generally devoid of over-the-top flashy pyrotechnics. Uncanniness is displayed mostly without overt special effects. Any attempt to make "The Three Nephites Movie" could be done with a fairly low budget. Someone successfully has a telephone conversation only to discover that the line has already been cut. Or the shack where the story subjects met an old man who seemed to live there is later revealed on inspection to show signs of not having been inhabited for years, as in "Tumble Down Cabin."

Following the good advice of creative writing instructors everywhere, the stories display a "show it; don't say it" strategy. We rarely get an Aesop's fable–like ". . . and the moral of this story is that the Three Nephites are real, and the gospel is true" type of interpretation served up on a silver platter. A few hard-to-square-with-normality details are provided, and then we are left to connect the dots on our own. As any good campfire storyteller knows, giving the audience minimal pointers as to how to imagine the horror on their own is a much more effective technique than lurid descriptions of gore. Perhaps so too are glorious otherworldly divine realities better obliquely alluded to rather than vividly depicted in photo-realistic detail. Things we imagine ourselves, rather than just have described to us, are much more frightening when we realize they are being made and happening in our own mind. In Three Nephites stories, tellers seem to presume the same is true for spiritual insight and religious awe. The pedantic phrase "and thus we see" can go in one ear and right out the other. Perhaps insight we glean by figuring it out ourselves, constructing answers in our own mind, can feel much more like our own convictions, rather than just someone else's, and can have a much more powerful and long-lasting impact.

One function of telling Three Nephites stories this way may be to model a hermeneutic method for recognizing providential activity in the world around us—not with thunderbolts and lightning but by inviting listeners to notice more subtle signs and wonders that might indicate Three Nephites activity. These tend not to wave a flag to draw attention to themselves, and they might take some thought and pondering to recognize. This is done not by providing a checklist of bullet points but by narrative example of possible signs and wonders. Attentive audiences will learn to pick up on "small proofs," such as grapes left in a car seat; weather unusual for the area, as in "The Grape Eater"; or a stranger knowing where a shovel was kept and using it tirelessly, as in "Shoveling Snow." Often in the narrative such "small proofs" are noticed only in retrospect, after events have been mulled over and considered from various angles to reveal their miraculousness. Sometimes details like she has been his wife for "65 years," as in "Elmer's Wife Prophesied," are included without any overt dot-connecting work present at all in the narrative about how this detail might show how a memory of a possible Three Nephites encounter was less likely an illusion or misremembered and more likely an actual visitation. A listener may come up in their own mind with "Well, then, how did he meet her if it was not really a Nephite?" or "I suppose I could go ask her as a second witness to this story I just heard."

Presumably, such evidence may not impress those who are not spiritually tuned in but, like Elijah's "still small voice," can be persuasive to those who experience and hear of them and partake of, and help construct Latter-day Saint methods of story interpretation that are just as much part of Latter-day Saint folklore as the stories themselves.[42]

Landscape, Local Knowledge, and the Significance of Detail

The "Grapes" narrative mentioned above contains another motif whose significance is not overtly mentioned and whose significance might slip by many readers. The storyteller mentions that it was cold and raining on the road between Miami and Globe, Arizona. To locals, this detail would jump out as quite noteworthy. The Valley of the Sun, including Phoenix and surrounding towns, is one of the hottest and driest places in North America. A story set in Seattle and told to Seattleites might not even bother to mention that it was chilly, wet, and overcast because of course it was. However, these same weather details in the desert setting of "The Grape Eater" foreshadow for the attentive reader further strangeness yet to come.

Understanding how shared local knowledge shapes what details might or might not appear in a story and how locals might interpret the significance of details that do or do not appear is also relevant to understanding the most common motifs of the vanishing hitchhiker type of Three Nephites story. When the Nephite disappears from the backseat of a car and is suddenly nowhere to be seen, readers in many parts of the country might not be particularly impressed: "Certainly, he could have darted behind a tree into the woods, ducked inside a building, or disappeared into a cornfield." On most drives, in most of the country, one or more of these possibilities pertain. But to inhabitants of the Intermountain West—the formative natural habitat of Mormons and Three Nephites stories—a very different mental image appears when one hears a story with a road trip setting. This driest of regions has some of the lowest population density rural areas of the "Lower 48." Between small islands of concentrated settlement are vast stretches, sometimes for scores of miles, of not a single tree, building, or stalk of corn anywhere to be seen in any direction to every horizon. Such a landscape would not be what comes to mind for people from other parts of the country. But to Mountain Westerners, this is the default mental image of interstate travel. A storyteller from Star Valley, Wyoming; Mesquite, Nevada; or Vernal, Utah would likely not bother including a landscape description in her narration. This is not because envisioning it is unimportant for the story to have its full intended impact but because, rather, she can rightly assume that her listeners in these towns have already envisioned the appropriate landscape to underscore the Nephite vanishing's miraculous nature.

Narrative Chain of Custody: PENs, FOAFs, and Secondhand Stories

Following "The Grape Eater," this volume's next narrative, "A Seminary Teacher's Student's Father's Story," is noteworthy for another reason. The story's careful and detailed presentation of a short two-step chain of custody involving known and trusted sober people underscores how proximity and familiarity can serve to make a story more believable.

Urban legends often begin with some variation of "I heard this from a 'friend of a friend.'" This is both an "opening formula" indicating that a narrative is beginning and a "validating formula" appealing to the authority of the story's custody chain back to eyewitnesses. This formula and its variations are so prevalent that the acronym FOAF (for "friend of a friend," as mentioned earlier) has come to refer not only to the formula itself but also to the type of story that this formula introduces.[43] The FOAF introductory formula can be misleading, since as the story passes from person to person, most of the ever-growing number of ". . . of a friend, of a friend, of a friend . . ." instances needed to accurately preface the story tend to slough off. This keeps the story a manageable length and free of cumbersome repetitions. However, this truncated reporting of narrative custody chains can also make it seem that the teller has far fewer degrees of separation from the action than they really do and hence were closer to the action than they really were. This, perhaps inadvertently, can increase a story's perceived credibility.

In contrast to FOAFs, the term PEN (for "personal experience narrative") refers to stories where the storyteller and the main character are the same person, or rather it's an eyewitness account. By far the majority of Three Nephites tellings one is likely to hear are FOAFs. Occasionally, one might hear a memorate/PEN from someone claiming to be an eyewitness to a Nephite encounter.

"A Seminary Teacher . . ." and "Elmer's Wife Prophesied" in this chapter are both examples of neither a FOAF nor a PEN but "secondhand stories," which occur when there really is only one degree of separation, rather than zero (as in a PEN), or at least three (as in an FOAF) between the teller and figures in the story. In each case, the narrator is careful to provide names for the figures in her story and to underscore a clear and short chain of custody from her own rendition of the events back to the originating memorate. Hereby, the narrators provide their stories with not only a richer texture but also a fuller flavor of validating verisimilitude.

But Was It Really One of the Three Nephites?

Building a sense of verisimilitude, or "having the features of the appearance of reality," might seem a pretty central task in most Three Nephites storytelling situations. Latter-day Saints could be presumed to draw on Joseph Smith's familiar wording regarding his First Vision in interpreting identity in Three Nephites stories—"I knew it, I knew that God knew it, and I could not deny it"—or to use a rote phrase from Latter-day Saint discourse once so common that it now often appears in self-deprecating parody as "I know beyond a shadow of a doubt with every fiber of my being." However handy and familiar these vivid idiomatic tools are, and however common the sentiments they express might be, such language is notably almost never used in telling Three Nephites stories. Instead, storytellers couch and hesitate like Samson's mother, who did not say, "I know I saw an angel!" but rather, "His appearance was like the appearance of the angel of God," perhaps being unsure if what she saw was actually what it looked like or only a simulacrum.

This a prudent tack to take. In the Latter-day Saint tradition, making authoritative pronouncements that an event has possible doctrinal or theological import for the whole church is the exclusive purview of the First Presidency and the Quorum of the Twelve Apostles. While personal revelation is urged for everyone, the scope of its claim on another's belief is limited to one's own stewardship within an orderly hierarchy. A too forceful claim that any narrative most certainly describes an angelic appearance may run afoul of a culturally and ecclesiastically appropriate sense of circumspection and propriety about such sacred matters.

So, as both a folklorist and a lay Latter-day Saint who has been tasked with writing this introduction, I am not inclined to opine on whether any of the following stories "really happened" or if one of the Three Nephites "really appeared," despite knowing many readers may want this. Following Hufford's experience-centered approach, I reckon many, if not most, of the accounts in this chapter could well be traced back to personal experiences that sure seemed like, or had the verisimilitude of, an angelic Nephite encounter to those who were there at the time. And just in case these stories are indeed a witness to marvelous works and wonders being afoot in the world, I always try to follow the relevant advice the Bible gives: "Let brotherly love continue. Do not neglect to show hospitality to strangers, for thereby some have entertained angels unawares."[44]

Vanishing Hitchhiker Nephites Stories

"No. Can I Help You?"

After the 1992 women's conference, my sister in law's next-door neighbor—no wait it was the neighbor's sister. . . . Anyway, she was coming home from the tabernacle in Salt Lake at the women's conference. She was on the highway driving and she saw a man on the side of the road and thought to herself, I should pick him up, but she thought, "That's crazy, because I would never do that." Then she saw him again and thought it was weird. But she had a feeling to stop and talk to him. So, she stopped and the man started walking towards her and he came up to her and then she said, "Can I help you?"

He said, "No. Can I help you?"

She was, like, "What's going on?"

Then he said, "I just want to tell you to have your food storage by December."

She said, "Wait a minute." And then she said, "Can I take you anywhere?"

And he said, "Yes."

So, she opened the other door to have him get in, and when she turned back, he was gone. He disappeared when she took her eye off him. She thought, "That was so weird!" She thought she was going crazy. While she was sitting there, she saw flashing lights behind her. It was a highway patrol man. He asked her if she was okay and she said yes. He asked her why she was sitting there and she said, "If I tell you, you will think I'm crazy." Anyway, she told him.

And he [the policeman] said to her that she wasn't crazy at all because hers was the tenth time that night he had heard someone tell the same story.

—Merilee Bateman Collins. Homemaker from New Orleans, Louisiana, Collected by Andy Collins in 1993. #1290

A Shabby Old Man

One night, a couple of ladies were returning home from a church meeting. The driver of the car was the wife of the Chief of Police. For some reason, and acting out of character, she stopped to pick up an old man standing alongside the road. It was a cold night in Cache Valley, and she felt it was the Christian thing to do.

The ladies visited with the old man, discussing the recession and how hard times were right now. The old man, who was bearded and dressed in shabby clothes, asked the ladies if they had their food storage. He said, "If you don't have a year's supply as counseled by the prophet before the end of the year, it will be too late!" When the ladies turned to tell him they had their supply, the old man had vanished.

Frightened out of their wits, the driver swerved back and forth as they searched the floor of the car looking for him. Just then, the car which had been following them for some time, turned on its red light. A policeman pulled them over. He asked the woman for her license, suspecting a drunk driver. When he discovered who she was, and she had told her story, the policeman told her he had seen three people in her car while he was following them. He also told the ladies that this was the third time he had stopped people with similar stories. The ladies drove him [the old man], convinced they had been warned by one of the Three Nephites.

—Dolores Booth. Homemaker from Malta, Idaho. Collected by Janis H. Warr in 1991. #1378

Such a Strong Feeling

One afternoon Brother Te'o was driving from San Francisco to Sacramento, California, on his way to a regional welfare conference. As he drove along, he noticed a shabbily dressed old man standing at the side of the road, trying to hitch a ride. But as it was his policy never to pick up hitchhikers, he drove on. A short while later, however, he had such a strong feeling that he should pick up that man that he turned around and drove back.

Soon after the stranger entered the car he asked Brother Te'o where he was going. He told him that he was going to a regional welfare conference, and the man said, "Oh, that's where I am going, too." They then began discussing the Church and the welfare program. After they had attended the conference together, the stranger asked if Brother Te'o could take him to San Francisco. Brother Te'o said that he would, and asked the man if he would like to come to his home for dinner. The stranger readily accepted the invitation.

When they arrived at the Te'o home, he asked if he might get cleaned up a bit before dinner. Then he went into the bathroom and closed the door. The Te'os prepared dinner, but by the time everything was ready the man had still not come out. They called to him, but there was no answer, and the door to the bathroom was locked. Soon they found a key and opened the door, but the man was gone, even though there was not another possible way out of the room.

—Jane Zobell. 1959. "*The subject was Eddie Te'o, a forty-eight-year-old Latter-day Saint, born and raised in Samoa of royal parentage. He told his friend, Jane, the story.*" Collected by Carolyn Roberts in 1962. #75

Footprints in the Snow

Another time when one of the Three Nephites appeared as a hitchhiker is concerned with a man who had to travel to Las Vegas on business. After sitting silently for several minutes, the hitchhiker, whom he had picked up, said to him, "Are you quite sure your wife's all right? Don't you think perhaps you should return to her?"

The man, without questioning the passenger, or even professing amazement, was immediately convinced that he should return at once to the side of his wife. Asking the hitchhiker what he would like to do, the passenger replied, "Oh, you can let me out here." The passenger got out and began walking over a hill as the man turned his car around. After he had turned around, the man began wondering about the knowledge of his passenger.

So, he alighted from the car and followed the man's footprints over the hill. Just on the other side of the hill, however, the footprints disappeared and the man could see no one, although the view was unimpeded for over a mile. The man went back to his car and drove home. When he got home, he was told that his wife was at the hospital where she was extremely ill, and that they had been trying to contact him.

—Collected by Don L. White in 1962. #85

Shoveling Snow

It was winter and my grandfather had been on a business trip to Hutchinson, Kansas, where he had interests in an oil well and refinery. He was caught unexpectedly in a snowstorm, which came up very quickly. The temperature of the air was intensely cold. The cars then did not have heaters, and grandfather had wrapped an army blanket around his legs and feet to keep out some of the cold. He even pushed on [the] accelerator and brake pedals through the blanket.

As the storm continued, the road conditions became worse; it was apparent that my grandfather would soon be hindered from driving. He felt it was best to drive on, however, in the hopes of finding a farm or place to stop. After driving at a snail's pace for some time, a man dressed in a dark suit and hat appeared on the side of the road. Grandfather picked him up. After a while the man told grandfather if he would stop and get the shovel out of the trunk in rear of car, he would shovel the snow on the road so they could proceed faster. They inched along the road in this fashion for several hours. It was apparent that nightfall was not far off. So, this gentleman told Grandfather that several miles down the road a large barn was located where he could stop for the night and be out of the storm.

Eventually, this point was reached, and at the place predicted, and according to the description given. When they reached the barn this man told Grandfather that help would come for him the following morning, the road would be cleared, etc. It wasn't until his departure that a clue was given to his identity. Then the realization came to Grandfather that he was one of the Three Nephites.

As Grandpa said later. He wore no heavy coat to protect himself from cold. He was able to shovel snow for hours with no apparent fatigue. He came in the spirit of helpfulness. His appearance was out of nowhere, and after he bade Grandfather goodbye—he left as he had arrived—Grandfather did not see him walk down the road. How did he know there was a shovel in the trunk? Finally, without his aid Grandfather would have surely frozen to death in the stalled car. The next morning, help came in the form of a farmer with his team who helped Grandfather take his car to the next city.

When this story was told to my mother she asked Grandfather what they had talked about. The man had admonished grandfather regarding the importance of keeping the commandments and living up to the principles of the Gospel.

—Helen F. Price. The story takes place in Vandes, New Mexico. Early 1930s. Collected by Margaret Price. #37

The Color of His Eyes

In 1939 Jack B. Trunell was driving a truck from the east coast to Salt Lake City. In Wyoming, just west of Cheyenne, he passed a man who was hitchhiking. Later at a road-side diner a few miles down the road the same man walked in, sat down by Dr. Trunell and asked if he might have a ride with him to Salt Lake City. Dr. Trunell said that it was okay. He noted that the man had brown eyes.

Dr. Trunell had been driving for several days and was without much sleep. He started down the long, winding canyon near Laramie and began to feel very groggy and incoherent. He glanced at his passenger who was gazing at him with a brilliant intensity. Dr. Trunell felt as if his sleepless condition would cause him to fall asleep if he wasn't careful. His passenger looked at him intently again and smiled and all sleepiness and fatigue was instantly lifted from him. The man smiled again and said, "Do you feel better now?" Dr. Trunell assured him that he did.

The trip to Salt Lake was completed without incident. Dr. Trunell let his passenger off at the Temple and at the time he did so noticed that his eyes were brilliant blue. He believes that this was one of the Three Nephites.

—Jack Trunell, 55. Doctor. 1939. *The collector of this story notes that they found the teller sincere and believable.* Collected by Gregory Vernon in 1966. #394

Coming Back to the Faith

Millie and George (made-up names) were a middle-aged couple who had gone a little to the wayside. When first married, they hadn't thought of ever having a cup of coffee or a shot of whiskey. But now, who's to say they were wrong to just calm their nerves by the coffee or the whiskey. In their younger years, they never missed a church meeting or calling. Now, it was harder to get up and wipe the sleep out of their eyes. It was much easier to stay in bed and let Priesthood and Sunday School go on without them. When it came time for Sacrament Meeting, Millie was too busy fixing dinner, and George, he was too tired from laying around all day.

This routine went on for quite a few years. One day as Millie and George were riding down a lonely Arizona road, they saw two men who were hitchhiking. Usually, they would never think of picking up hitchhikers, but something told them to pull over and pick up the two men. The two men were dressed nicely and looked as if they hadn't walked even a mile. When asked where they were going, they said that they were going anywhere Millie and George were going. Then, they began to talk of things which were very extraordinary and unusual. They told Millie and George that they were living in the last days when the Savior of the world was to come again. They told of the great destruction that would come to the wicked if they did not repent. They told them of the wonderful day when Jesus Christ would again come and never leave His brothers and sisters again. They talked on about all that was to come for the world and all its inhabitants. Finally, they told Millie and George that if they didn't repent, they were going to be two sad people. If they kept on as they were, they would be very unhappy and discontented when they didn't obtain the degree of glory they wanted. It was those little things that were bringing them to destruction. Millie and George just sat there wide-eyed and listening to each word spoken by these two strange men. They couldn't bring themselves to turn around and look at the two men because they knew within what they said was true. Millie finally got up enough courage to turn around to ask the men how they knew so much about she and her husband's personal lives. When she turned around, the two men were gone, and they didn't leave even a hint that they had been sitting in that back seat.

This experience shook George and Millie greatly. From then on, they gave up their habits and shortcomings. Millie and George, to this day, believe those two men who brought them to the truth were two of the "Three Nephites."

—Alice Wilson, 18. Student. *The storyteller expressed belief in the Three Nephites but not this story nor many others that are told. She said, "To be a good Mormon, one doesn't have to believe these stories. Many people make them up just to attract attention."* Collected by Jan Wanlass in 1969. #440

Suicide by Serial Killer?

A young married couple had just had a terrible fight. The husband got in his truck and left. He started driving towards the desert, where he would be out in the middle of nowhere. He was so upset at the argument that he planned to take his life. While he was driving out on this long stretch of desert, he saw a man walking on the side of the road. The man did not look like an honest character and the young man that was driving the truck picked him up half hoping that this stranger would do him in so he would not have to take his own life. So he stopped and asked him if he would like a ride.

The stranger accepted. As they started to talk the young man that was driving told the stranger of his fight that he just had with his wife.

The stranger told the young man that if he would go home everything would be just fine with his wife and they would have many happy years of marriage. Then the stranger told the young man that he needed to get out. The young man stopped at the side of the road and let him out. The stranger told him to turn around and go straight home. As the young man was turning his truck around he decided he could not leave the stranger out in the middle of the desert. But when he got his truck turned around the stranger was gone. The young man felt uneasy that he could not see the stranger, there was no place for the man to go for miles. He could not figure out where he went. When he got home everything was fine with his wife. And just as the stranger had told the young man, they lived many happy years of marriage.

—Stanford Williams. 58. Retired national guard officer from American Fork, Utah. "*Stan heard it from a friend that he was in the National Guard with. Stan likes to tell this story whenever he has the chance. When I asked him to tell me a story, he was very eager to repeat this one to me again because he felt it was the best story he had to tell. I think he likes to tell it because it leaves the listener and the teller with a good feeling of peace due to the happy, but mysterious ending.*" Collected by Tara C. King in 1990. #900

Elmer's Wife Prophesied

Elmer lived and worked in Utah around the 1920s and was a member of the LDS church. He was engaged to be married and went to visit his fiancée. When he arrived, she told him that she was not going to marry him and in fact, she was going to marry someone else. Elmer was devastated. He left her house and went straight to a liquor store. He bought some hard liquor and decided that he was going to drink the liquor and drive up over mountains into the next town where he was going to be working for a while. His plan was to crash his car and kill himself.

While driving up into the mountain he saw a hitchhiker along the side of the road. Elmer had not seen any other cars on the road, so he stopped the car and asked the traveler where he was going. The hitchhiker said he was trying to get to the very town in which Elmer was headed. Elmer gave the man a ride and during which they had a conversation about what had just happened with Elmer's fiancée. As they drove, Elmer calmed down. Before they reached town, the traveler asked to be let out of the car. He got out and Elmer looked behind to watch him walk away and the hitchhiker was nowhere to be found. Elmer went into town and a few weeks later he met Lois Ann, his bride of over 65 years.

—Tina Ballenger, 55. Legal secretary from Boise, Idaho. Collected by Katy Ballenger in 2000. #1592

Too Late!

My cousin's cousins were coming down to Salt Lake for some church meeting. It might have been Conference. And they saw this hitchhiker, and they picked him up. He got in the back seat, and they started talking, and he found out they were Mormons and everything. And he asked them if they had their food storage. Or it might have been, "Do you have your two years' supply?" And they said, "no." And he said, "It's too late." And they turned around and he was gone.

—Paula Wright. Provo. Collected by Chris Borg in 1975.[45] # 554

Tumbled-Down Cabin

Brother Howard was driving home from a long trip on a lonely road. He saw an old man with a white beard walking along the side of the road. Since it was raining hard and getting dark out, Brother Howard picked him up. They traveled a ways to the man's house where the old man convinced Brother Howard to stay the night.

In the morning, Brother Howard continued his trip only to discover a wash-out in the road not far from where he spent the night. Had he continued his travels the night before, he would probably have been killed. He returned to the house of the old man only to find an old, tumbled down, uninhabited cabin. Brother Howard interpreted this as a saving of his life by one of the Three Nephites.

—Terry Lahde Johnson, 24. Works for Utah Wildlife Resources Department from Orem, Utah. *The collector remembers that this story was told in the early 1960s to "strengthen faith in the church."* 1976. #742

A Dead Man in Your Car

Oh, yes, I've heard of the Nephites lots of times. I've never seen one, but I certainly wish I had. There was one in New Mexico. My sister was living down there in Lourdsville [*sic*] and she read this in the paper and she thought it was so interesting she remembered it. Some people were going to El Paso, going along the highway there, and they met a little old man on the road. They picked him up and took him quite a ways. When he got out he said, "What can I do for you?" and they said, "Nothing." Then he said, "Well, just ask me anything you want to know, and I'll tell you." Now, who else in the world could that have been but one of the Nephites, to know so much?

And they said, "Well, when will the war end?" That was two or three years ago—while the war was going on. He said, "The war will end in July." So they asked him how he knew that, and he said, "I know that just as sure as you are going to have a dead man in your car before you get home."

Sure enough, before they got to El Paso they came to an Ambulance that was broke down, and they took in the sick man from the ambulance. But before they got to El Paso he was dead. So, the old man was right. But they forgot to ask him the year.

—Mrs. Parley Bryan from Tooele, Utah. Collected by Hector Lee in 1945. #1186

The Grape Eater

Roland was on the bread delivery route, headed towards the small town of Miami, Arizona, from Globe, a twenty-minute drive. It was almost dark and it had started to rain. Roland recalls that it "was getting very cold, especially in the bread truck because there are no doors on the bread truck." Roland was thinking about his wife, who had just passed away, when he saw a traveler on the road. The traveler was wearing old white pants and a long white, almost see through shirt. Roland pulled to the side of the interstate and offered the man a ride. (By now it was pretty dark and raining hard.) The man accepted, and sat in the seat next to Roland, smiled, and ate grapes. The man asked Roland about his wife.

Roland said, "My wife just passed away Christmas day."

The man looked at Roland and said that it was important and symbolic that she left this world on that day. The man then said, "She's very happy now, and she looks forward to seeing you." Roland looked to the seat where the man had been sitting, but he was no longer there, just his grapes on the seat. Roland said, "I think I dumped in my shorts right about then." They had been travelling over fifty miles an hour the whole way.

—Roland Roth Corriveau, 68. Bread deliveryman from Globe, Arizona. 1987. *Roland said that he calls this story a "Nephite Story" because the man looked "like a warrior, not like a heavenly angel." The collector did not record whether they asked Roland if he had seen a heavenly angel to make this comparison.* Collected by P. Paul Corriveau, 1992. #1260

A Seminary Teacher's Student's Father's Story

As a young married man, my student's father was totally inactive in the Mormon Church. He was a heavy smoker. He did not attend nor participate in any way, in spite of the efforts of his wife to try to get him to attend with her and their small children. One day in the early spring while he was plowing his land in preparation for planting, his plow broke down. He couldn't repair it and was forced to drive about thirty miles to a neighboring town to buy a part to fix the plow. He drove over and bought the part he needed and was returning home. At a junction of two major highways which he passed going over to get the part, he had noticed a hitchhiker. He was a clean-cut looking young man with blond hair and somewhat shabby clothing and was carrying a small suitcase.

As my student's father passed the same junction on the way back home, he noticed that the same young hitchhiker was still there. Even though he never made it a practice to pick up hitchhikers, he had a strong feeling that he should pick up this young man. He stopped and picked him up and explained that he would only be going as far as his farm which was about 23 miles from the junction. The young man seemed very grateful to get a ride that far. They began talking together as they rode along through the rolling farm country. The young man was coming from Montana and was headed for California. He had been on the road for many days and had been supporting himself with occasional odd jobs. He mentioned that he had met several Mormons in his travels and said he was impressed with what good people they were. He asked the father if he were a Mormon. The father replied that he was one, but not a very good one. At that moment he was smoking a cigarette, so that fact was obvious. He felt very embarrassed at having to admit to his inactivity in the Church.

There followed more conversation from the young man in which he told the father how precious it was to have a family like his and how important it was to raise them with righteous principles in their lives. The young man based what he said on experiences with his own family and on people he had met in his travels. As the conversation continued, my student's father experienced a profound feeling of the precious thing he had in his family and in the Church even though he was not active. He could see clearly for the first time the error of his life as it then was. There was born in him a desire to improve and do better. He looked over at the young man with his blond hair and sincere face and realized that he was probably unaware of the feelings he had prompted within the older man.

At length they came to the point where the driveway of the farm joined the highway. My student's father pulled his car off the highway and onto his own gravel road and stopped. He told the young man that this was as far as he was going. The young man thanked him very much for the ride. He got out of the car taking his suitcase with him. He waved and started back toward the highway. The father put the car in gear and started up his road. He looked into the rearview mirror to see which way the young man would turn when he got back to the highway. To his amazement, there was nobody in the rearview mirror. He stopped the car and put it in reverse and backed up to where he had let the young man out. He walked the few feet back to the highway and walked out into the middle of it and looked both ways, but there was nothing to be seen. He walked across the highway and up onto the railroad tracks which run parallel to the highway. He even walked across and down to the river on the other side of the tracks. There was nobody to be seen anywhere. The young man had completely vanished.

My student explained that this experience was a turning point for her father. He never smoked another cigarette after the one in the car that day. The next Sunday he went to Church for the first time in years and he had remained active in the Church always after that. He was convinced that the young man was one of the Three Nephites who had been sent to reach him in a way that nobody else could have done. The depth of the effect of the experience was shown by his Church activity and service which had begun then and continued for more than 20 years.

—Female. Seminary student, 17.[46] Small agricultural community in Southeastern Idaho. "*This story was shared with me in confidence by. . . . while I was her Seminary teacher in a small agricultural community in southeastern Idaho. She told me about this experience which had happened to her father because she wanted me to know why she had such a great love for the Church and why she felt so strongly about keeping the commandments and staying faithful in the Church. This experience was held in great respect—almost in awe—by her family. They felt that it was a direct manifestation to their father that had changed the course of his life and the course of the lives of the whole family as well. She felt that largely because of this experience her father had changed his life to one of activity in the Church and had served in many positions in the Church. Her siblings had also grown up active in the Church largely because of this experience of her father."* Collected by a male university student in 1988. #1356

Inversion

Jay Fowler had just returned from Korea in April of 1959, and he was going from Provo to Salt Lake. Many people had passed him up probably because he was hitchhiking, so he felt that he would kneel down and pray for a ride to Salt Lake City. This fellow had a lot of faith, and after praying he started walking with joy in his heart. Soon an old man in a black car picked him up and took him right where he was going. This man just happened to be returning to Provo, fortunately, after a few hours. This was just ideal for Jay because he wanted to return at the same time. As Jay thanked the gentleman kindly and turned around for a moment, he turned back around to find neither the man nor the car in sight.

—Jay Fowler. Somewhere between Provo and Salt Lake City. 1959. Collected by Janet Seeley in 1961.[47] #175

2

The Worldwide End of the World

CHRISTOPHER JAMES BLYTHE

The Church of Jesus Christ of Latter-day Saints is a millenarian faith. The very name of the church positions it within the end times—the latter days. Unlike some mainstream Christian eschatologies, which can be vague and on the periphery of everyday belief and practice, Latter-day Saints emphasize their faith's role in preparing the world for the Second Coming. The central place of global missionary work is in response to a belief that "this gospel shall be preached unto every nation, and kindred, and tongue, and people."[1] The performance of temple ordinances is likewise in fulfillment of scriptural passages about a last-days temple and the coming of "Elijah the prophet before the coming of the great and dreadful day of the Lord . . . [to] turn the heart of the fathers to the children and the children to the fathers."[2] Latter-day Saints tend to think of events involving the establishment of the United States, the establishment of their own church, events involving missionary work, and global war as apocalyptic. For two hundred years, Latter-day Saints have expected the return of Christ to occur if not in their own lifetimes, then in those of their children or grandchildren, but the signs of its coming have been unfolding for the entirety of that time and before.[3]

Thus, it won't come as a surprise that the Three Nephites are apocalyptic figures. According to their origin myth, as explained in the Book of Mormon, Christ made them immortal in response to their desire to "live to behold all the doings of the Father unto the children of men, even until all things shall be fulfilled according to the will of the Father, when I shall come in my glory with the powers of Heaven."[4] Until then, the Three Nephites would perform many "great and marvelous works . . . before the great and coming day when all people must surely stand before the judgment-seat of Christ."[5]

There is an important parallel between the Latter-day Saint legend of the Three Nephites and the medieval legend of the Wandering Jew. This latter figure, an Israelite contemporary of Jesus, was said to have persecuted (or at least been impatient with) Christ in connection with his crucifixion. As a result, he was cursed to live until the Second Coming. According to a thirteenth-century account, the wanderer had become a pious man traveling and performing good works, "always looking forward with fear to the coming of Jesus Christ, lest at the last judgment he should find him in anger."[6]

While there are obvious differences between the Wandering Jew, who was cursed with longevity, and the Three Nephites, who were desirous to live to serve until the Second Coming, they both exist in legend cycles in part as reminders of the coming end. They both appear with an assumption that they are paving the way toward Christ's return. As a fictionalized Nephite declares in Michael Allred's *Madman* graphic novel, "I am one of the three. I am Nephite—I wait for the end."[7] Indeed, the Three Nephites are always apocalyptic. Whether they are performing missionary work or hitchhiking to promote food storage, the audience knows where the story eventually will end.

Latter-day Saint apocalypticism begins with an emphasis on the New World. America was the Promised Land much as Palestine had been declared the Promised Land in the Bible. As such, the Book of Mormon presents the future European discovery of the New World among a small series of significant events leading to the establishment of the last-days Zion. The prophet Nephi sees a vision of "a man among the Gentiles, who was separated from the seed of my brethren [then in the New World] by the many waters; and I beheld the spirit of God, that it came down and wrought upon the man; and he went forth upon the many waters, even unto the seed of my brethren, who were in the promised land."[8] Latter-day Saints generally assumed that this figure was Christopher Columbus.[9] They saw confirmation for such an idea in Columbus's own claim to have been divinely led to the New World. Not surprisingly, Latter-day Saint holy figures became entangled in the miracle stories of Columbus's voyage.

On July 4, 1854, LDS apostle Orson Hyde spoke of Moroni, who in life was a Nephite but not one of the Three Nephites, as an angelic messenger who guided Columbus to the New World.[10] According to Hyde, Moroni "was with Columbus and gave him deep impressions, by dreams and by visions, respecting this New World. Trammelled by poverty and by an unpopular cause, yet his persevering and unyielding heart would not allow an obstacle in his way too great for him to overcome; and the angel of God helped him—was with him on the stormy deep, calmed the troubled elements, and guided his frail vessel to the desired haven."[11] Moroni ensured the arrival of Europeans to the Americas, an event that would lead to the reintroduction of Christianity in the Promised Land and ultimately paved the way for the rise of the Latter-day Saint tradition centuries later.

Some Latter-day Saints, like other Americans, read (or misread) Washington Irving's four-volume fictional work, *History of the Life and Voyages of Christopher Columbus* (1828), as an accurate account of Columbus's voyages. As a result, a fascinating passage in which Columbus encounters an unusual indigenous group in Cuba has gained attention:

> Here, a party was sent on shore for wood and water; and they found two living springs in the midst of the grove. While they were employed in cutting wood and filling their water-casks, an archer strayed into the forest with his cross-bow in search of game, but soon returned, flying with great terror, and calling loudly for aid upon his comrades. He declared that he had not proceeded far, when he suddenly espied, through an opening glade, a man in a long white dress, so like a friar of the order of St. Mary of Mercy, that at first sight he took him for the chaplain of the admiral. Two others followed, in white tunics reaching to their knees, and the three were of as fair complexions as Europeans. Behind these appeared many more, to the number of thirty, armed with clubs and lances. They made no signs of hostility, but remained quiet, the man in the long white dress alone advancing to accost him; but he was so alarmed at their number, that he had fled instantly to seek the aid of his companions. The party all hurried to the ships.[12]

In 1909, E. D. Partridge, a professor at Brigham Young University, identified this scene as an account of the Three Nephites in an article in the LDS *Improvement Era*. As Latter-day Saints retold this story over time, the Three Nephites became more than a curious sighting: They came to intervene for the safety of the explorers. This is the case with "The Three Nephites Attempt to Lead Columbus to Water," included in this chapter.

Patriotic Stories from America's Founding

Latter-day Saints have considered the founding of the United States, where the LDS Church would be established, as a key last-days event. As such, Latter-day Saints have an affinity for patriotic miracle stories. One early example can be found in the same July 4, 1854, discourse by Orson Hyde quoted above. Hyde referred to the angel Moroni's role in guiding "the destinies of America." Specifically, Moroni "was in the camp of [George] Washington; and, by an invisible hand, led on our fathers to conquest and victory; and all this to open and prepare the way for the Church and kingdom of God to be established on the western hemisphere, for the redemption of Israel and the salvation of the world."[13] This story of an ancient Nephite aiding in the Revolutionary War does not appear in any collected Three Nephites stories; however, two other stories appear in Wilson's collection.

The first is a Latter-day Saint spin on a narrative first introduced in George Lippard's *Washington and His Generals: or, Legends of the Revolution* under the heading "The Speech of the Unknown." According to that text, when the Continental Congress met to sign the Declaration of Independence, there was a great hesitation at signing the document for fear of reprisals from the British. An unknown figure arose to assuage the group's worries with a rousing speech. The signing began in the wake of this discourse. Lippard notes only that this unknown patriot was "a tall slender man . . . dressed—although it is summer time—in a dark robe."[14] It was a small step for this unknown patriot to become one of the Three Nephites in Latter-day Saint legend as he became in "Three Nephites and the Declaration of Independence," which follows later in this chapter. A second story, "Three Nephites Captured in Painting," confirms this story by identifying the Three Nephites in John Trumbull's famous painting of the signing of the Declaration of Independence.

Georgia Pillar

The state of Georgia is also home to a significant Three Nephites legend with apocalyptic dimensions. This legend cycle involves a large cement pillar in Augusta, Georgia, the remnants of the city's historic marketplace. A local legend states that the pillar was once the subject of a prophecy concerning the town. According to a 1970 newspaper article, "An itinerant preacher, legend says, was refused permission to preach at the market in 1829 and he threw a curse on the market, saying a great wind would destroy it except for the pillar."[15] In 1878 a tornado demolished the marketplace, leaving only the pillar.

As with other legends of mysterious figures, the story of the nameless evangelist begged to be incorporated into Three Nephites lore. Like vanishing hitchhikers or the unknown patriot, this preacher's divine authority and mysterious lack of identity and backstory made him an ideal candidate for being one of the Three Nephites. In at least one item in the collection, the pillar is explicitly prophesied to stand until the Second Coming.

The preacher's anger with the people of Georgia is explained in different ways depending on the account. In this chapter we have included one entry that posits that the Nephite preacher was outraged by the murder of a slave. This likely developed from a local legend that the pillar was a "whipping post" rather than a pillar in the marketplace. Another interpretation is included in the story "Georgia Pillar Marks Site of Persecution." This story is much closer to the standard legend; however, the preacher is substituted in part with a set of Mormon missionaries who are "beat up and . . . ran out of town." It is then that "a man in a suit with long white hair"—implicitly a Nephite—arrives to pronounce judgment on the people of Augusta if they won't repent. This story builds on the memory of Southern persecution against missionaries in the late nineteenth century. Indeed, the American South was the most severe site of violence against Latter-day Saints. Historian Patrick Mason has found 336 such incidents occurring between 1876 and 1900.[16] For Latter-day Saints, it would make complete sense for this angered prophet in Georgia to have had in mind the persecution of his fellow preachers when he pronounced judgments on the community.

While I would not consider stories of the Georgia Pillar as traditionally apocalyptic, they focus on divine judgment. One of the most basic ideas of LDS apocalypticism is that the deeds of the nation would lead to its collapse and that this would occur only after they had been warned of the impeding judgment. Stories associated with the Georgia Pillar have all the essential motifs of Latter-day Saint apocalypticism, even if they only sometimes include reference to the Second Coming.

Native American Encounters with the Three Nephites

One of the key elements of apocalyptic belief laid out in the Book of Mormon is the mass conversion of Native American peoples. It was not unusual for Latter-day Saints to expect that the Three Nephites would play a role in their conversion. For instance, on February 7, 1875, the apostle Orson Pratt preached a sermon in which he declared:

> They should be instruments in his hands in bringing these remnants to the knowledge of the truth. We hear that these messengers have come not in one instance alone, but in many instances. Already we have heard of some fourteen hundred Indians, and I do not know but more, who have been baptized. Ask them why they have come so many hundred miles to find Elders of the Church and they will reply—"Such a person came to us, he spoke in our language, instructed us and told us what to do, and we have come in order to comply with his requirements."[17]

That one or three mysterious visitors appeared to predict the coming of Latter-day Saint missionaries is a prominent legend cycle that has endured for more than 170 years. In February 1855, Ute leader Arapeen wrote to Brigham Young about how he had seen "three personages and there [*sic*] Garments were white as Snow and as Brilliant as the Sun and bye and bye all good People would Appear as they did."[18] Latter-day Saint missionary George Washington Hill reported that the Shoshone chief Ech-up-wy had likewise been visited by "three strange men" with an "Indian complexion," who encouraged him to accept the missionaries' instructions.[19] This theme subsequently became a regular part of missionary folklore.

After the initial report from Arapeen, most of these stories describing the initial interactions between Natives and missionaries are largely told from the perspective of non-Native Latter-day Saints. This is certainly the case in Wilson's collection. A typical scenario includes a missionary explaining Christ's organization of a church in the Americas. When the missionary mentions "twelve apostles" or the Three Nephites, the Native reveals that this is a closely guarded secret among their tribe. Native esotericism is common in Latter-day Saint folklore, particularly the claim that vestiges of Book of Mormon histories are preserved among the private teachings of a particular tribe. Other stories about the Three Nephites appearing to Natives move beyond conversion narratives to include divine warnings or other interactions.

The Three Nephites and the Atom Bomb

Like other American apocalypticists, Latter-day Saints were primed to think of World War I and II in the context of the last days. Different miracle stories have circulated at different times, including the protection of a Latter-day Saint temple during the attack on Pearl Harbor. The single example of these miracle stories involving the Three Nephites is a story recorded in 1990 about one of the Three Nephites leaving the plans for the atomic bomb at a gas station in the Mojave Desert with directions for it to be delivered to a "certain scientist." The account refers to the weapon positively as the "bomb that ended the war." In contrast, in 1946 J. Reuben Clark of the LDS Church's First Presidency, delivered a major sermon at the October 1946 General Conference condemning the attack as the "crowning savagery of the war."[20]

The Three Nephites Defend the Nation of Israel

From the origins of the tradition, Latter-day Saints have believed that Israel would again be established as a Jewish homeland. The Book of Mormon itself prophesies a future when there would be both a New Jerusalem established in the New World and when Jerusalem "after it should be destroyed it should be built up again, a holy city unto the Lord . . . and it should be built unto the house of Israel."[21] In 1841 the apostle Orson Hyde traveled to Jerusalem and dedicated the land "for the gathering together of Judah's scattered remnants according to the predictions of the holy prophets."[22] Latter-day Saints subsequently interpreted the founding of Israel in 1948 as an important event in the last-days chronology.

The story that appears here involves the Israeli military being outgunned and outmanned by their Arab enemies. When all hope seems lost for the Israelis, the Arab military inexplicably surrenders. The captives would later declare that a mysterious man or three appeared to "warn them to surrender or face annihilation." In some accounts, they were shown a "phantom army" ready to fulfill the promise.[23] In these instances the story echoes a vision recorded in 2 Kings 6 when the prophet Elisha's servant fears the size of the Syrian army. Elisha assures him that "they that be with us are more than they that be with them," and then the servant sees a vision of an angelic army—"the mountain full of horses and chariots of fire."[24]

Like the story of the unknown patriot and the Georgia Pillar, the story had its origins outside of the Latter-day Saint tradition before it was incorporated into Three Nephites lore. In this case, the story first appeared in a California-based periodical, *The Jewish Hope*, and then was picked up in an influential Latter-day Saint text, Joseph Fielding Smith's *The Signs of the Times: A Series of Discussions*.[25]

The Wilson collection includes thirty-three accounts of this legend, with the majority dating to the 1960s and 1970s. As Wilson noted, this story "has been applied to most Arab-Israeli conflicts—1948, 1956, 1967, and 1973."[26]

The Worldwide End of the World Stories

The Three Nephites Attempt to Lead Columbus to Water

On the second voyage where Columbus came in there to Florida, he ran out of water and so he sent his men in to get some buckets or some wooden kegs, whatever they carried it in, to hunt for some fresh water. They started right in and maybe hadn't walked for an hour or maybe a half hour and they saw three men coming toward them, all three of them dressed in white robes, each one of them had a staff. And they had white beards and everything was white. Next, following along, were a group of Indians peacefully coming towards them to lead them to where the water was. As soon as they got too close Columbus' men were scared to death and wheeled around on their heels and went right back to the boat. Columbus was put out over it so he stayed there and told his men they would have to go back and get the water somewhere on the land. When they went back they never saw them again.

—J. Bert Sumsion. Springville, Utah. Time the story took place: 1493. *Sumsion "felt that the three men in this story who appeared to the men during one of the voyages of Columbus were the Three Nephites." He acknowledged having read the account in Washington Irving's book.* Collected by James D. Browne in 1969. #0247

Three Nephites and the Declaration of Independence

When Thomas Jefferson had drafted the Declaration of Independence and all the big-whigs were gathered together to consider its content, and vote on whether or not to pass and sign the famous document, there was a lot of debate on whether or not it should be passed. The sides seemed to be split right down the middle, and it looked as if the document might be disregarded as nonsense, and Jefferson might be sent to draft something different, which could have conceivably changed the state of things here in our beloved country. Well, anyway, as they were counting up the vote by a show of hands, what they had feared would happen did: the vote was split right down the middle, until a solitary hand raised itself in the back of the assembly of notables and big-whigs, that indicated it was in favor of passing the Declaration of Independence. Now, nobody knew who this guy was, but seeing as he was dressed to kill (in those days at least) with powdered wig and all, they counted his vote, and even allowed him to sign the document itself. It turns out that this man just plain disappeared after a while, and his signature was mysteriously missing from the original document on past review, but by the time anyone found that out, we were well into the war, and it didn't really matter by then, so they just let it pass. Now everyone who knows, knows that that person was one of the Three Nephites who was given by God eternal life, so that the future of the world might be vicariously taken care of through the hands of God's chosen.

—Dayle Perkins. St. George, Utah. Time the story took place: 1776. *While Perkins was a local bishop earlier in his life, at the time of this recording he had ceased believing in his faith. This item was reconstructed from the memory of his son, Todd Perkins, who was then a student at Dixie College and had also come to discount his childhood faith.* Collected by Todd Perkins in 1992. #1414

Three Nephites Captured in Painting

As you can see, this is the signing of the Declaration of Independence. Well, see in the back at the doors how there are three guys standing there, apart from everyone else, just watching them sign? See how their clothes look a little different? I heard this story from my stake president. During the signing of the declaration the founding fathers realized that they were basically signing a death sentence, and they started to have second doubts. They knew they were probably gonna get destroyed by the British, and this was basically an executioner's list. But as they were about to give up, three men walked in through [the] doors. They addressed everyone powerfully and said, "Men, you must not quit, you have to go through with this. The future of the whole world depends upon this. The future of God's kingdom rests upon this. If you sign this paper it will be a victory for America and a victory for God! We will not let you fail, we will block these doors until you all sign." After that they all got super pumped and could tell that these were not ordinary men, but sent by God, and you know how history goes after that. So, the Three Nephites helped save America before it even began.[27]

—Dirk Wilkins, 21. Missionary from Utah. Time the story took place: 1776. Collected by Thomas Goodwin in 2018. #1664

Three Nephites and the American Flag

Here is a story that was told to me the other day by my dressmaker, Mary Miekle, who lives in the Kimball Apartments. She says a Dr. Horne's wife is telling this story, and I understand that she copied it from a book in the Library of Congress in Washington, DC. The book is *The Mysteries of Our Flag*. The character is described only as "the Professor." He was the key man in bringing together the colonies and giving them the idea of liberty and the making of the flag. He gave them the idea of the flag. (Betsy Ross only followed his directions; she was merely the instrument in making the flag.) The running story of these conferences is that a man with long white hair known to the conferences as "the Professor" was present at the meetings. Each of the thirteen colonies was supposed to send to the convention a representative to contribute an idea for the flag. As each presented his ideas, the Professor would criticize them and point out why they were not just right. Some were too much like the old country from which the people of the colony came; some were too French or too German or Norwegian—or whatever they represented. The old country influence was so predominant, he said that the conference should not select any one of them. But from the ideas they brought forth, he found the right idea for the flag. Betsy Ross followed his instructions, but he did the thinking on it. After the flag was made, the conference wanted to give him a banquet because he had been so helpful. During the banquet he partook only of grain and fowl food. And during the banquet he disappeared. The men at the banquet became so curious about him that they went to the place of the lady with whom he stayed. She said she knew very little about him except that he was the finest man she knew. She said that his diet also consisted of food from grain and fowl.

—Mary Miekle. Dressmaker from Provo, Utah. Time the story took place: 1777. Collected by Hector Lee in 1945. #1203

Georgia Pillar Marks Site of Persecution

A few years before my mission, there was a town in Georgia where the missionaries were getting beat up and were eventually ran out of town. A few days later, a man in a suit with long white hair came into town and told the people, "If you don't let the missionaries back into this city, this whole section of town will be destroyed and the only thing left standing will be this pillar and whoever tries to knock it down will be destroyed." They didn't let the missionaries back in, so, just like the man said, that part of town was destroyed and the only thing standing was the pillar. The pillar was called the "pillar of prophecy" from then on.

Later, they rebuilt that part of town. In order to widen the street, the pillar had to be torn down. Because of the prophecy, no one wanted to do it. So they hired a black man for $500 to do it. When the man raised up his sledgehammer, he fell over dead. The people didn't know what to do, so they prayed about it. A man came along and told them that they needed to build a platform, put the pillar on it, and roll it back from the road. The people did this and widened the road. The pillar is still standing today.

—Marion P. Thatcher, 85. Contributor's grandfather from Arizona. *Marion "firmly believes that one of the Three Nephites was involved."* Collected by Mark Thatcher in 1989. #0911

Pillar Marks Slavery Atrocity to Stand until Second Coming

Back in the 1800s a slave owner had a plantation on this spot. One of his slaves had tried to run away. The slave was captured and returned to the plantation. The owner wanted to use this slave as an example to discourage future runaways.

The slave was tied to one of the pillars that made up the front of the mansion. While the slave owner was preparing to whip the runaway a preacher walked up. The preacher said if the owner committed this injustice the plantation would be wrenched from his hands. He said that nothing would be left but the pillar to which the slave was tied. The preacher told the slave owner that the pillar would stand until Christ's Second Coming as a testimony against the slave owner.

The slave owner ignored the preacher. The slave was whipped to death and shortly thereafter the civil war broke out.

The owner lost his plantation, the mansion was burned, and the slaves were emancipated but the pillar still stands today in the middle of the sidewalk in Augusta, Georgia.

—Elder Monty Hewett. Mission district leader in Augusta, Georgia. *While in this telling he does not refer to the preacher as a Nephite, the name he gives the pillar implies as much.* Collected by Melvin Jepson in 1981. #1454

Preacher in Georgia Was One of the Three Nephites

A few weeks later I was talking to a Mormon family about the pillar. They told me that a patriarch in the LDS Church from South Carolina told them that the preacher was one of the Three Nephites.

—Elder Monty Hewett. Mission district leader in Augusta, Georgia. Collected by Melvin Jepson in 1981. #1455[28]

Three Nephites Prepare the Utes to Meet with George Washington Hill

My Great, Great Grandfather, George Washington Hill, came out west with the Pioneers about 1850. He and his family settled in Franklin, Idaho. He spent several years on missions to the Indians living in Northern Utah and Southern Idaho, among other things, building Fort Limhi and establishing the town of Washakee [Washakie].

He was very much beloved and trusted by the Indians he visited and taught; and there are many stories about his missionary successes and adventures. One in particular had to do with the intervention of the Three Nephites:

The story goes that he was (as happened very often) visited by a representative of a Ute Indian tribe who told Brother Hill that he and a large part of this tribe (it seems like it was most all of them) wanted to be baptized. Brother Hill told the man that he would first like to teach the people the Gospel, then he would be glad to baptize them. The visiting Indian said that would not be necessary because they had already been taught for the past several weeks by three men.

The "three men" were the Three Nephites; and they had been preparing these Indian people so that Brother Hill could baptize them.

—(FIFE Archive) Steve Marti. Utah State University Student. Estimated time the story took place: late 1850s. Collected by Lin Tsai in 1990. #1366

Secret Tradition of Three Nephites Preserved among Natives

A missionary was serving his mission up in Canada. He and his companion were teaching the chief of a certain Indian tribe.

When they got to the part in the Book of Mormon that talked about Christ's visit to the Americas, they began discussing the twelve apostles that the Lord had chosen among this people. To the surprise of this Elder, the Indian chief already knew the names of the twelve Nephites chosen to be apostles. He also knew that three had been chosen from among these twelve to remain upon the earth and prepare the world for the Second Coming of Christ.

This story had been passed down from chief to chief since the time of Christ's first appearance to the Nephites. When the missionary inquired as to the names of the three who remained, the Indian chief said that he knew their names, but could not reveal them because of an oath that he had made to only tell his son, who would be the next chief.

—Holly L. Allen, 24. BYU student from Portland, Oregon. *Allen heard the story from a seminary teacher and notes, "I do not know whether or not to believe this story; I have heard other variations, and it seems to be told frequently in Seminary and at Firesides."* Collected by Holly L. Allen in 1997. #1596

Chief Tuba Meets with One of the Three Nephites

Well, the story was told to me by my grandfather James Henry Johnson. This happened to his father Benjamin Samuel Johnson in late 1800, about 1860, when he was called by Brigham Young to go down into Northern Arizona and colonize with a bunch of different Saints. And so they went down and established a small settlement two miles north of [the] Hopi Indian Reservation. The chief of this tribe was named Tuba, T-U-B-A. Chief Tuba was a real good man and I believe eventually joined the church as well as many of his people. My great grandfather became familiar and quite a good friend of Chief Tuba and one day he went to visit him. He was sitting outside of his tepee, or perhaps a hogan, I am not sure in this case. At any rate, he was outside sitting down and great grandfather came up to him and sat down with him. He said, "Chief Tuba tell me a story, something that happened to you a long time ago." The chief sat there and he thought awhile and didn't say anything for quite awhile and finally said, "When I was a young man and I had just become chief and I was really troubled because my people had become so wicked and constantly going to wars and stealing . . . and this sort of thing." They weren't peaceful and he was really troubled by it and he kept trying to persuade them to live righteously but they wouldn't listen. And now at this part I don't know if he prayed about it and asked the great spirit to help him or not, but at any rate he was again sitting out in front of his tepee one day and he said a man dressed in a long white robe, an old man, approached him and came up and asked him, "Chief Tuba, why are you so sad?" He proceeded to tell the story about how his tribe wasn't living righteously and then this man proceeded to tell him that he was to teach his people how to plant corn and . . . live as normal, live as, I can't think of the term, but anyway, live as farmers, if you wish instead of constantly being on the warpath and killing and so on and he promised him and he said, "Chief Tuba, if they do this they will have a happy people, if they refuse to, you will see drought and famine and most of your tribe will be destroyed." Then he asked for some food and Chief Tuba went into his tepee or hogan to bring out some food and when he returned the gentleman was gone. And as it so happened Chief Tuba went to his tribe and told them precisely what he had learned and the young warriors of the tribe laughed and refused to obey him. That fall, or that summer, they went on the warpath again and didn't plant any corn or do anything, and then there was a drought and eventually over several years most of his tribe was reduced or destroyed by war or famine. Eventually, they came around and started realizing what Chief Tuba had told them and they stopped warring and started planting corn and their crops, and from that time on they were a happy people.[29]

—John Kenneth Johnson, 27. BYU student from Spanish Fork, Utah. Estimated time the story took place: 1860. *The story's collector noted that "Mr. Johnson believes this story very much because it was passed down through his family and he has no reason to doubt its truthfulness."* Collected by J. Howard Anderson in 1969. #311

A Nephite Brings the Formula for the Atom Bomb

In the early 1940s this guy went into a gas station out in the middle of nowhere and gave the gas attendant a stack of papers with formulas written on them. He then told the attendant to deliver them to a certain scientist at a certain time and place. The gas attendant in the course of the conversation turned around for a minute, and when he turned back, the man had disappeared. The formulas supposedly turned out to be the formulas that made the bomb that ended WWII. The man was thought to be one of the Three Nephites.

—Cindi Hook. BYU student. Time the story took place: early 1940s. *Hook "heard this story when she was 16 from a friend while attending Youth Conference (an LDS Conference for youth 14–18 yrs. old) in Lake Forest, Illinois. The friend told it to a group of girls one night for entertainment."* Collected by Tiffany Andrews in 1990. #908

Nephites Appear on Arab-Israeli Battlefield

I got this story from my cousin who received it in her Book of Mormon class, about an incident over in Israel after the war in 1950 between the Arabs and the Israelis. The Israelis were very weak and they were about to be overcome by the Arabs, who had a tremendous army behind them. They didn't know what to do. And all of a sudden the Arabs turned back and they left. The Israelis were able to keep hold of the city they were fortifying. Later, I think it was the President of Israel, asked the Arabs, "What happened? Why did you turn around and flee?" The Arab General said, "Well, all of a sudden there appeared to us three men in flowing white robes and these multitudes of armies behind them. And they said, 'If you don't turn back you will be destroyed.'" And so they turned back and apparently this was—we can assume that it was the Three Nephites. This happened another time when they were fighting the Arabs in another situation. This story is known all over Israel. . . . It's common knowledge.

—Peggy Wilder, 20. BYU student from Salt Lake City, Utah. Time the story took place: 1950. *Wilder heard this story from a cousin, who had in turn heard it in a "Book of Mormon class" in connection with a conversation about "Israel and modern-day prophecies about it." When asked if Wilder believes this story, she simply responded, "yes."* Collected by Becky Blackwell in 1970. #0474

Nephites Lead Army in Arab-Israeli War

A little over two years ago there was a great battle in the Arab-Israeli war. The Israeli troops were poorly equipped, having very few guns and little ammunition. The Arabs were well equipped and well trained. When the battle began there was little hope for the Israeli army.

As the war progressed the Arabs won position after position. The Israelites fought hard but their numbers were too few. The battle continued until the Israelites had reached their last stronghold, which was an old brick wall outside of the city. When all appeared lost to the Israeli generals, the battlefield became silent, and then all of a sudden the Arab troops turned heel and ran away from the battle.

The Israeli army recovered from their shock and pursued after them. After everything had quieted down the story of what had taken place was told by one of the captured generals.

"As the Arabs were making ready for their last assault on the Israeli position the battlefield became silent. Over the heads of the Israelites was a bright light and then the sound of thousands of men charging. The last thing we saw was the light become three men and the Israeli troops coming after us."

And so the Arab-Israeli war was won by Israel with the help of the Three Nephites as they helped restore the Jews to the land of their inheritance.

—John Seymour, 19. BYU student. *Seymour recalled hearing this story from a classmate in LDS seminary, a program of religious instruction for Latter-day Saint high school students, but his own attitude toward the story is "passive."* Collected in 1968 by John Seymour. #0286

3

Proclaiming-the-Gospel Stories

Three Nephites Serving Missionaries in All the World

JILL TERRY RUDY

Three Nephites proclaiming-the-gospel stories portray ways that those involved in missionary work of the Church of Jesus Christ of Latter-day Saints receive aid from unique beings well prepared to assist them. The stories follow a pattern that usually includes these elements: Someone providing missionary service faces trouble, encounters a stranger who gives exactly what is needed, senses divine care, and receives confirmation of their mission when the helper vanishes without a trace.[1] Happenings in these stories are aimed at helping two groups: people who have not yet joined the church and missionaries. Some Three Nephites actions are aimed at preparing people to be baptized. Most stories, however, focus on interactions between at least one of the Three Nephites and full-time missionaries set apart from their usual pursuits and relationships to share the gospel message. Interactions in the stories between missionaries and the Three Nephites involve service that resolves the missionaries' physical, mental, emotional, and spiritual struggles. This chapter introduction focuses on structural, contextual, and thematic patterns that link these Three Nephites stories with familiar storytelling conventions and historical details associated with missionaries and missionary work.

Once people recognize the pattern of these stories in formal structure and themes, they can become volunteer story researchers, or narratologists, and predict the outcomes.[2] As Arthur W. Frank observes, "People's sense of how plots will probably go reflects and generates their everyday common sense of which actions lead to which consequences, whether in stories or in life."[3] This implies that people not only predict a story's ending but also perceive some life experiences according to preset storytelling schemas.[4] In these stories, being a missionary brings with it the difficulties of finding people to teach and facing the discomforts and dangers of homesickness, rejection, and emotional or physical injury. Receiving aid from a Nephite brings the consequences of enjoying sustenance, protection, and converts. The problems and resolutions indicate the values of the missionary storytellers and their various audiences. Bert Wilson calls this the "value center" of the stories and the groups that share them. He notes that collecting and analyzing stories shows what values may stay constant because stories reflect and adapt to changing social situations and cultural priorities.[5] Proclaiming-the-gospel stories indicate that missionaries value having their message and sacrifice be accepted by others and be pleasing to God.

Stories afford human beings a measure of time travel because stories share actual and fictional happenings (narrated events) during storytelling situations (narrative events). Richard Bauman observes that "part of the special nature of narrative is to be doubly anchored in human events."[6] This double anchor refers to what happens in the *story*, including the plot, dialogue, settings, and characterizations, and to what happens in the *storytelling scene*, wherever and however people gather to relate stories. While the reality of the narrated events in Three Nephites stories often stretches everyday possibility, the resolution makes for satisfying storytelling because after being in some peril, missionaries end up receiving much-needed assistance. Storytelling sessions about how the Three Nephites serve missionaries occur during training meetings, church classes, late-night storytelling sessions, missionaries' letters home to family and friends, podcasts, comic books, folklore classes, and academic books and journals. The stories thus reach other missionaries, future missionaries, missionaries' families, church members, folklorists, and potentially anyone who appreciates a satisfying and intriguing story. The reception of the storytelling also deserves much consideration because all stories depend on performance, a teller taking accountability to an audience for a display of communicative skill.[7] Although scholars Austin Fife and Hector Lee assumed Three Nephites legends would, like the popular concluding motif, simply disappear,[8] Wilson's collection demonstrates the Three Nephites stories' persistent capacity to meet human needs for entertainment and instruction.

As Eric Eliason explains in chapter 1, "Vanishing Hitchhikers," Three Nephites stories have been studied as supernatural religious legends by folklorists because the orientation toward reality in the narrated event occurs in historical time and in recognized geographic locations (not long ago and far away like fairy tales). Legends involve happenings that stretch the possibilities of reality, actions often associated with the Three Nephites when they exhibit extraordinary aura, strength, longevity, and vanishing ability.[9] Legends also are often told as something that happened to someone unknown or tangentially acquainted with the storyteller, the "friend of a friend" (FOAF). However, Three Nephites stories that connect closely with a storyteller's personal experience portray genre conventions that folklorists call "memorates," stories of personal spiritual encounters.

Proclaiming-the-gospel stories include both legends and memorates as well as secondhand stories, where the experience happened to someone close to the narrator. In most situations, belief as reported by the teller to the collector tends to be stronger with close associations, as noted in the contextual information included with the stories. Elliott Oring discusses this continuum of proximity as "distancing," which encompasses "degrees of separation between a narrator and the presumed source of the narrative."[10] For Oring, this involves the narrator's ethos, and "the more unambiguous the source of a narrative, the more believable the narrative is likely to be. Likewise, the closer the connection of a narrator to his or her source, the more credible the account is likely to be."[11] This bears out in many proclaiming-the-gospel stories. However, Tom Mould recognizes in his study of Mormon personal narratives of revelatory experience that the "continuum of attribution and authority is critical," and "secondhand stories allow for more dramatic experiences to be shared without the dictum for humility" on the part of the narrator.[12] Two stories in this chapter that portray more dramatic encounters through this secondhand association include "Stranger Gives a Teaching Referral" and "'I Met One of Them.'" All the Three Nephites stories included in this chapter confirm the worth of the missionaries and those they preach to because the troubles they face are noticed and resolved through divine intervention and personalized service.

Three Nephites stories about proclaiming the gospel take part in the distinctive mission history and methods, or "missiology," of the LDS Church. Leaders and missionaries since the nineteenth century have perceived their mission to preach "truths restored by the Prophet Joseph Smith" and have "functioned under the prophetic and scriptural injunction to take those newly restored truths to the whole world."[13] The church presents itself as an *organizational* restoration of the primitive Christian church, with authorized prophets and apostles, and as a *spiritual* restoration, bringing angels and miracles back to the earth.[14] Missionaries have served and preached with a distinct perspective and purpose of proclaiming a restored gospel that resonates with the Christian call to mission.[15] The LDS Church's commitment to proselytizing underscores a mission's significance for most Christian churches and many individuals.[16]

As documented in the William A. Wilson collection, the oral Three Nephites storytelling tradition portrays detailed situations where these special messengers promote missionary work, from the nineteenth to the twenty-first century. The service rendered by the Three Nephites in proclaiming-the-gospel stories shows miracles uplifting and preserving missionaries and, by extension, supporting the Latter-day Saints' call to conduct missions. Church leaders Dallin H. Oaks and Lance B. Wickman emphasize that this missionary work involves "the spiritual duty to witness of Jesus Christ and his gospel."[17] They note two restraints on this witnessing duty: "profound respect for moral agency" of others to choose their own religious practices and "the law," which may restrict or prohibit proselytizing in various areas.[18] Missionaries cannot force their message on people they meet, and they cannot control the actions of others that unintentionally—or intentionally—cause them harm. The trouble faced in many of the proclaiming-the-gospel stories relates to respecting the agency and choices of others. Stories presented in this chapter portray the Three Nephites as intelligent, courageous beings who use their expansive skills and abilities to teach, support, and uplift other missionaries who seek to bring souls to Christ.

The suspenseful elements of missionary work that require help from the Three Nephites make for fascinating stories, especially because proclaiming the gospel involves nothing less than the salvation of souls and often involves peril and sacrifice. Mission practices since the nineteenth century center on missionaries called and ordained by church authorities to leave their families to preach in an assigned area for periods ranging from around twelve to thirty-six months. With the commission to preach to all the world, geographic areas have ranged from North America and the British Isles to Scandinavia, Europe, and the Pacific Islands and then extended to South America, Asia, Africa, and Russia.[19] Most early missionaries were married men who, following New Testament injunctions, traveled and lived without purse or script, relying on strangers and God to provide physical support.[20] Eventually, the LDS Church developed a system of financial support based on the missionary's own savings and the contributions of family and church members and standardized a daily schedule of study time and going out to find, teach, and serve people willing to listen. Some women accompanied their husbands on early missions, and unmarried women started receiving official mission calls in 1898.[21] Taking literally the charge to go to *all* the world, LDS missiology links local and foreign members in organized mission units, including companionships, and ideally seeks unity and belonging among all peoples. In these labors, missionaries require support in grappling with rejection, living frugally, and overcoming those who would persecute and harm them. This work involves dangerous situations likely unencountered in the missionaries' previous life experience with the aid received from the Three Nephites helping with fears of the unknown, loneliness, failure, and responsibility to be emissaries of Jesus Christ.

As with most stories in this collection, those selected for this chapter portray the Three Nephites in action, using their powers to find, rescue, heal, and succor their peers in the taxing and dangerous ministry of taking the gospel to all nations. In these stories three vital themes emerge: The Three Nephites *prepare* the way for missionary work by going ahead of other missionaries and teaching in isolated areas.[22] They *protect* missionaries by preaching and singing in street meetings, doing work on cars, rescuing missionaries from traffic accidents, performing surgery, and intimidating potential evildoers by their size and aura. They *preserve* missionaries in their physical and emotional struggles by causing gas stations to appear in a desert or delivering necessities from home. In the stories, the Three Nephites' deeds provide service both mundane and miraculous.

Preparing the Way

Finding people who want to learn about the Church of Jesus Christ of Latter-day Saints remains an ongoing difficulty of proclaiming the gospel. The duty to preach the gospel may be accepted, but the gospel message cannot be forced on anyone without violating that very message. Since the nineteenth century, approaching individuals personally, often called "tracting," has been a significant finding approach for missionaries.[23] This one-on-one, unsolicited contact with strangers to share a personal conviction requires courage and tenacity. Such tracting involves approaching people on the street, at their front doors, on public transportation, and in other settings like markets and local businesses, where missionaries may be inspired and expected to initiate a conversation on spirituality and the gospel of Jesus Christ. The process is ripe for recurring rejection, which may involve subtle turndowns, angry verbal refusals, and even physical force. Thus, finding acceptance becomes one of the first and recurring challenges of missionary work, which in proclaiming-the-gospel stories is helped along when one or more of the Three Nephites already prepared the way by making contact, asking questions, or giving detailed doctrinal and church-related instruction. Closer proximity, or narrative distance, between the people who experience the narrated events and those who tell and record them tends to invite more reverence. Often, stories told as something that happened to a FOAF or an unknown person question or mock the reality of unusual events in the story, while stories told in the first person or by a close acquaintance or descendant accept the reality of unusual happenings. Stories of preparing the way portray this receptive range. Narrative distancing relates with the truth value accorded the story and its reception as something wonderful rather than something laughable. In these stories, what matters is finding people prepared to accept the gospel message and being watched over by God's messengers, the Three Nephites.

Protecting

Proclaiming-the-gospel stories show the Three Nephites meeting the missionaries' needs for security in the face of daunting challenges. Wilson writes that "few themes have been more popular in Mormon folklore than that of divine protection of missionaries."[24] This popularity echoes centuries of storytelling traditions. Canonical scripture tells stories of prophets, their families, and other believers who experience verbal abuse, harassment, bullying, beatings, imprisonment, and even martyrdom. Christian story traditions also include "Lives of the Saints" stories told and recorded in the medieval church and other hagiographies of devotees who suffer for the gospel under mundane and miraculous situations. According to the Book of Mormon account, the transformed Three Nephite apostles survived several attempts to harm them in their first extended ministry;[25] they serve as unifying ministers who welcome believers and who have power within themselves from God, as they "did play with the beasts" and "smite the earth with the word of God" to overcome their persecutors.

Contemporary proclaiming-the-gospel stories show the Three Nephites as highly capable of serving and saving other missionaries and no longer needing to be rescued themselves. The Wilson collection includes stories from earlier eras when missionaries need protection during street meetings and face difficulties of preaching to hostile crowds or malevolent people. In terms of storytelling drama, rescue from the dangers of automobiles and accidents make for the more compelling stories in this section even though many LDS missionaries still walk, ride bicycles, or travel by public transportation. I include two variants of one story, "Help When Car Runs Out of Gas," told by the same narrator to two different collectors, in order to show how the "twin laws of folklore," as discussed by Barre Toelken, relate to the adaptability of these stories. The twin laws simply mean that some elements remain the same while others display dynamic change. The version told to a mere acquaintance involves more details than the one told to a friend.

Some protection stories depend on the striking physical appearance of one or more of the Three Nephites. This is a shift from the stories documented by Austin Fife in which the Three Nephites invariably were old men wearing beards. In these more recent protection stories, the messengers appear as incredibly muscular, strong men who intimidate by their size and appearance, whether they hold weapons or not. A small cycle of these stories relates to the protection of the Missionary Training Center, where the protectors are identified as Nephite warriors—not necessarily the Three Nephite apostles—while a larger cycle centers on the protection of female missionaries (once known as "lady" missionaries and now called "sister" missionaries). Wilson attributes these sister missionary–protection stories to increasing numbers of female missionaries in the later twentieth century and the pronounced threat of sexual predation.[26] Just as a general history of LDS missions remains to be written, the experiences of sister missionaries deserve more study for their unique history and contributions.

The Wilson collection has thirty-seven versions of sister missionaries receiving divine protection from attack by a serial rapist/murderer involving all of the Three Nephites. Another thirty-seven stories are told with one or two of the Three Nephites standing guard. Wilson notes that only one story was collected before 1980 and that a similar story was collected by a student at a Methodist college in the 1990s, where the divine assistant was seen as the Holy Comforter, granted to those who wish for Jesus to accompany them.[27] In 2008 Wilson attributes the concern for safety with more women serving missions at the end of the twentieth century. Most versions of this story were collected between 1989 and 1998, a period before the policy change in 2012 that allowed sister missionaries to serve at age nineteen. Because this sister missionary–protection story was not collected more often when even more women were serving missions, future research could explore cultural concerns about assaults against women in the 1990s, after the execution of serial killer Ted Bundy in 1989, and the assurance of protection this story provides.

Because personal experience and news accounts readily confirm instances when missionaries have succumbed to emotional and physical harm, the persistence of Three Nephites protection stories offers a counterbalance offering that sometimes divine intervention happens, and even if not, missionaries are sacrificing their everyday lives back home to share a message of hope through teaching the doctrine of Christ.

Providing

While protection stories remain popular because of their dramatic effects and thematic reassurances, stories of preserving missionaries by providing them with food, clothing, and words of encouragement resonate with a pleasing, if often unexpected, connection between home and the mission field. In these stories usually only one Nephite appears to make a request from home and then delivers the needed item. The missionary and loved one realize later, when together again, that the loaf of bread or pie given at home to the needy stranger provided sustenance for the needy missionary far away. The messenger's ability to travel extreme distances quickly makes these stories as compelling as the coincidence revealed in the end that the items came from the missionary's home. Homesickness and missing out on comforts of familiar food, surroundings, communications, family, and friends affect all missionaries at some point during their months away from their everyday lives. While preparing and protecting stories magnify the significance of the missionary work by assisting or rescuing the missionary, these providing stories amplify God's care for missionaries and their loved ones during their sacrificial offering of time together. Receiving items from home, by way of one or more of the Three Nephites, assuages some loneliness, preserves physical and emotional well-being, and fills needs in an intriguing and simply reassuring way.

On several public occasions, notably in "The Study of Mormon Folklore" and "Teach Me All That I Must Do,"[28] Wilson asks whether the sensational occurrences in the Three Nephites stories overshadow key principles and values of church members. Our study of this collection confirms that most of the sensational story elements simply affirm divine concern and service offered through the Three Nephites and their extraordinary abilities. Rather than detracting from the call to love and serve others, the proclaiming-the-gospel stories show this charge in action, specifically as many of the stories lead people to a better way of life. As described throughout this book, Three Nephites stories may conclude with a coda, a parting statement that draws out a lesson or principle. Note how many of the preparing-the-way stories in this chapter end by mentioning baptism, conversion, and salvation. Many of the protection stories, however, finish by reemphasizing the reality and special feat of guarding and saving the missionaries from harm, even if the helper has vanished and has not been seen again. The providing stories present the Three Nephites as special mediators between home and the mission, offering comfort and service to meet basic needs for food, clothing, and care. Contextual phrases documented by well-trained folklore students offer a narrator's disclaimer or testimony about the veracity of the occurrences. These codas and contextual information offer commentary on, and usually affirmation of, the value of proclaiming the gospel, serving a mission, and saving souls, because the Three Nephites contribute their unique aura and service to this cause.

Three Nephites Missionary Stories

Answered Prayer for True Religion

I worked in Cambridge, Illinois, on my mission. And there was a couple that came out and played the piano for us, out in Cambridge, Ill. She played the piano and he just attended. Their conversion was very spectacular, or at least extraordinary. One evening they went into their living room and knelt down and prayed to know the truth about religion. Which church to join. They prayed very earnestly. When they got off their knees, a knock came at their door, and three fellows called on them. The three fellows told them that they were there to teach them the true gospel of Christ. These three fellows taught them the gospel in six different visits. They then instructed them to go to Rock Island, Ill. They told them to go to the branch in Rock Island, and look up the church. They told them the address of the church, and where to find it. They told them to go to the branch president (they gave the name of the branch pres.) and ask for baptism. So this couple came to church one morning, and asked for baptism. This was the story they told. We had no missionaries in the area, no members had called on them. There were some members scattered, but none close to them. They were baptized and were very stalwart in the church. He was a very humble man. The last time I heard they lived in Rock Island.

—Male. Cambridge, Illinois. *This story documented in 1962 gives a second-hand account where the collector hears the story from the people who experienced the Nephite visitation. This visit provided them gospel instruction and explicit details about finding the LDS church to request baptism.* #34

Swedish Farmhouse Family Prepared

[Robin's] Grandfather was on a mission in Sweden. The work was hard and the people were not very interested in what the missionaries had to tell them. He knocked at a farmhouse and explained who he was and what he was doing. The people asked him in and were glad to see him and his companion. The people said that only about an hour before, there had been three men that came to their door and asked to teach them about the Mormon Church. The people said they were not interested and slammed the door in their faces. Then they decided that their actions had been too abrupt, and they opened the door to apologize, and the three were gone. The land was flat, and there was no woods or brush to obstruct their vision, but they could not see the men anywhere, they had apparently disappeared. Robin's Grandfather was able to convert this family to the church. He feels that the three men were the Three Nephites, and that he was inspired to go to this house at that particular time.

—College freshman, male. *This story was told to the storyteller by his grandfather as a testimony. The grandfather met and taught the people who experienced the Nephites visit. While the storyteller does not believe all Three Nephites stories, he does believe this and many others to be true. An earlier item in the Wilson collection, there is no data about when or where this was documented.* The story happened in 1929. Collected by Elbert Pratt. #379

People Prepared in Kentucky–Tennessee Area

I'm stretching my memory beyond its legitimate bounds, but I do remember as a seminary student someone reading a story of a group in—it seems to me it was in the Kentucky–Tennessee area somewhere. When the missionaries arrived, that is the first missionaries of the church arrived, in this area and began holding meetings, they found some people who said, "Yes, we've heard of the church." In fact, they knew quite a bit about it, and some, in fact, were ready to be baptized; they were really converted to the doctrine. And it turned out that an old man had been proselyting in that area some years before, certainly before any missionaries from the church had been sent into that area. An old man had been proselyting there and had actually converted many people.

—Astronomy professor, male. Bloomington, Indiana. *Johnson heard this story in seminary, a church program of religious study for youth 14–18 years old, in Bear River, Utah, in 1945.* Collected by Bert Wilson for his initial Three Nephites collection submitted to Richard Dorson. #226

"The Man Said You Would Be Here"

Brian strongly believes in spiritual experiences and that we can get help from the other side when we need it. Brian's mission companion at this time was Elder Steve James. He was a good, hard-working missionary, but over a period of about three months, he was often too sick to go out and work. One day Elder James was very discouraged because he couldn't be out working. He had a feeling that he should kneel and say a special prayer that Brian and his temporary companion would be helped in their work. At the same time Brian was praying in his heart that the spirit would help them. As he and his companion were walking down the street Brian got a strong feeling that they should turn up a road and when they got to a certain house the spirit told him that he needed to knock that door. Brian had learned by this time that when the spirit told you to do something, you just did it. Brian knocked on the door which was quickly answered by a boy of about 17 or 18. He introduced himself and his companion and told the boy they were representatives of the Church of Jesus Christ of Latter-day Saints. The young man cut him off and said, "I know, the man said you would be here." Brian asked the boy, "What man?" The boy then described a tall, older gentleman with light skin, light hair, and brown eyes. Brian then asked if the boy knew the man's name or if he had ever seen him before. The boy replied that he did not ask the man's name and had never seen him before. Brian is not completely sure that the man was one of the Three Nephites, but he does know that the boy was very, very ready to receive the gospel, and that he was waiting for the missionaries to visit him that day.

—BYU law student, male. Provo, Utah. *This is retold from her husband's mission experience in Dey Som Peratos, Costa Rica, earlier in the 1980s.* Collected by Brook Boggess for an Introduction to Folklore class in 1989. #909

Stranger Gives a Teaching Referral

Two missionaries were really having a hard time in their area. They were working hard but weren't finding much success. One morning before leaving their apartment they prayed to be led to a family that was prepared for them and were interested in the church. Before they were even done praying they heard a knock at the door. It was an elderly man, who gave them a note card and without saying anything turned and left. The missionary was really quite stunned. He looked down, noticed the card had a name and an address on it, then looked up to ask the man about it, but the man was nowhere in sight. Both missionaries went out and looked around, but couldn't find him anywhere. The missionaries thought they would check the name on the card and ask them who the man was. The address was a few miles out of town and back in some trees so the missionaries had to really look to find it. When they got there the people had no idea who the man was, but after talking to the missionaries for awhile decided that they wanted to hear more about what the missionaries did. The missionaries began teaching them and the family was soon baptized. Neither the missionaries nor the family ever saw the old man again.

—BYU folklore student, male. Provo, Utah. *This story was shared by church members in Denham Springs in 1989, during [Todd] Robison's mission to Louisiana. He explained, "The father of the family told this story. He seemed to really believe that it was one of the Three Nephites who delivered the note."* Told and collected by Todd Robison. #1309

"I Met One of Them!"

I asked Robert to tell me his conversion story. This is what he related to me: He was an 18-year-old young man working at Frye's Electronics in Anaheim, California. The employees at this Frye's are very culturally diverse with people from different backgrounds. On a certain day, a man entered the store and began to go up to each employee and speak to them. He asked each of his féllow employees where they were from, and when he was told, he spoke to them in their language. The man did this about 7 times. Some of the employees spoke back to him and others laughed and snickered. Robert was amazed at the man's knowledge of so many languages. When the man worked his way down to where Robert was working, Robert left his post (he called it the cage) and said to the man, "I sprecken zee Deutsch." This was meant to be a joke. The man then said, "I sprecken zee Deutsche too," and then began to speak perfect German. Robert told him that he was just kidding and he really doesn't speak German. But Robert asked him how he knows all these different languages. The man said, "I know more languages than you know even exist." When Robert pressed for more information, the man said, "Go home and Google the word 'Nephite.' I am one of them." Then the man left the store. Robert returned to his work area and tried to remember the word Nephite but couldn't. He wrote down Nephilon or something like that. He couldn't remember the word. Two years later, the missionaries were teaching him and asked him to turn to 3rd Nephi. When he heard the word Nephi, he remembered the man from the store, and he promptly told the missionaries, "Nephite. I know that. I met one of them!" I can't imagine the shock the missionaries felt.

—Attorney, male. Anaheim, California. *Eric Eliason received this story in an email from Dale R. Atherton, who heard it from the man who experienced meeting a Nephite. Atherton and another church member were visiting the man's family, recent converts to the church. Atherton presents himself as a skeptic of faith-promoting stories, but he writes to Eliason, "I want to pass this by someone who has experience in Mormon folklore. I googled it and saw your name and figured you'd be the perfect person to give me an honest evaluation here. I don't want to spread false stories." Eliason responded, "You have sent me probably the most straightforwardly believable one that I've heard. And hearing a story like this so close to the people to whom it happened is unusual."* Collected by Eric Eliason. #1503

A Gift and a Mystery

I was working out in the oil fields in the middle of nowhere Texas. The only thing you could see for miles was the site I had been assigned to. Everything else was flat for miles. One day while I was eating my lunch, two young men in white shirts and ties came up to me. One of them handed me a book. He said that if I'd read the book, it would change my life. The other did not speak. Now this was strange for many reasons. We were out in the middle of nowhere, first off. Also, I couldn't tell how they'd gotten here. There was no car or anything. Nevertheless, I accepted the book and started to read. I heard the lunch bell ring, indicating I had to get back to work. When I looked back to thank the two young men for the book, they were gone. Now I remind you, you could see for miles without anything getting in the way, and I only looked up for a minute, but the two young men were gone. The next time I saw young men in white shirts and ties offering me a book that would change my life, I knew exactly who they were because I'd already read the book a couple of times.

—Folklore student and software trainer, male. Provo, Utah. 2016. *For an introductory folklore class, Stirling Miller documented this story that he heard at a dinner provided by an unnamed church member on his mission in Austin, Texas. This was the conversion story of the member who experienced the visitation and joined the LDS church.*

The collector records that he "typically retells the story when the concept of the 3 Nephites comes up in various conversations, or when he feels spiritually inspired to share it." Collected by Stirling Miller. #1513

Saved by Singing at Street Meeting

Elder Parry and I were very undecided whether to hold a street meeting, as we two had never held one before together and only twice with all four elders present. We had knelt down and had prayer before we left our room, which was our usual practice. We walked to the corner of the street in front of one of the banks where we usually held our street meetings. It was raining and cold. I was not very enthusiastic about holding a meeting, being new in the work. But few persons were on the streets within a radius of many blocks in every direction. I felt that it was perfectly useless to hold a meeting on the street under those conditions. Neither one of us could carry a tune, but we stepped out on the corner and proceeded to sing the song: "Oh My Father."

We were just about through the last verse when I noticed a gentleman to the right of me about ten feet away, at the side of an automobile. He was taking off his cap and gloves. He was of a very small build, about five feet eight inches tall, light complexioned, slightly bald, about fifty years of age, and dressed very neatly but not elaborately. He came over to us and asked, "Do you boys mind if I help you sing?"

From that time on he took complete charge of the meeting and assumed the responsibility. Elder Parry asked him, "Are you a member of the Church?" The stranger replied by saying: "I am acquainted with this work." He then suggested that we sing, "Love at Home," which was recorded in the small booklet that contained the popular Latter-day Saint songs. One of these small booklets was given to him. We all listened to the beautifully clear tenor voice which ran out for blocks in its sweet harmonious strains. At the time we first started to sing, there were only two or three people listening by the side of the bank building, on the sidewalk. When he had finished singing this song, a fair-sized crowd had assembled of some twenty persons, which was the largest that had ever gathered in that town before. He stepped to the curb and gave a five-minute talk to the people assembled on and about their "Love at Home." The crowd gave rapt attention while he was speaking but was less attentive while we spoke to them. After making the very effective remarks, he stated to the crowd, "Now one of the brethren will speak to you," at the same time turning to Elder Parry. Elder Parry then stepped forward and spoke.

While Elder Parry was speaking, the stranger stepped to me and said, "We will sing this song, then you can speak," pointing to the booklet "Glorious Things of Thee are Spoken." I looked at the name of the song and said, "I do not know it." He said, "You should, they play it while they pass the sacrament." He then hummed the tune to me, which I afterwards learned was the same tune that was used originally in singing this song, and not the modern tune used at the present time. While Elder Parry was speaking, several in the crowd were talking which seemed to disturb him. The stranger walked over to them and said something which I did not hear, but they were very attentive after he had spoken to them.

After humming the tune of this song to me, he turned his face towards the west as though he was looking at someone and said, "Hello," at the same time walking no more than fifteen feet in that direction, the crowd being several feet to the north, and all of a sudden he completely vanished from sight. I was watching him closely all the time, observing his actions and taking note of what he said. After the closing remarks, Elder Parry and I walked around the town to see if any individual could be found who coincided with the appearance of this stranger, but no one knew of him before or since. This happened in Medford, Oregon, in 1927.

—Male. Salt Lake City. *This is an early documented item with little contextual information. Although presented as a first-person account, the relationship between the contributor and the collector is not described. The collector mentions [that] the story also was told by President Sloan of Portland, Oregon, in 1938*. Collected by Carole Lee at BYU in 1962. #9

Out of the Crowd

There were two missionaries in a big city. They were teaching on the bad side of town. One day a crowd gathered around them in the street. The crowd began to throw sticks at the missionaries. This crowd was serious. They meant to kill the missionaries. The crowd trapped the missionaries; there was no way they could get away. Suddenly everything froze and a man was standing with the missionaries in the middle of the crowd. He said, "Follow me," and led them through the frozen crowd. Then he told them to go away and not look back. The missionaries walked away, but one elder looked back at the crowd. Right away the crowd moved and began chasing the missionaries. But the elder got away thanks to the Nephite.

—Male. Provo, Utah. *[Debra] Pearson describes the storyteller as a recently returned missionary who served in Brazil. He heard the story in the Missionary Training Center, "told in a group of elders." He "believed the story when he first heard it," but when asked at the time of collecting, "he hesitatingly said yes."* Collected by Debra Pearson for American Folklore class, winter semester 1982. #884

Missionaries Protected from Gang

This missionary and his companion were teaching a family who was really interested in the church and were about to be baptized. The family lived on the other side of a really rough part of town so the missionaries had to walk through the bad neighborhood in order to get to their house. The missionaries had been warned that they should be careful in the neighborhood and to never walk there after dark because so many bad things happen.

But one day the missionaries were at the family's home and the family had a concern about their baptism. So the missionaries stayed a lot longer than they planned to in order to help resolve the family's concerns and answer their questions.

The missionaries finally left, well after dark, and were walking home through the bad neighborhood when they saw a big gang of guys blocking the street ahead of them. Some of them had knives and they all looked very threatening. The missionaries were pretty scared but said nothing. As they got closer, they noticed the gang all started staring very blankly around, acted like they didn't notice the missionaries, and casually moved out of their way. When the missionaries passed, the whole gang ran off down the street.

The next day they went back through the neighborhood to visit this family again. As they were walking, a couple of younger boys came up to them and one said, "You're the guys who were walking through here last night, huh?" When the missionaries said "Yes," another boy asked them where the other guys were, "the ones who looked like they were kind of glowing," he said. The other boy then said, "yeah, the ones with the swords."

—BYU folklore student, male. Provo, Utah. *Todd Robison reports that he heard this story at church while visiting relatives in California when he was "about twelve years old." The speaker shared this story as part of his missionary homecoming talk. The collector reports, "I thought it was a really good story and it made me want to be really good so that I could go on a mission and have experiences like that."* Collected by Todd Robison. #1303

Missionary Bikes Protected from Gang

There were two elders who were tracting a particularly rough neighborhood. Missionaries who worked the area in the past had experienced problems with gangs in the area. The gangs would steal or vandalize their bicycles and basically harass the elders. Knowing of these problems and having seen the gangs, the elders offered a little prayer before leaving their bikes locked in a rack. They asked that the bikes not be tampered with and be able to return home safely. The elders then left their bikes and went about their work. When they returned to the bike rack, standing behind the bikes were three big burly guys. As the missionaries approached the bikes the three vanished into the dark of the night. The bikes had been guarded and were not altered in any way.

—BYU advertising major, male. Provo, Utah. *The storyteller served in the Denver, Colorado, mission in the 1980s and was the collector's roommate. He said, "The story was told throughout his mission as a faith builder." The collector confirmed, "I don't know for sure if this particular incident actually occurred but I do admit that it is inspirational."* Collected by Corey L. Beebe for a BYU introductory folklore class in 1990. #1337

Missionaries Don't Drink Poisoned Milk

There were two missionaries tracting one day. They knocked on the door of one gentleman's home who appeared to be interested and invited them in. The man was very hospitable and asked the two elders to sit down for a moment while he fetched them a glass of milk. The man served the milk and one elder attempted to take a drink. The elder felt some sort of distinct restraining force, like an invisible hand, holding back the glass of milk so that he could not bring it to his lips. The elder was quite alarmed and felt very strongly they should leave. Though they felt awkward, the two missionaries politely excused themselves and left. The man looked perplexed but made no objection. Later that day the missionaries happened to pass the police station and were shocked to see the picture of the same man on a "wanted" poster. The poster claimed that the man was being sought for repeated murders which he had committed by giving people poisoned milk.

—BYU electrical engineering major, male. Provo, Utah. *Collected for introductory folklore class in 1992. Josh Heiner served in the Philippines Tacloban mission and heard this story in the Missionary Training Center in 1990. He records that it was told by "Elder Healy, a dynamic storyteller and favorite instructor of all the missionaries." These stories "strengthened his belief in missionary work and the miraculous occurrences which seemed to accompany it." Notice the "wanted poster" motif that also appears in protecting sister missionary stories.* #1499

Missionaries Saved from Hanging

This is a story that happened to my father's father when he was on his mission in Mexico in about 1916 or so. He and his companion were in an area where there was lots of political strife and anti-American and anti-Mormon feelings.

And one day while they were out tracting they were attacked by a mob who took them back to prison. They got put in jail. And I can't remember what the charges were or anything, but they had a trial and they were convicted. And they were sentenced to be hung. And while they were being led to where they were going to hang, out of nowhere there appeared this, this American-looking man. And he went up to the main leader of these Mexicans, this Mexican group. And my grandpa said that he talked fluent Spanish to him. And talked to him for a bit and convinced him that my grandfather and his companion were innocent. And miraculously they let my grandpa and his companion go, didn't try to oppose him or anything. And as my grandfather and his companion and this man who had come in and negotiated their release . . . were walking down the road, Grandpa turned to thank him and he was instantly gone and my grandpa looked all around and couldn't see him anywhere. And so to this day my grandpa thinks it was one of the Three Nephites and that he came and miraculously saved them.

—BYU history major, male. Provo, Utah. *The storyteller first heard this story from his father at a Sunday dinner where "his father was trying to express the great importance of genealogy and knowing your an-*

cestors." He "believes that the man was one of the Three Nephites and said his grandfather knows it was." Collected by Todd Robison for introductory folklore class in 1992. #1300

Missionaries Saved in Snowstorm

This is a story about two elders in a small branch in northern Minnesota. They were out working one day. And there was a big snowstorm, and they were driving back from an appointment or something. And there was a lot of snow on the ground, and it was snowing really hard out. And their car went off the road and got stuck. And they decided it would probably be in their best interest to get out and walk, because they didn't think anyone would see their car off the side of the road. So, they got out and started walking. And they had been walking for quite a while and they were getting really tired and really cold, and probably . . . They weren't very close to anywhere and they were getting really worried that they were going to . . . to die.

And then, a guy drove up to them and he said, "Hey, do you need a ride?" and they said, "Yes, we do," and they got into the car. They were so tired and cold they just kind of fell asleep in the back seat. They woke up, ya know, when the guy stopped. He drove them up to a gas station so they could call and get a tow truck and find out about, ya know, getting a ride back to their apartment and stuff. As they walked in the store the store manager, he goes, he asked them what they were doing out walking out in a big snowstorm like that, and they said, "Well, we weren't walking. That guy that just drove off, he dropped us off." And he's like, "What are you talking about there hasn't been a car here for at least an hour." And they went outside and there weren't even any tire tracks or anything.

—BYU pre–physical therapy major, female. Provo, Utah. *The storyteller interviewed two sister missionaries for a high school class project, and they told her this story and "several faith promoting stories." She reported that "she really liked the story but wasn't sure if she believed it or not."* Collected by Todd Robison for an introductory folklore class in 1992. #1304

Injured Missionary Pulled from Traffic

Steve, my priest quorum advisor, when I was a priest, told me this story in class once. He said that he and . . . well he went on his mission to Japan, and he and his companion were riding their bikes down the street and I guess it was a really busy street, a lot of traffic. The streets in Japan were really small. So it was real tight. And they were riding their bikes, and he was in the front and his companion was behind him. And they were riding along and all of a sudden he heard screeching of tires and stuff, and he turned around and his companion was . . . he couldn't see his companion. And he knew that his companion wrecked or had been hit by a car or something. And so he turned and came back, and his companion was laying on the sidewalk and his bike was underneath some car and all crunched and stuff. And he took his companion . . . got there and took his companion to the hospital and everything. Later that night, I guess he wasn't hurt very bad, just bruises and stuff, he got released from the hospital and everything. And that night Steve was talking to his companion, and he asked him about the accident. And his companion said that he had just been riding along and had been bumped or something by a car and had wrecked in the street. And he was kind of just laying in the street there next to his bike, and he looked up and saw a car coming and he was too weak or too in shock to move. And he knew he was going to be run over, because the traffic was so bad. About that time, somebody grabbed him and pulled him out of the street and pulled him up on the sidewalk and he, while he was laying there saw the guy but because the sun was shining just right he couldn't really see his face very well. And then his companion, Steve, came and was there and took him to the hospital. And he said that as he got up, as Steve got him up, he looked around to see the man and couldn't see him anywhere. And he never did see the man again.

—University of Wyoming finance student, male. Cody, Wyoming. *The storyteller heard the story eight years before. He said that he "couldn't remember why the story was told at the time but said that he believes that it did happen."* Collected by Todd Robison for BYU introductory folklore class in 1992. #1302

Help When Car Runs Out of Gas #1

This is a story concerning the Three Nephites that happened around Pineridge, South Dakota, in 1967. This event happened one evening during the fall months. We had been out working in the country and we had come in to take some Relief Society sisters to, ah, Relief Society there at the church which was located about a mile out of town, and we had been working that day and hadn't been able to fill up our van with gasoline. As we was driving back to the church to the town we was about three-fourths of a mile out of town, our van ran out of gas. And as it ran out of gas at that moment we had looked in our rear view mirror to see if any cars were coming, besides checking the road ahead of us that we were in hopes that a car might be coming so we could have 'em help us, umm, have 'em push us in to town. And as we looked we noticed that no cars were coming at either direction so we got out of the van and closed the doors and as, just as we stepped out of our van we noticed that there was a car parked directly behind us and the bumper of that car was matched directly to the bumper on our van. As I went back to talk to the person that was in the car, umm, his—as I went back to converse with him he turned his head the other direction so I wasn't able to see his face directly but, the person had a very large build. He wasn't fat in any way. He just had a large constitution, large facial features, he was fairly elderly, and had a deep voice and as I went back to my car he said to get into the van I'd push you into town. And so we hurried and got in the van and he pushed us into town. There, ah, where, ah, the service station was located—and as he had pushed us in and we'd coasted off the road into the service station, I turned around to wave at him and thank him for his help and just as I turned around, just about one or two seconds after we had left contact with the bumper on his car, he was gone. We had a good view of the road in all directions so if he had sped up or slowed down or turned in any direction we would have still been able to see him but, he had completely disappeared. And he had just gone like into nowhere, like he had appeared there when we were needing a push. That's, uh, about all there is to the story. It's quite a peculiar incident and there's not too much more to be said about it.

—BYU student, male. Provo, Utah. *[Robert] Call reports that the storyteller "wouldn't let me use the story unless he was assured that my professor believed in the stories." He told the story on the way to a campus event.* Collected by Robert M. Call at BYU in 1969. #314

Help When Car Runs Out of Gas #2

This incident happened in the fall of 1967 in Pine Ridge, South Dakota. My companion and I were working out in the country for a family all day and one evening, so we had to go into town, the reservation community, to pick up the sisters for Relief Society. We had a Dodge van on our mission in this area so that we could pick up the different members of the church to take them to various meetings because very few of them had any means of transportation. We'd been working all that day, we'd started about six in the morning, and we hadn't come in from the country until about seven, and it was getting kind of late for Relief Society, and our van was getting quite low on gas, so we decided to pick up the sisters and take them up [to] the church then fill up with gas later. We came back, drove around, picked up all the sisters that were going to Relief Society that evening, and drove them up to our chapel, which was about a mile from the town. On the way back from the chapel about a half a mile from town, our van ran out of gas. It was pitch black at this time, the sun had gone down, and as it ran out of gas we drove her over to the side of the road, and we looked around, both in front of us and in back to see if any cars were coming. No cars were coming so we got out of the van and started locking it up. We noticed there was this car parked right behind us. We hadn't seen the lights at all coming back from behind us because it would have been very evident to us because of the glare that would have existed. So, not thinking too much about the incident at the time, we went back and talked to the person in the driver's seat. As we went back to talk to him, it was an older car, I don't know the kind of car or the year, so we went back and talked to him. As I stuck my head through the window, he turned his head sort of the other direction, so I couldn't directly see his face. He wasn't a real old person but he was well aged. He had a big build, he wasn't fat but he was just of a big constitution. As I started to talk to him, he said jump in the van and he would push us up to town to get some gas. Because of our situation we weren't going to argue with him any, so we went up and jumped in the van and he proceeded to push us into town. As we got up to the town, up to this service station that was still open, we had enough speed going and so we waved him off, and you know, that he could just slow off and we could just coast into the service station just by our own momentum. As we waved him off we turned around to thank him and to wave him goodbye. As we did this he wasn't there. We had a clear view of the road both ahead of us and to the rear and both sides, and there wasn't a car going either way or coming either way. So we proceeded to drive in at the time. We didn't really think about the experience because of the present situation until later. As I thought of it I remembered the stories I heard about the Three Nephites and their existence and the things which they have done to further the work of the Lord here upon the earth and I believe that this man that helped us was one of the Three Nephites.

—BYU Animal Science major, male. Provo, Utah. *[Robert] Peters did not know the storyteller previously. The storyteller reports he shared the story "in our church meeting—to emphasize that . . . prayers for those serving on missions are really helpful in that our Father in heaven cares a lot for those who are in his work, and by this experience I hoped to emphasize it." This version has more detail than the one collected by Robert Call (#314).* Collected by Robert F. Peters at BYU, spring 1970. #453

Gas Station Appears in Desert

Out in the middle of some desert in New Mexico, these two lady missionaries were driving from their old mission home to a new one. Apparently, they didn't check their gas before leaving. Half way there they ran out of gas, got out, and started pushing the car. All of a sudden, there was this service station they hadn't seen before. They pushed the car in, filled it up, and left. Upon arriving at the new mission home they had three quarters of a tank left. One of the missionaries asked them how they made the long trip on one quarter a tank of gas. They replied, "Oh, we stopped at a gas station about half way." The new missionary said there are no gas stations between here and there. A month later they traveled the same stretch of road again but saw no service station.

—BYU pre-med student, male. Provo, Utah. *The storyteller heard the story from his uncle who was in the New Mexico mission at the time of this story, around 1950. He "finds it hard for himself to believe this story."* Collected by Larry Meyers in April 1969. #531

Car Off the Road

I was sitting in a stake conference about five years ago and the stake president asked a newly returned missionary sister to speak. And so she stood and told her experience about what happened to her while she was on her mission in Canada. . . . She was with her companion. It was a rainy day and there was a lot of mudslides and everything. And they had to be somewhere and they were driving on a mountain road. There was a lot of mud and so they were kind of in a hurry and while they were driving up there they had somehow slid off the road and were stuck in the mud. And they had to be to, I believe, it was a baptism. And so they went out and tried to push themselves out of the mud and everything and it didn't work and they were just getting all muddy. And so they said a little prayer and the next thing they knew a white car with dark tinted windows and no license plates pulled up behind them. And a man got out wearing all white and he had white hair. And got out and lifted the car out of the mud back onto the road. Without saying a word, got back into his car and drove away. She said that her stake president told her that it was an angel of light or one of the Three Nephites.

—Sears Telecatalog Center supervisor, female. Provo, Utah. *The story was told during a work break. The storyteller "believes this story to be true because she heard it from the person who experienced it." The story was initially shared in Simi Valley, California, earlier in the 1980s.* Collected by Wayne Reading for BYU introductory folklore class in 1989. #932

Missionaries Rescued from Car Accident

This sister missionary said that she and her companion were in a really bad car accident. The car was completely totaled, but neither she nor her companion were seriously hurt. She said that she didn't remember much of what happened at first. She and her companion were kept overnight at the hospital and that night she sort of had a dream or vision or something. She witnessed the entire accident from outside the car. She said she could see that they were being protected during the crash, by what she thought were angels. The angels had their arms around her and her companion shielding them from the crash itself.

After the car stopped she noticed it was on fire and then noticed two men who came up to the car. Each one helped drag one of the sisters out of the car to a safe distance away and stayed with the sisters till someone else arrived. Then she said they were gone. The sister missionary talked later with the people who found them first and they told her that no one was at the scene of the accident when they arrived.

—BYU freshman, female. Provo, Utah. *The storyteller heard the story from two sister missionaries after she accompanied them on a teaching appointment in Minnesota. The sister who had the experience initially told the story to [Todd] Robison's consultant.* Collected by Todd Robison for a BYU introductory folklore class in 1992. #1301

Skillful Surgery after Automobile Accident

Two missionaries had an automobile accident in rural Argentina. One walked away with only a few bruises, but the other had completely lacerated his face on the broken windshield. Anyway, the one left to find somebody to help, and soon a doctor showed up and took the injured missionary to the local hospital. Once the missionary was in stable enough condition to travel, he was rushed to a modern hospital in Texas where he could be worked on by a plastic surgeon. However, when the surgeon removed the bandages from the missionary's face, he found that the doctor in Chile had done just as skillful a job as he would have been able to do. Impressed by such medical skill and amazed that it was to be found in Argentina, the surgeon contacted the rural hospital and asked to speak to the doctor. However, the man wasn't to be found, and, in fact, nobody had even heard of his name. It was assumed that the doctor was actually one of the Three Nephites. . . . The missionary insisted that the history was true, since his friend had been in Argentina at the time. Nobody questioned its veracity.

—BYU senior advertising major, male. Provo, Utah. *Kyle Curtis, the collector, describes a storytelling session "in the hall after class in the Missionary Training Center." The Spanish-speaking missionaries shared stories about Chile and Guatemala, then one shared this story about Argentina. Curtis shares that the missionaries, including himself, "were impressed and reassured at the spiritual power and protection" expressed in this story. Other stories shared later were "regarded as swapped tales, and nobody really believed them."* Collected by Kyle Curtis. #1482

Two Nephite Warriors Guard MTC Companion

One night this missionary decided to sneak out of the MTC [Missionary Training Center] without his companion to go see his girlfriend who was attending BYU. After being with his girlfriend for a few hours, and it being very late at night, he decided he had better go back before someone noticed he was gone.

Since the MTC is locked up at night and has security guards roaming around, he decided to sneak over the back gate. Upon coming to the gate, he noticed there were two Nephite Stripling Warriors in front of each dorm entrance. This gave him an eerie feeling, but he knew he had to get to his room.

Upon coming up to his building he noticed only one warrior guarding the entrance. After building up enough courage, he walked past the warrior and on into the building. When he entered his room, he found the other warrior at the bedside of his companion. Also, after entering the room the warrior left and went back to the entrance of the dorm. The warrior was there to be with the other missionary since the other one had left him alone.

—BYU student, male. Provo, Utah. *This story was submitted to an English 115 writing class. The collector heard the story in a testimony meeting at the MTC, where it was shared as a personal experience of the missionary who snuck out of the MTC. The Nephites are described as warriors and not as the Three Nephite apostles.* #952

Three Nephites Guard MTC Doors

One night, the first councilor to the mission president left the MTC quite late. When he went out the doors, he saw three big men standing as if guarding the doors to the MTC. He ran back in and told the mission president, but the mission president said he already knew about them and told him they were the Three Nephites guarding the MTC because there had been some problems with evil spirits.

—Male. Logan, Utah. *The storyteller served a mission in Japan and was at the MTC in the summer of 1982.* Collected by Jim F. Lundberg for a Utah State University History 423 class. #1401

Sister Protected Walking in a Slum

The story I'm about to tell you was related to me while I was on my mission in California and would have been during the period of 1934 and 1935. One evening, in visiting a home, a lady by the name of Mrs. Caldwell, who was a member of the church, told us this incident. It had happened to her some years before when she herself had been a missionary in one of the eastern states. . . . She said she felt like she was between a three-way squeeze. She hated to leave the companion alone [who was ill] and she had been told that she should not go down in that area without an escort; she knew that if she didn't go that woman [a new convert to the church whose husband worked the night shift] was going to be left alone all night. She couldn't get out of bed, there was two children there, one of them very ill, and she really needed help. . . . So, at the suggestion of her companion they both knelt down; she knelt down by her bed. First her companion prayed and then she prayed, and their prayer was that in some way she would be protected after she had left the train, that in some way as she went the four blocks down in this slum area [she would be protected].

I remember her face that night as she told us so sincerely that, "I have never prayed harder in my life that the Lord would help me, and protect me during those four or five blocks that I had to go in that terrible slum area." She said as the streetcar stopped and she went toward the curb, a gentleman, an older gentleman with a beard, very quietly said: "I've come to take you to Sister so and so's home." She said she had such a funny feeling that she couldn't ask questions. All of a sudden she knew that the Lord was helping her. She said that as they went down the street nobody seemed to bother them, but she said she saw many things that would have terrified her had she been alone. They went down the four blocks, turned up the half a block into the porch, and when they came to [the] porch she turned to him and said, "Thank you." She said they had said very little to one another on the way down. She asked him to whom she owed this gratitude. He just smiled and said, "You will be safe now." And she said, "I turned to open the door and when I turned around he was gone."

Now I was very curious and I said, "Who do you think it was?" And she said, "Don't laugh. I think it was one of the Three Nephites." Then she said, "Girls, just so surely as the Lord hears prayer, he answered our prayer that night. I had to have help, and we told the Lord there was nobody to help me unless he sent aid, and he sent aid."

Now there was nothing dramatic about the way she told the story. It was very simple. There was a reason for her going. She was going because maybe there would have been serious results had she not gotten to the home, because she said she was up most of the night with the little baby and the mother, but she said, "Never have I been more thankful, and never have I ever had anything that gave me a stronger testimony that God lives, that the Book of Mormon was true, because," she said, "the Three Nephites were promised they should stay, as was John the Beloved." And she said, "All my life nothing could make me believe that one of them hadn't helped me out."

—Female. Payson, Utah. *This early item has little contextual detail. However, the storyteller told the collector, "I wouldn't want to be telling it to somebody who would smile at it and laugh . . . because I'm just so sure that the incident did happen to her."* Collected by James D. Brown in 1969. #237

You Will Be Watched Over

My missionary son, Todd, was serving in a very dangerous area of the town he was in. In fact, they wouldn't let him or his companion out of the house at night for fear of what would happen to them. A very special, but scary, thing happened to them. Two sister missionaries . . . came to a small, dirty house. They decided to try this one last house before they went home for the evening. They weren't sure if they should go or not but they decided that they would go. They went up and knocked on the door. After a few minutes a man came up to the door. This man was very dirty. He had a fully grown beard and it looked like he hadn't bathed for weeks. The sister missionaries asked the man if he would like to learn about the Mormon church. He said, "No" very quickly and told the missionaries to hurry and leave, then he slammed the door.

Two male missionaries, [the narrator's son and his companion], had seen the sister missionaries go up to this man's door so they followed the sisters, without the sisters knowing, because they didn't feel good about them going alone. The male missionaries saw the man and were relieved as they saw him slam the door.

A couple of days later the male missionaries were in the post office. They saw the man's picture on a wanted poster and right then and there they knew why they had the bad feeling. This man was the most wanted man in the United States. He was wanted for raping and murdering many,

many women. Immediately the male missionaries called the police. The police went to this man's house and this man was still there. They arrested him. As they were taking him to jail, one police officer asked him why he didn't invite the sister missionaries into his house and rape and kill them. The man replied, "I would have, if it weren't for the three men standing behind them."

—Nurse, female. Bountiful, Utah. *The Three Nephite[s] story of men standing behind, and protecting, sister missionaries from a serial murderer, sometimes including the wanted-poster motif, became popular in the late 1980s. This version is fascinating because the mother reports in a church testimony meeting that her son saw the incident firsthand and reported the rapist/murderer to the police. The mother lives near the collector's parents, and the collector reports, "Being an actress, she loves to talk in front of people. Her first son is on a mission and she is very proud of him and loves to talk about him whenever she gets the chance."* Collected by Marci Larson for an introductory folklore class in 1987. #845

Three Big Men Behind Them

There were two sister missionaries out tracting one day and they were just about to finish for the day. One of the sisters was in tune with the Spirit and the other wasn't. The sister who was not in tune with the Spirit wanted to go to one more house. The sister that was in tune felt that they should head back home. The sister not receptive to the Spirit finally talked the other sister missionary into going to one more door. They walked to the next house and knocked on the door. A man in his 40s answered the door. They gave their approach and he invited them into his house. They spoke with him for awhile and then left. Before they left they gave him a card of how they could be reached. A few weeks later this same man gets charged with the rape and murder of several women. As the police search this man's house they find the card the missionaries had left. The police were surprised that he had not harmed the two sister missionaries. When the police got back to the jail they asked him why he hadn't hurt or killed them. He responded, "There were three big men behind them. I wasn't going to do anything to them."

—BYU sophomore, female. Provo, Utah. *The storyteller heard the story from a roommate when they were "talking about religious stories that they had heard." The roommate believed the story, and the storyteller "felt that it could have been possible. It made her curious as to where the Three Nephites were today."* Collected by Richard Persson for a BYU American folklore class winter semester 1990. #896

Two Guys Dressed in White Behind Them

There was this guy in Brazil who the police had been looking for a long time, and these two sister missionaries knocked on this door [of the house] in which this man lived. They, of course, didn't know that this man was wanted for mass murder, rape, crime. He was a very dangerous man, but for some reason, he let them in and listened to their discussion on the church. He was just totally friendly, just like a normal person. And so, these sisters kept teaching him the discussions but then all of the sudden the police just totally broke in and just attacked the place and hand cuffed this man and were actually quite violent with this man. And the two missionaries were like, "Hey, what is going on?" The police were very protective of the girls and were wondering what the heck they were doing with this guy. Anyway, the police took this man to jail, and he had to talk to this psychologist who would ask him certain questions. And he asked the murderer, "Why didn't you just attack these girls and rape or do something to them since you had the perfect opportunity to do so?" He said, "Well how could I when there were two guys dressed in white standing there behind the girls protecting them?" This story would probably mean more to those who are familiar with the Mormon church. Most likely, the two men protecting the sister missionaries were two of the Three Nephites who were left on the earth by their own will to bring the souls of men unto Christ.

—BYU student, female. Provo, Utah. *The storyteller heard the story from her aunt who served a mission in Brazil. [Michael] Brober and the storyteller had been discussing "mind boggling things" when he heard the story. The collector puts the truth of the story in quotation marks, suggesting sarcasm and that events inside the story are unlikely to have happened.* Collected by Michael Brober for his BYU first-year writing course, taught by Jill Terry (now Rudy), spring term 1989. #1330

Two Gigantic Men Brandishing Swords

There were two sister missionaries out teaching, one dark and stormy night in a shady part of town. As they were going from door to door they came to a house where a man in his mid-forties let them in. Unknown to the sisters, he had been suspected of murder and rape. Fortunately an elderly woman, next-door, saw the missionaries enter the house. Knowing the man's intentions, she phoned the police fearing only that they would arrive too late. When the police arrived they broke in prepared for the worst. Instead of seeing the carnage and gore that was expected, they saw the two sister missionaries standing, unruffled, inside the door.

The killer was crouched in a corner away from the missionaries. The police arrested the man and took him to the station for questioning. The suspect was severely shaken but the police were able to calm him down enough to talk. The police were curious as to why he didn't attempt to harm the sisters. The suspect told the police that before he could do anything two gigantic men dressed in breast plates, helmets and animal skins appeared in front of the sisters brandishing swords. These two giant men didn't allow the killer to touch the girls or even move. Elder Berg [the storyteller] then said that these men must have been Nephite warriors. He also said that they were similar in size and appearance to Mormon and Moroni as depicted by an artist in the Book of Mormon.

—Missionary, male. Independence, Missouri. *[Eric] Lapine heard the story from the storyteller at home in Missouri, where he was serving as a missionary in Lapine's local congregation. They had been sharing spooky stories of mission encounters on a "dark and stormy night." Notice this story version is not identified with a specific location, just a "shady part of town."* Collected by Eric Lapine for his BYU first-year writing course, winter semester 1988. #1331

Stranger Warns Missionaries away from Investigator

Two missionaries met a lady and set up an appointment to teach her for the first time. They didn't talk to her much, they just made the appointment and then left. The next day they were walking to the appointment and on the way an older man stopped them. They had never seen the man before, but he called them by their names, their full names. This shocked the missionaries because he even used their first names which missionaries use very little on their missions. The man talked with them a while and then warned them not to go to the appointment with this lady, made sure they understood the importance of what he said, and then said goodbye to them and left. The missionaries looked at each other a second then looked around the corner to see where the man had gone, but they didn't see him anywhere. Both the missionaries knew that for some reason they really trusted the man and felt a good spirit about him, so they didn't go to the appointment. A few days later they passed by the lady's house and noticed it looked vacant and there was a for sale sign in front of it. They never found out what would have happened if they had gone to their appointment and neither one of them ever saw the man again.

—BYU illustration student, male. Provo, Utah. *The storyteller was soon to be a missionary in Argentina, and he heard the story when a group of friends "were talking about missions and missionary work." He thought that "his friend brought it up to illustrate the idea that missionaries will be helped in their work if they are willing to listen and know when they are being helped." He told the collector that "he thought the man could be one of the Three Nephites and his friend who told the story didn't say one way or the other."* Collected by Todd Robison for BYU introductory folklore class, 1992. #1306

Two Large Men Walking Behind You

Another story of sister missionaries in some mission in Mexico. There was a certain part of their area that they avoided walking by every night, for it was extremely dangerous. One night, however, they were forced to walk that way to avoid getting home late. There were many creepy men on the path, but none of them did anything to them. The next day they walk that path during daylight (safe hours), and a man pulled them aside to ask them about the church and what they shared. He said to them, "Last night, you have no idea what all the guys were thinking to do to you. Horrible things. Then out of nowhere there were suddenly two large men walking behind you, watching over you." Two of the Three Nephites?

—Student/web developer, Missionary Training Center employee, male. Provo, Utah. *[Donald] Ford asked his coworkers "if they had heard any interesting stories involving missionaries" and the consultant later emailed him this story.* Collected by Donald Ford for introductory folklore course, winter 2016. #1506

Australian Missionary Greeted and Sent to Hotel

Grandpa Nash went to Australia on a mission when he was a young man. He left San Francisco in the summer of 1905, and it took him four and a half months to reach his destination. In the city of Sydney, no one was aware that he had arrived, he hadn't been able to contact anyone from the boat. When he had gotten his luggage, a man said to him, "You're Brother Nash, aren't you? Arrangements have been made at (such-and-so) hotel, which has a telegraph so you can call your mission president." He then handed him the address and helped him to load up a dray cart. Grandpa placed his briefcase in the cart and turned to thank the man, but he was gone. Nash was in Australia for three years and never heard from, nor saw, the man again, no one else had ever heard of him before.

—Dentist, male. Laguna Niguel, California. *The collector's father told her this story about his grandfather, Grandpa Nash. He heard the story directly from his grandfather just before his grandfather gave him his patriarchal blessing, a statement of Israelite lineage and a life blessing.* Collected by Janece Hoopes for introductory folklore course, fall semester 1987. #890

Suit to Needy Missionary

A young missionary had left his family in order to fulfill a mission for the Mormon Church. After he had been away from home for a while he needed a suit very badly, but could not afford one. When he was downtown one day, a man whom he had never seen came up to him and told him that he had a suitcase for him from his family. The missionary found a new suit in the suitcase and when he turned to question the stranger, he found that the stranger had disappeared.

The missionary also learned that his family did not send the suitcase to him. The missionary believed the stranger to be one of the Three Nephites.

—Male. Jackson Hole, Wyoming, 1957. *This story has little contextual information and is affiliated with the University of Utah Marriott Library, Manuscript Division, Special Collections.* #1011

Bread Delivered in England

This story was told to a seminary class which I was in during my senior year in high school. The teacher, Brother G. Osmond Dunford told it. He said he heard it a number of years before from a man who he happened to be talking to, but he couldn't remember who it was. The man allegedly read it in a family diary or history of some kind. It took place in about the 1870s in a house northwest of Payson. The teacher didn't say whether he believed it or not, he just simply told it to us.

The story went like this. There was a man called on a mission to England who had a wife and children. He was required to leave them home, and they were having a difficult time getting enough to eat themselves when one night a knock came on the door and a stranger (a man) asked if the lady had any food that she could give to him. She thought to herself of the difficult time she was having just feeding her children in her husband's absence and explained this to the stranger. He seemed pretty determined so she finally gave him a loaf of bread and since it was a wintry night she wrapped the bread in a handkerchief to protect it. She told the stranger good bye and never saw him again.

One day after the husband came home from his mission, he and his wife were going through his missionary bags and papers when a handkerchief fell out. To the surprise of the wife it was the same handkerchief that she had wrapped the loaf of bread in a year or so before for the stranger. She asked her husband about it and he said that one night when he was cold and hungry he wondered where he was going to get a little to eat when a man stopped him on the street and asked him if he would like a loaf of bread. He readily accepted the bread and thanked the man for it.

When the couple thought back to the time when the strange event occurred it was on the same day. They felt that it had been one of the Three Nephites or someone else of similar status because there wouldn't have been time for the man to have traveled to England between the time he got the bread from the missionary's wife and the time he gave it to the missionary. There may have been some more details, but this is the story as well as I can remember it.

—Male. Spanish Fork, Utah. *Sterling Hill heard this story in 1961, but no collection date is given.* #271

The Apple Pie Incident

One day Janice's grandfather—my great grandfather—and his companion were proselyting in a southern town. The townspeople became angry and ran them out of town. After this they walked a long way without any food. Finally they came to a corn field and were so tired and hungry that they fell to the ground. As they rested there my great grandfather noticed a paper bag a little ways off. At first he thought that it might be a trap set by some of the townspeople who hated them. Finally his curiosity got the best of him. He walked over to it, looked inside and found an apple pie. Both he and his companion noticed how delicious the pie was, very different from the apple pies they'd had in the South up till then. In fact, it was just like the pies his mother made back home. He didn't think anything about this incident until he returned home from his mission, when his mother told him about some apple pies that she had made one day. She had put them out on the porch to cool, but when she went back to get them one was missing. Come to find out, this occurred the same day that my grandfather found the apple pie in the cornfield. Commenting on this story my mother said that to this day they are unsure of what really happened. But they say it could have been one of the Three Nephites, or maybe just chance.

—Collector's mother, female. Spanish Fork, Utah. *This story is about John Tanner who served a mission in the southern states.* Collected by Cynthia Nelson, BYU English graduate student. #825

The Loaves of Bread

This woman's husband was on a mission. In those days a lot of men would go on missions and leave their families behind. She was baking bread one day when a stranger came to the door and asked her for something to eat. She said, "I just put the bread in the oven, but if you wait a little bit, I'll give you some." He said no, that she should take the bread out right then. She told him she had just put it in the oven, but he asked her again to take it out immediately. So, she opened the oven and the bread was done. She gave him two loaves, and he left. A few weeks later, she got a letter from her husband. He wrote, "We were walking down the road one day, and we were starving. So we knelt and prayed for food, and this man came up and gave us two loaves of bread. They were warm, and they tasted just like yours."

—Beaver High School English teacher, male. Provo, Utah. *The storyteller is the father of the collector's roommate. He told this story when [he] learned that Mooney was taking a folklore course while he was visiting his daughter. He heard the story from his grandmother, and the incident "supposedly happened to one of his ancestors."* Collected by Catherine Mooney for introductory folklore class, fall semester 1987. #894

The Handkerchief

In the late 1800s Jean's great grandmother's son was sent to serve a mission for the LDS (Mormon) Church in South America. Through letters the family could tell that this son was doing a wonderful job on his mission. Towards the end of the son's mission they did not hear from him as often because he was busy and did not have enough money to send a letter. In the last couple of weeks of his mission the son and his companion were out of money. They went an entire week with no food. They were hungry and prayed that Heavenly Father might send help for them. One day there came a knock at this son and his companion's door. It was an older gentleman. He had a loaf of fresh bread wrapped up in a handkerchief and offered the loaf to them. The young men thanked him and graciously accepted the offer.

Jean tells that the son comes home from his mission. As he and his mother were unpacking his things from his mission they come across this handkerchief that the stranger's loaf of bread was in. The mother was astonished when she saw it and asked the son where he had gotten that handkerchief. The son related the incident of the man coming to their door when he and his companion were hungry and gave them the loaf of fresh bread that was wrapped in the handkerchief. The mother started to cry. This had been her handkerchief. She then told the son that one day a stranger had come to their door and told them that he was hungry and wondered if they had any food to spare. The mother had just finished baking some bread. So she took a loaf and wrapped it in the handkerchief and gave it to him. The mother watched the stranger walk down the road when she decided to go and invite him for dinner. She grabbed a hat to go out in the sun to invite the stranger. But when she got outside there was no one in sight. It was if he had vanished into thin air.

The mother and the son were both amazed. They shared the description of the stranger with one another and realized it was the same man. They humbly came to the conclusion that the stranger had been one of the Three Nephites that are wandering the earth today to serve others in need of help.

—Mother and PTA president, female. Lehi, Utah. The storyteller told this story at a family gathering on a Sunday afternoon. The collector does not describe her relationship to the storyteller but explains that she "had always been impressed by this story and felt that it contributed to her religious beliefs." Collected by Tara C. King for an American folklore class at BYU, winter semester 1990. #899

Package from Boyfriend

Well, Sister Brown told me this. I think it's the only Three Nephites story I heard as a missionary. Some sister in our mission had not received any mail for a long time, especially from her boyfriend. She was really upset, and it was bothering her even while she worked. You know how that goes, and she was a good missionary and everything. But one day, it was like a Saturday or sometime when the mail would not be delivered, a guy came to the door with a package. He wasn't dressed in a uniform or anything like that, just normal clothes, and the package was from her boyfriend. She and her companion decided it was one of the Three Nephites.

—BYU English major, female. Provo, Utah, early 1990s. *[Joi] Gardner records that "one of [the storyteller's] companions shared this story with [her] at a time when she had not received mail for quite some time. The missionary obviously believed the story and shared it as a means of extending hope. [She] accepted the story as the truth, but hardly expected the same thing to happen to her."* Collected by Joi Gardner for her American Folklore class, winter semester 1993. #1312

A Sweater Delivered in Alaska

My uncle Jonas went to an Alaskan mission, like before there were ever missionaries there. He got some special call by the Twelve or something. Anyway, now this gets confusing so I'll go over what happened here in Utah and then what happened up there. But you have to remember, they happened pretty much at the same time, what I mean is that when it happened down here, it also happened up there. Anyway the story goes that his companion had written home and asked his mother for a very thick sweater to keep him warm. The mother started knitting a sweater and it took her like two weeks, I guess it was a real good one.

Anyway, right after she had finished, like right and directly after she finished, there was a knock at the door. Now this was winter time here remember, anyway, there was a nice looking guy at the door but he was without any kind of jacket so the lady invites him in to warm up. He sits and chats while he is warming up, now I can't remember if he asked to be let in or not but anyway, after some time he is ready to leave and is walking to the door and the lady gives him this sweater that she has been working on all this time. The guy thanks her and leaves and the lady is trying to figure out how she can make another for her own son. I guess there was a money problem that I forgot to mention.

So, that is the story down at this end. Now, up in the frozen north, on the very same day, the Elder is tracting in a town he has never been in, knocks on the door, is invited inside to warm up and talk. As he leaves, the guy who let him in, says here, this looks like it is just your size, and throws him a sweater. Well wouldn't you know it, when the Elder got home and started unpacking his stuff, he pulled out this sweater and his mother asked where he got it. He explained what happened and she explained what happened and they both knew, after all that what it had to be. Anyway, one of the Three Nephites is the only explanation I have heard to go along with that story.

—BYU student, male. Provo, Utah. *The storyteller told this story that happened to his "father's older brother's companion."* Collected by Dan Knudson for introductory folklore class in fall semester 1991. #1429

4

Mix-ups, High Jinks, and Jokes

Humorous Three Nephites Stories

JULIE SWALLOW

Where is the line between faith and gullibility? Latter-day Saints navigate living in a secular, rational world while at the same time believing that "with God all things are possible."[1] In 2021 Elder Ronald A. Rasband, a Latter-day Saint apostle, talked about miracles in a worldwide conference address. He unequivocally stated that miraculous events are taking place all the time; noticing them is a matter of perception. He explains:

> Miracles, signs, and wonders abound among followers of Jesus Christ today, in your lives and in mine. . . . Some suggest that miracles are simply coincidences or sheer luck. But the prophet Nephi condemned those who would "put down the power and miracles of God, and preach up unto themselves their own wisdom and their own learning, that they may get gain."[2]

Note that, according to Elder Rasband, supernatural events aren't just frequent; they "abound" in everyday life. He suggests that pride or ingratitude may account for a reluctance to acknowledge the hand of God in the quotidian. Members are actively encouraged to consider divine intervention as a possible explanation for a myriad of daily small events. Was finding your lost keys lucky or inspired? Sitting on a flight next to someone who can make an important business connection for you could be a coincidence, but it could also be a sign that God wants to help you succeed. Not surprisingly, this has led to a series of stories in which members see evidence of the divine . . . mistakenly.

Here is an example told by Julie Lewis Aagard at a family Sunday gathering:

> This guy I know from my home ward is an electrician for the church and is really involved in installing electrical things in the temple. So, one day he's at one of the temples and he was doing some electrical work. In order to do it, he had to lift a panel out of the ceiling and go up into an attic. Then, of course, he had to climb back out of the hole and put the panel back. As he came down and out of the ceiling, one of the female temple workers saw him. And he just put the thing back in and went on his way. So then he's in the temple later on that day or maybe someone else told him about this later, but he heard that there was this wild Three Nephites story going around in the temple that this woman temple worker had seen one of the Three Nephites climb out of the ceiling in the temple. She obviously thought he was one of the Three Nephites because she didn't see him go up.
>
> —Julie Lewis Aagard. Math teacher. *She heard the story in her ward from the man it happened to.* Collected by Anna-Lisa R. Aagard in Orem, Utah. 1992. #1286

Those listening to the story "responded very enthusiastically." Folklorist Elliott Oring would suggest that this group of Latter-day Saints was finding humor in an "appropriate incongruity."[3] Oring, who writes about the reasons why funny stories regarding religious experience arise within groups who take their religious practice very seriously, explains: "Any organization, whatever its goals, must depend upon people who are inept, foolish, or weak—at least some of the time. This is, perhaps, the most fundamental incongruity that conditions religious humor: the irreconcilability of the ideal and the real, the quest for perfection within a material world."[4] Within Bert's Three Nephites collection, thirty-seven of the stories are clearly intended to get a laugh by exposing the potential pitfalls of believing in signs, wonders, and miracles.

The majority of the humorous stories in this collection play with the pattern of the standard Three Nephites story. As discussed in the introduction, Bert explained that Three Nephites stories "almost always have the same narrative structure: someone has a spiritual or physical problem, a stranger appears from nowhere, the stranger solves the problem, the stranger disappears, usually miraculously."[5] These parodies generally involve a case of mistaken identity like the one above, in which an ordinary mortal is thought to be one of the Three Nephites, allowing listeners to laugh at someone who *is* credulous enough to believe so.

Sitting in a conference for LDS educators in 2019, I was surprised and delighted when the presenter, Gerrit Dirkmaat, started with a story about mixed-up identity. His energetic delivery captivated the audience; the story got them laughing and engaged. It was the perfect icebreaker—just what the speaker wanted before he launched into his presentation. But the humor would make sense only to an audience acquainted with Three Nephites stories and their structure. Following is a transcript of the story taken from a video of the lecture, which has been edited for clarity and length:

> I have a story that I tell sometimes to try to demonstrate that you never really know where attacks on your faith are going to come from. . . . When I first was working on the Joseph Smith Papers project, . . . I moved to Utah and we were building a house and our house wasn't done when it was supposed to be. . . . So we lived in this place temporarily. . . . And one Sunday, I went to church and it was Fast Sunday. And I'd love to tell you I was paying rapt attention to everything that was being said but . . . I was changing my quarterback out of my fantasy football lineup. . . . Someone gets up and starts sharing their testimony and immediately I realize this guy's either *not* a member of the church or he's, like, brand new—like "missionaries just toweled him off out of the font" member . . . —because he was using words and phrases that were off. . . . He goes down and he's sitting with a whole group of people roughly the same age, and the next person in their group goes up and he has a whole stack of papers. He gets up and he begins bearing his "testimony."[6] This testimony is essentially a refutation of everything the Latter-day Saints believe, right? "We know there's some people here who think that Joseph Smith could have seen God, but the Bible says, 'No man has seen God at any time.' So if anyone tells you that, they're obviously a liar." And he continues to go down this road. . . .
>
> I went from not caring at all about my sacrament meeting . . . to being really, really, really angry, like, "How dare you come into my sacrament meeting that I clearly care about?" But he just kept going. Now, our bishop was gone; he was out of town. Our first counselor was gone; he was out of town. Our second counselor had just been called to be the second counselor the week before. This is literally his first sacrament meeting. . . . [The second counselor] gets up, whispers to him. Nothing happens. . . . . Then they send the little deacon runner to go find, I think, the stake president. [And the guy at the pulpit] just keeps going: "We know that there are people here who think that someday they become like God but Isaiah said that, that no man could become like God. There's only one God and so anyone who is telling you that, they're a liar." . . . The stake president finally comes in. Hears what's going on. Whispers to the guy, I'm sure, saying, "Hey, this is not appropriate." [The guy] looks at [the stake president], shrugs his shoulders, and keeps right on going. . . .
>
> Finally this guy runs out of material, and it's clear that the plan is they're just going to keep going. . . . And so . . . when this guy finished, before the

other one could get up, I ran up to the pulpit. And I got there, and then I just filibustered the whole rest of [the] meeting. I gave like a 35-minute testimony. . . . I do church history. I was working for the Joseph Smith Papers, and I went through some historical points to refute the things that were being said. And when I finished, I got the sign from the stake president, [who moved me aside] and closed the meeting. . . . I was kind of embarrassed about the whole thing. I went to my Sunday School class and I could hear . . . the voice of the stake president as he was going around these classrooms looking for someone that he thought was named Dirk Moss. Now, I think it's because my last name's Dirkmaat. And he asked the second counselor, "Who *was* that?" "Oh, that's Brother . . . ah . . . Dirk, Dirk Moss." So he thought my first name was Dirk and my last name was Moss. And so he's wandering [through the building] and he's, like, "Is there a Brother Moss in here?" . . . And everyone's, like, "I don't know who you are talking about." . . .

And I could hear him as he eventually comes to the stage and knocks on the door. . . . [He asks] the teacher, "Do you have a Brother Moss in your class?" . . . But then he sees me: "Brother Moss!" And he comes over and he sticks his hand out. "Brother Moss, it's so good to get to talk to you." And now at this point, when someone has called you the wrong name, like, thirty times, you don't want to say, "Well, actually my name is Gerrit." You just let it go, right? And he's, like, "Brother Moss, I just want to thank you for getting up there. How did you know the things you were talking about? I have been a member of the church my whole life and you were telling things about Joseph Smith's life that I've never even heard before." And I was, like, "Oh, just lucky, I guess." . . .

But the funniest part of it is something that I don't even know whether or not it happened. And that is that we immediately thereafter moved out of the ward. I don't even know if we ever actually went back to church there. And so what I want to believe is that that stake president went back and he looked on his records and there was no Dirk Moss: "There has never been a Dirk Moss. Not in my stake. He seemed to know everything there was about Joseph Smith. He was there by himself. No one knew who he was. Then he was gone." So if you ever hear a story coming out of Layton, Utah, like Three Nephites. . . .[7]

When Dirkmaat said "and there was no Dirk Moss," the group erupted in laughter. They understood that he had potentially been mistaken for one of the Three Nephites without Dirkmaat's specific reference to them at the end of his story.

Note how Dirkmaat highlights each of the expected tropes in a Three Nephites story that members of a ward might draw on to conclude that the stranger *may* have been a Nephite: He seemed to know everything there was to know about Joseph Smith. He was there by himself. No one knew who he was. Then he was gone. The element of "disappearance" is important to the story because that is part of what convinces people to believe that the unidentified individual is one of the Three Nephites.

Folklorist Peter Narvaez explains that parodies usually serve one of two functions: humor or self-reflection.[8] In most cases it seems that Three Nephites stories are meant simply to be funny. They are often used in the way Dirkmaat uses his story: a way to show that the speaker is part of the community they are speaking to. However, occasionally the story is told to underscore the peculiar worldview of some members within their Latter-day Saint community, thereby distancing the teller from gratuitous superstition. For example, in the story "Phony Three Nephite Story" in this chapter, a sealer is locked out of the building. Members visiting the temple see him waving at them from above, and, rather than coming to a more obvious conclusion that he is locked out, they decide they have seen a heavenly visitor. In the case of the "Mysterious Rider," neighbors decide that one of the Three Nephites has been passing by their home rather than the obvious explanation: It's just a person riding a horse. When I asked Stacy Nielsen Patton about this family story via text, she wrote, "It's funny when you think about the story in their family . . . how many testimonies that it might have strengthened." She is amused that the experience may have inadvertently bolstered someone's belief in God. Stacy recognizes that the event could also have given birth to a specific genre of Latter-day Saint narrative: the faith-promoting rumor.

Faith-promoting rumors are stories that are shared to either confirm or reinforce the faith of fellow LDS Church members. Folklorist Eric Eliason calls faith-promoting rumors "stories of unknown provenance that some Latter-day Saints are highly suspicious of and some embrace without too much thought." Eliason feels that most members are somewhere in the middle of the extremes. Whether or not they decide to believe "depends on who they hear it from, depends on if they had breakfast that morning. There are lots of factors that influence belief: how well it's told, the authority figure who told it."[9] Because members refer to these stories as "rumors," it allows them to hold out the possibility of belief while at the same time allowing themselves the space to reject the stories as fiction. Eliason tells of a man he knew in his ward in Texas who, upon hearing anything during a church meeting that seemed suspiciously like a faith-promoting rumor, would lean to his wife and say, "Well, maybe one of the Three Nephites told him that." For this couple, who chose to view the world with a relatively high measure of skepticism, the Three Nephites were shorthand for anything false.

The range of responses to faith-promoting rumors is evidenced in a story told at Brigham Young University in 2020. Angelica, a young college student from Philadelphia, was part of a group at a "casual church gathering" who were swapping "crazy stories from church." She joined in by sharing an experience she had in her congregation back home:

> When I was younger, there was a brother that served in our ward. His name was Brother Hope. He was the nicest, nicest brother and he would always serve those around him. And he would teach us how to play piano and he was really, really nice to all the young women and young men in our ward. He was something of a celebrity in our ward. And one day, one of the young women came up to him, and he was the ward clerk, and she was like, "I think you're one of the Three Nephites. You're just too fantastic and wonderful, it just makes sense." About a week after that we had not seen Brother Hope at all and it's a tale that we believe that Brother Hope is one of the Three Nephites.
>
> —Angelica Santiago, 20. Philadelphia, Pennsylvania. *Told via voice recording while Santiago was serving a mission in Massachusetts.* Collected by Rebecca Haymore in 2020. #1684

In response, the group "laughed in surprise." Laughter wasn't the response Angelica was expecting. She said that for her religious community in Pennsylvania, it was a "tale that we believe." In contrast, Rebecca Haymore, who collected the story from her friend for a folklore class, indicated that those listening to the story "were not sure whether or not to believe her story but agreed that there were some interesting circumstances." Rebecca and her friends treated the story as a faith-promoting rumor, allowing themselves to both find it funny *and* hold out the possibility of its truth.

Mistaken-identity stories derive their humor from the gullibility of other members of their faith community; the teller of the story has the satisfaction of knowing what *really* happened. As Oring explains, "The joke is a kind of *reductio ad absurdum* that tells us when a particular line of thought or behavior goes beyond the pale. A repertoire of jokes delimits the boundaries of a world within which the ordinary, aware, and reasonable person can be expected to think and live."[10] Perhaps, as Narvaez suggests, parody stories are shared among Latter-day Saints to inspire a form of self-reflection about Three Nephites stories generally, encouraging listeners to approach them cautiously rather than wholeheartedly to avoid making a laughable mistake.

Two of the stories included in this chapter can be classified as "true" jokes because they include a punch line. Oring gives an excellent definition of the punch line and its role in jokes:

> The punchline is a device that triggers the perception of an appropriate incongruity. It reveals that what is seemingly incongruous is appropriate, or what is seemingly appropriate is incongruous. In any event, the recognition brought about by the punchline must be *sudden*. The punchline must bring about an abrupt cognitive reorganization in the listener. As such, the punchline is not a necessary element of humor but a literary device that characterizes the particular form of humor we label "joke."[11]

In this chapter, "Chevrolet" and "Damn Nephite" both include punch lines. The stories rely on a basic understanding of the Three Nephites story cycle and their narrative structure. They both adhere to the traditional and "appropriate" formula of a Three Nephites story until something "incongruous" happens. In "Chevrolet" the expected big reveal isn't the name of the Nephite but rather the name of an automobile manufacturer. In "Damn Nephite" listeners might get more of the joke if they are familiar with the incredible farming abilities the Nephite demonstrates on the Whitmer farm. But if not, they can still appreciate the appropriate incongruity of an unfulfilled promise from a religious leader while at the same time relishing the use of a taboo word.

There are a few examples of people using their knowledge of the Three Nephites to trick or abuse Latter-day Saints. I have categorized these as "Nephite as Prank" and "Nephite as Weapon." The prank section includes a few versions of stories about Ithimer Sprague—a man who went to great lengths to convince his fellow community members that Nephites may be visiting their town—in addition to stories in which one church member uses the Three Nephites to mess with another member's mind. In contrast, the stories in the "Nephite as Weapon" section are examples of people outside the faith community using their knowledge of LDS doctrine to hurt Latter-day Saints either emotionally or financially.

Occasionally, strangers are called Nephites in jest. I've labeled these "Honorary Nephites Stories." The tellers know the people aren't Nephites but take pleasure in the similarities between their situation and their understanding of the Three Nephites story formula. Jason Wheeler, whose family camping trip was saved by three men, said of the experience, "We don't necessarily think this is a Three Nephite experience but what is funny about it is that the conversation came up. That this is such a part of our culture that [my wife] Kara jokingly said, 'These three guys are like the Three Nephites. They were there when we needed them and then they just kind of disappeared after that. You know and we didn't see them again'" (#1680). Latter-day Saints are more likely to assume God intervened in their lives through the kindness of other human beings rather than sending supernatural beings to the rescue. But that doesn't stop Latter-day Saints from finding amusement in entertaining other possibilities.

In 1984, in an article titled "The Seriousness of Mormon Humor," Bert urged people not to make any broad conclusions about what members of the Church of Jesus Christ of Latter-day Saints do and don't find funny. He wrote:

> It would be a mistake to assume, then, as folklorists and others often do, that what is true of one Mormon will be true of them all or that most Mormons will respond in similar ways to the telling of Mormon jokes. It is impossible to stereotype Mormons. Each person must be viewed as an individual in some ways separate and distinct from all members of the group.[12]

He did, however, suggest that in looking at what makes LDS Church members "laugh the hardest . . . we may learn in the process to recognize those things most Mormons feel most deeply" because jokes are "a barometer of those concerns engaging the minds of people at any particular moment."[13] Dirkmaat's "Dirk Moss" story is an example of one that many members of the LDS faith might find funny. Humorous Three Nephites stories highlight the challenge of being a believer while navigating a secular world: Leaning too hard on the rational can blind you to the divine, while an unquestioning embrace of the seemingly miraculous can make you a sucker. When faced with the tension between the Sunday discourse of miracles and the realities of modern life, sometimes all you can do is laugh.

Stories

MISTAKEN IDENTITY

Phony Three Nephite

This man went to the Los Angeles temple early in the morning. He performed many marriages for young couples, and had gotten into the habit of stepping out onto a part of the roof for a few moments before the ceremony began to gather his thoughts. This marriage was going to be a rather early one, and he had gotten there particularly early so that he could spend some time alone. No one else was there yet. He walked out onto the roof for a while, but then he noticed that it was starting to get late. He went to open the door, but it was locked. He walked out to the edge of the roof and waved his arms to get someone's attention so that they could let him in. People were now starting to arrive. All that day people were talking about seeing one of the Three Nephites on the roof of the Los Angeles temple.

—Manavee Anderson. Computer programmer. *Heard from her father who knew the man it happened to.* Collected in 1997. #1607

Visitor Mistakenly Thought to Be a Nephite

My father was traveling, and he stopped at the home of some friends. He knocked on the door, but no one was home. The table was all set, so he had something to eat and then left. Later the friend said she knew one of the Nephites had been at her house. He was so clean and neat and had done up his dishes. Father hated to tell her it wasn't a Nephite.

—Mrs. F. Barker. Taylorsville, Utah. *Heard story from her father.* Collected by Cynthia A. Techmeyer in 1973. #1031

Nephites in the Church Meeting

It was the designated "preparation day" for the mission and my companion and I were in our grubby clothes. Late in the afternoon, we remembered that we had a meeting. We were late for the meeting so we didn't have time to change into our suits. We grabbed our bikes and pedaled to the chapel arriving late for the meeting. Because the meeting had already started we quickly entered the back of the room speaking to no one. About halfway through the meeting we discovered that we were in the wrong meeting so we quietly slipped out. The week following, the Bishop—who was presiding over the first meeting—stood up and informed the ward that 2 of the 3 Nephites had visited their meeting. *Paul ended the story remarking that he hadn't realized that he looked like a Nephite.*

—Paul Bird. *Event happened on his mission in Houston, Texas, in 1977. It was told in an Elder's Quorum meeting and was "received with great laughter."* Collected by Kent Stone in 1991. #1323

Grocery-Carrying Nephites

There are some missionaries who are at a service project and they were in a triple companionship at this time. And they were in Salt Lake area so, of course, everyone there is Mormon. As they were driving home, they saw this old lady trying to move her groceries in and for whatever reason they didn't have their name tags on. I can't remember why. They were in normal clothes cause they had just gotten done with a service project. They stop, jump out, and help this lady bring in all her groceries (*some chuckling*) and they go to get in their car and this old lady's so happy that someone helped her and says, "Oh thank you guys! Where are you from?" They had all gotten in the car and their windows were down and they start to back up when one missionary in the backseat leans out and says, "We're the Three Nephites!" (*Lots of laughter*) And they have a good laugh about it. In Utah missions, they cover stakes instead of wards so they get ready to go to their next church meeting that Sunday. They go to the ward they're supposed to [go to] at this fast and testimony meeting and these three missionaries watch as an old lady walks up and starts to [bear] her testimony about how the Three Nephites helped her carry in her groceries. (*Lots of laugher*). So they left the ward early cause they didn't want to run into any trouble. I love that one. I can so see that happening. Only an LDS missionary would be dumb enough to say something like that.

—Josh Camp. Collected by Anna Camp in 2017. #1538

"I'm One of the Three Nephites, I Guess"

Mr. Gammet, when he was in his thirties, was called to be the stake president in Salt Lake, much to his surprise. Feeling extremely unprepared and nervous he traveled to a certain ward house where he was to give his first talk as a stake president.

He arrived at the ward house, greeted the bishopric, and sat down. He didn't know what to make of their inquisitive looks but chalked it up to his newness. As he looked at the program though, he noticed that the ward number did not correspond to the ward to which he had been assigned; in fact, this ward was not even in his stake! By this time the meeting had already started and he couldn't very well just up and leave. Embarrassed beyond belief and not knowing what to do, he took the opportunity during the invocation to quietly slip out a side door. He then found the correct building address and made it (if not a little bit late) to his first talking appointment.

A week or two later, stories started percolating through the stakes that a particular ward had been visited by what many argued was one of the Three Nephites. Apparently, an unidentified man had greeted the bishopric, looked over the congregation, and then disappeared during the invocation. The ward took it as a sign that they were just being checked up on. To this, Mr. Gammet just laughs, "I'm one of the Three Nephites, I guess."

—Darrel Gammet, 54. "*Since it was over the phone I couldn't see his facial expressions, but his voice resonated with a kind of mischievous delight. I got the idea, however, that he didn't often tell this story and chose his contexts carefully. I guess he didn't want to burst anyone's bubble.*" Collected by Keith Johnson in 1997. #1572

Mysterious Rider

The action takes place when my father's family lived near the end of a little road by the fields outside of Murray. Jim was a rough and ready kid. Although he was only sixteen, he worked as a bouncer in his father's bar. Evenings when he didn't have to go to work he'd walk over to my grandparents' place to see my father. He'd usually come over before dusk, I suppose after he got his chores done. One day, he got a new horse, a race horse of some kind. Being the wild young man that he was, Jim would ride it everywhere just as fast as he could possibly make it go, as if he were in the Grand National Steeplechase.

Now Jim had a new way to get over to my grandparents' house. Every evening he'd ride up the road at his usual break-neck speed. My grandparents' house was the last one before the fields, and Jim would hardly slow down to turn into the little land which [led] past their house into the back of the yard where the garage was located. He'd ride right into the garage, and tie up his horse there and then walk into the house to see my father. He usually wouldn't leave until after dark. No one thought anything of it until several days after Jim started doing this. My grandparents' neighbor came over and [was] talking to my grandmother, and she asked her if she had seen anything unusual the past couple of days. My grandmother said no, she hadn't. The neighbor said that the past several evenings just about dusk she had seen "a mysterious rider" come charging up the road in front of their houses on a horse, riding very fast. She would see him turn in and dash down the little land that was between the two houses, and then just disappear. My father, listening to her tell this to his mother, noted to himself that at that time of the evening it would be getting a little difficult to see, and her vision would be additionally obscured by some trees scattered about the little field that lay between their two houses. My father also noted that she probably hadn't seen Jim walk into the house because he had been tying up his horse. It also probably never occurred to her that anyone would put a horse in a garage. She reported that she had become very concerned about this "mysterious rider" that was racing into my father's yard every night, to see who it was and where he went, but the rider always disappeared, "horse and all." He couldn't have gone across the fields because she would have seen him. She had looked both ways up and down the lane, and hadn't seen him. But she had seen and heard him race up the road and down the lane, where he would disappear. She then confidently assured my grandmother that it was one of the Three Nephites.

—Stacy Nielsen submitted two versions of this story in 1985. One as told by her grandmother, Retha Peterson Nielsen (#1397), and this one, with "more details" as she had heard it from her father. The story took place in Murray, Utah, around 1946. #1398

JOKE

Chevrolet

A Mormon driving in his truck through a desolate area in southern California came upon an old man by the side of the road. He stopped and gave the man a lift. The old man asked to be let off at a point just as desolate as the one where he was when he was picked up. When the Mormon dropped him off the old man handed him a large round silver thing, rounded on one side—kind of convex. He told the Mormon to keep the object on a shelf for three years and after three years to look at it and he would find the old man's name written on it. So the Mormon put it on a shelf and just left it there for three years, not thinking much more about it. Then three years later he remembered what the old man had said and went to the shelf to get the round silver thing. As he rubbed the dust off it, sure enough, he found a name: "Chevrolet."

—Gary Flood. High school English teacher. Collected by Lynn Pugmire in Provo, Utah, in 1969. # 393

Damn Nephite

My great-uncle Byran had a farm out in Corin[n]e. One day his bishop called him in and asked Uncle Byran to send his two sons on mission, but he told the bishop that he couldn't run his farm without the help of his sons so he couldn't send them. The bishop promised Uncle Byran that if he would have faith and send his sons on missions, the Lord would send the Three Nephites to help him run his farm. Finally Byran sent his sons. One day as he was coming home he could see that the cows had gotten into the neighbor's field, the horse had gotten into the grain, and just about everything had gone wrong. Byran turned to his wife and said, "It's those damn Nephites; they don't know a thing about farming!"

—Ronald V. Canfield. Applied Statistics professor at Utah State University. The collector writes, "*We most often hear [this story] when my father tells it to LDS friends who are visiting. It is always told for entertainment and gets a good laugh.*" Collected by Canfield's daughter, Lisa Canfield, in Logan, Utah, in 1984. #1400

NEPHITE AS WEAPON

Worthless Wheat

He [Brother George Quincy Cannon] related one such story which occurred in Mesa, Arizona, a town heavily populated by Jews and Mormons. It seems a couple of Jews bought several tons of surplus wheat and then originated and circulated the rumor that the Three Nephites had appeared and given warning of immediate famine. These two merchants as well as other merchants in town were soon cleaned out at huge profits. Even the other Jews in town, noticing the activity of the Mormons, began to get worried and made large purchases of food. Later the entire episode was exposed as a hoax and the Mormons found themselves robbed of their money and nothing to show for it but some moldy, worthless wheat.

—Brother George Quincy Cannon. *Since several of the other missionaries had received letters with similar messages, the group of elders sought George Quincy Cannon, their mission president, for an answer. Brother Cannon knew of many stories purposely perpetrated by Jewish merchants acquainted with Mormon doctrine.* Collected by Sandra Swapp in 1961. #134

"It's About Me"

I remember laying in bed in an old apartment in Novosibirsk, listening to the various stories being told and occasionally adding my own to the conversation. Eventually the conversation turned to missionary "trolls," or people who seemed to derive great enjoyment out of heckling, tricking, or otherwise spiting the missionaries. At one point a story was shared about a missionary companionship (not one that I knew directly, naturally) being approached by a Russian man who claimed to be one of the characters from the Book of Mormon. He came up to the missionaries and said something along the lines of "Hey, that book you've got there—it's about me." The startled missionaries, somewhat dubious, then allowed the man to take a copy of the Book of Mormon they had been holding. He promptly turned to Third Nephi, pointed to a verse about the Three Nephites, and said, "Yep! Here I am!" and then walked away laughing, leaving the confused and disappointed missionaries behind, shivering in the cold.

I think the story really resonated with the Russian/Kazakh–serving missionaries, because it typified the type of treatment they received on a daily basis—the general consensus among missionaries was that if anyone ever approached *you*, it was probably because they wanted to mock you or to take your money.

—Erick Hansen. Collected by Erick Hansen in 2017. #1523

NEPHITE AS PRANK

Ithimer Sprague (Version 1)

One of the most interesting stories we tell here is in connection with the town of Washington. There was one young Danishman by the name of Ithimer Sprague. He was a young fellow in his teens, apparently not very attractive to the young people, and they generally didn't invite him out to their parties. He was under training as a carpenter, and decided there was a way into the society in Washington, and he made a pair of boot soles that he could put on his hands and make back-tracks. When there was a party or a shower, he would manage to be around the building during the evening and put these backward tracks around that were disturbing evidence of visitors, and he always managed the next day to call someone's attention to the fact that giants had been here again, and the entire community got so stirred up about it. Some of them decided they were getting visitations from one of the Three Nephites, so they held a mass meeting and required everyone able to attend the mass meeting, and they said if there wasn't someone there that knew about them they would send a runner to Brigham Young for help, or move in a body to St. George. At the meeting the young lady that Ithimer Sprague had been courting noticed him, that he didn't say anything and sort of laughed when they were talking about the tracks—he'd put his hand up and smile [in] back of it. So after the meeting she went up to him and said, "Ithimer, you may walk home with me tonight." And then on the way home she said, "Aw, now, who was it?"

—Miss Mable Jarvis in St. George, Utah. Collected in 1939. *Incident is said to have taken place in the late 1860s.* #1063

Ithimer Sprague (Version 2)

I just remember a little [about Ithimer Sprague]—about him going up to the cemetery pretending to be one of the Three Nephites, trying to deceive them that way. He used to live up here a couple of blocks.

Ithimer had unusual large feet and they used to make fun of him quite a bit for having those large feet. Finally he got so he'd make a little fun over it for hisself. He made some shoes that was much larger than his feet and put them on and went around town, different places. He'd take as large steps as he could, to raise a little excitement. Thought it was pretty good and continued it.

Finally people began to surmise what it could have been. Some had one idea, some another, some thought it was one of the Three Nephites. He went up around the cemetery and built fires and got gunny sacks, burlap. Afterwards some thought someone had been camping there. He got a stick so he could take larger steps. They had spies out on the road, some this way (pointing), and some out here, different places. It seemed as though they would just miss him. After a long while, before they found out who it was anyhow, he told them—let them know at last who he was.

—Calvin Hall. Collected in Washington, Utah, in 1939. #1082

Nephite or Real Estate Developer?

When I was in India there was a guy who came scoping out land for the church to invest money in and to buy. I was in the mission office at the time and so I got to ride around with him with my companion. He was talking to our mission president about a meeting he had recently been in with the First Presidency. I asked where he was from and he said he didn't really have one place he called home and that he just traveled around for the church. I also asked about what it was like having his job for the church and he mentioned that it was easy to know which area were good to invest in if you watched development in an area long enough. And then I asked about his wife and how she felt about him traveling all the time and he said that she had passed away. I apologized and he said, "It's to be expected. . . . It was a long time ago, I'm one of the three Nephites." But he had a dead serious expression on his face when he said it. Then he chuckled and changed the topic. I know that he was just kidding and more likely than not he is not one of them. But that would be a great job for one of them to have for the church. Watch development of cities and purchase land in up-and-coming area[s] based off how they have seen things grow in the past.

—Carons Dean Mills. Collected by Rebecca Marilyn Lyons in 2017. #1541

The Nephite Test

Whenever I meet a missionary, an unsuspecting missionary, I tell them that I've heard that there's one of the Three Nephites who appears younger than the others, who disguises himself as a fellow missionary. He inserts himself into the mission field and he is that *one* missionary, that one companion that every single missionary gets, the one companion who they just *hate*. This is his holy mission to . . . test the patience of the missionaries to make them stronger for having overcome their irritation with that one companion who they really hated. So I convince them that this one companion who everyone talks about—the one companion they hated—is, in fact, the same companion and he has been everywhere. . . . It's total baloney but it's nice to see the strange looks on their faces.

—Dorie Mae Cameron. Collected by Rebecca Marilyn Lyons in 2017. #1542

HONORARY NEPHITES

Missionaries Find the Nephites

It was really funny. We found and talked to these three guys and they were super spiritual and it was really funny. It was this amazing conversation with these three guys. They were pretty young. They obviously lived out of their car. So we could never find them again. But occasionally we'd see their car around town and be, like, "It's the Three Nephites! We found them!"

—Margueret Betbeze, 22. *Served her mission in Washington State.* Collected by Katie Krumholtz in 2019. #1674

Who Saved Our Camping Trip?

We had taken the kids one Saturday for a short hike up towards Lake Blanche and we'd hiked about maybe a mile of it and the trail didn't seem too bad and all of the kids did well, including Ani. We thought maybe we will come back next week. The next Friday, I got off of work early and we headed up the canyon with all of our gear and Ani fell asleep in the car on our way. And so we got to the parking lot and she woke up incredibly grouchy and not cooperative. We started off not well and we started hiking this hike and we didn't realize how steep it was going to get as we got near the end. And so what ended up happening was Ani refused to walk and so we tried to have her on my shoulders for a little while but with the backpack and everything that was a challenge and we were not making very fast progress. And so I finally said to Kara, "I'm going to walk ahead with [the three older kids] and then I'll drop my bag and run back and pick up Ani." So Kara was walking slowly with Ani. We went about a mile up the trail. I left [the three kids] there and sprinted down the mountain and piggy backed Ani up the next mile. So we did this a couple of times—this kind of leap frogging. And it was a lot slower than we thought it would be. It was getting dark and we needed to set up camp and make dinner. And so as I was coming back down after dropping my bag off one time to meet up with Kara, I come around the corner running on the trail and there are these three men there with their teenage daughters and Ani is on the shoulders of one of these guys. Anyway, they really helped us out because they carried Ani basically the rest of the way up to the campground and we were able to get up there right as the sun was setting and get our camp set up.

Obviously, we don't necessarily think this is a Three Nephite experience but what is funny about it is that the conversation came up. That this is such a part of our culture that Kara jokingly said, "These three guys are like the Three Nephites." They were there when we needed them and then they just kind of disappeared after that.

—Jason Wheeler, 39. Architect. *He says he has told the story several times, just with family. They like to laugh about the nature of the experience.* Collected by Julie Swallow in 2020. # 1680

5

"That Your Joy Might Be Full"

Three Nephites Stories as a Reflection of Latter-day Saint Priorities

JULIE SWALLOW

Although it may not always be obvious, service is foundational to the stories in the previous chapters. A Latter-day Saint listener would understand that the vanishing hitchhiker is serving by reminding those he meets to follow the words of church leaders who have encouraged members not only to prepare for seasons of financial hardship but also to perform missionary and temple work. LDS listeners would also understand that creating democracy, spreading the gospel, and protecting Israel are part of the larger mission of preparing the world for the second coming of Jesus Christ. Missionaries consecrate eighteen months to two years of their lives serving the Lord. Church members would see the encouragement and protection of those missionaries, as well as assistance in the conversion process of the people they meet, as important acts of service.

As discussed in the prologue, Bert was concerned that his vast collection of Three Nephites stories was an academic misrepresentation of the Latter-day Saint religion he was spiritually committed to. He felt stories of supernatural beings helping individual church members may suggest to those outside the religious culture that Latter-day Saints are only interested in "what God can do for them."[1] However, he believed deeply that the Church of Jesus Christ of Latter-day Saints "is primarily an *other*-centered religion whose members are encouraged to sacrifice their own interests to devote themselves to the service of others."[2] In his 2007 address at the Leonard J. Arrington Mormon History Lecture Series, he explained that LDS devotion is manifest in temple, genealogy, and missionary work. It also comes in the form of humanitarian service manifest through donations of time and money to people in need around the world, regardless of their religious affiliation. He asserted that "once one understands that service is a vital and central part of LDS belief, then those dramatic tales of divine intervention take on an entirely different character. They can be seen not simply as accounts of how God has helped individuals with their personal problems but as behavioral models urging individuals to help others as God has helped them."[3] Jill, Eric, Chris, and I believe Bert's collection stands as a monumental tribute to the *other*-centeredness of the LDS faith and its members. And we are not the only scholars to take note of the way in which Three Nephites stories are both a reflection of and a model for practicing members of the faith.

In 2015, Jad Hatem, a Lebanese poet and philosopher, wrote a book titled *Postponing Heaven: The Three Nephites, the Bodhisattva, and the Mahdi*. In it, he analyzed 3 Nephi in the Book of Mormon and compared the three men who asked to remain on earth to other religious figures who consecrated their lives to the service of humanity. For James E. Faulconer, a Latter-day Saint scholar who wrote the foreword to the English translation, Hatem's book was revelatory. It "turned the Book of Mormon account of the Three Nephites from something I paid little attention to into a central metaphor for Christian Life."[4] Hatem's scholarship helped him understand that "whereas Christ died for others, making it possible to return to the Father, the Three Nephites are preserved to bring the rest of humanity to him. Mormonism, therefore, understands Christian life as an imitation of the Three Nephites, even if only implicitly."[5] However, the supernatural elements of the Three Nephites stories may blind both scholars *and* LDS practitioners to their true cultural significance: their role as behavioral models for discipleship. In many of the stories in this chapter, the supernatural aspect is incidental. Simply helping a confused family catch a flight or brushing a hospital patient's hair on Christmas morning are what makes the mysterious stranger an everyday hero. Certainly, there are miracles performed by the Nephites that are beyond human ability (e.g., raising the dead, getting a car with no engine to drive for miles), but anyone can be of assistance to strangers, offer comfort in time of need, or participate in family history. That is the real message of these stories: Disciples of Christ serve.

The service stories are organized into the following categories: *Comforting*—offering emotional or physical comfort during a difficult time; *Rescuing*—saving from harm; *Providing*—bringing needed food or skills at a critical moment; *Healing*—offering relief from physical injury; *Warning*—giving or attempting to give information that might help them in the future; *Protecting*—preventing harm or injury; *Genealogy and Temple Work*—providing assistance with family history work; *Generosity Testing*—seeing if the person is willing to share what they have; and *Traveling Mercies*—offering any of the previous types of assistance to a traveler. Like most Three Nephites stories, many could be placed in several of the categories. Is helping a runaway bride fix a flat tire and eventually find a good husband a traveling mercy or an example of offering comfort? I placed it in the "Comfort" category because the flat tire was incidental to the larger issue—choosing a spouse. Most of the categories are self-evident, but three of these categories require a bit of background knowledge: *Healing*, *Genealogy and Temple Work*, and *Generosity Testing*.

Healing

In the Wilson Three Nephites collection, the Three Nephites heal physical ailments in a variety of ways. They expertly perform medical procedures or do triage, leaving the surgery to doctors. Other times they simply provide medication or tell someone to do something seemingly unconnected (like bury the ax head that injured them) to find relief. They also administer healing blessings using the priesthood.[6] The Church of Jesus Christ of Latter-day Saints' Gospel Topics manual defines the priesthood as follows: "the power and authority that God gives to man to act in all things necessary for the salvation of God's children." Latter-day Saint men who have been ordained to the priesthood frequently provide sick individuals healing blessings, typically upon request.[7] The variety of methods the Nephites use to heal is fascinating; they don't always rely on miraculous healing powers, but the healing is always miraculous.

Genealogy and Temple Work

Members of the Church of Jesus Christ of Latter-day Saints are encouraged to be involved in family history research. They believe that knowing one's family history gives people a stronger sense of self. It can help members be more resilient because they can draw on the strength their ancestors showed in times of trouble as they face their own hardships. Most importantly, it creates a feeling of connection to those who have gone before because members are interested in more than just birth dates and death dates; they try to come to know their ancestors by looking for stories and photographs where possible. Members take the names of deceased family members they find while doing genealogy to the temple and perform ordinances vicariously for them. Because they believe these ordinances are necessary for salvation, members want to give everyone in their family line the opportunity to receive them. Temple ordinances include baptism, confirmation, initiatory and endowment, and marriage sealing. Marriages performed in the temple are believed to create a bond between husband, wife, and children that will last throughout eternity. Members who do genealogy and temple work feel they are doing a sacred service for those who died before being able to perform the ordinances for themselves in this life. Those who are no longer living can choose whether or not they want to accept that service. In a 1994 meeting commemorating the one hundredth anniversary of the Genealogical Society of Utah, Gordon B. Hinckley, then-president of the Church of Jesus Christ of Latter-day Saints, explains ordinances for the dead as follows:[8]

> That which goes on in the House of the Lord, and which must be preceded by research, comes nearer the spirit of the sacrifice of the Lord than any other activity of which I know. Why? Because it is done by those who give freely of time and substance, without any expectation of thanks or reward, to do for others that which they cannot do for themselves and for which they expect no thanks or recompense.[9]

Members engaged in genealogy and temple work are not only trying to save souls; they are also forging an eternal link among family members past and present. After church members perform their own ordinances in the temple during their first visit, every subsequent visit is a loving act of service.

Of the 120 stories we have about genealogy in this collection, 62 percent appear to be direct variants of a story connected to Henry Ballard, an early LDS Church leader who received necessary family information from the miraculous delivery of a newspaper. Story #1220 in the "Doing Genealogy" section of this chapter is very similar to what can be found in the autobiography of Margaret McNeil Ballard, Henry Ballard's wife. She wrote her version of the story in 1917, and this seems to be the first written record of the Three Nephites being specifically named as the mysterious strangers:

> On May 17, 1884 the Logan Temple was dedicated. The second day after the dedication President John Taylor said that all members of the Church who were worthy and who desired to go through the Temple might do so the next day. My husband, being Bishop, was very busy writing out recommends to all who wished to go through the Temple when my daughter came in with a newspaper in her hand and asked for her father. I told her that her father was very busy, but to give the paper to me and I would give it to him. She said, "No, a man gave the paper to me and told me to give it to no one but father." I let the child take the paper to her father and when he took it and looked at it he was greatly surprised for he saw that the paper had

> been printed in Birkshire [*sic*], England, his birthplace, and was only four days from the press. He was so amazed at such an incident that he called Ellen and asked her where the man was who had given her the paper. She said she was playing on the sidewalk with other children when two men came down the street, walking in the middle of the road. One of the men called to her saying, "come here, little girl." She hesitated at first for there were other little girls with her. Then he pointed to her and said, "You." She went and he gave her the paper and told her to give it to her father.
>
> The paper contained about sixty names of dead acquaintances of my husband, giving the dates of birth and death. My husband took the paper to the President of the Temple and asked him what he thought about it. President Merrill said, "Brother Ballard, that was one of the three Nephites or some other person who brought that paper to you for it could come in no other way in so short a time. It is for you to do the work for them."
>
> My husband was baptized for the men and I for the women and all the work was done for them. Again, I felt the Lord was mindful of us and blessed us abundantly.[10]

It is interesting to note that in this version and the one collected by Bert, the Three Nephites are the first possible explanation for this inexplicable event. In the many versions of this story, most keep the important details: Two men deliver a newspaper from a faraway location; it's dated a few days earlier; it contains family history names; the men aren't seen in the town by anyone else. Tellers often don't connect it to the Ballard family. They do, however, frequently include the detail that an outside authoritative figure (such as a church leader) identifies the strangers as Nephites. Other stories that seem to be variants of the Ballard narrative include a newspaper, often from far away, that has needed information, but the narrative itself is quite different from the original. While it is possible that these stories are not connected and that newspapers were a popular means for the Three Nephites to provide people with important genealogy information, the prevalence of this detail suggests that many of these stories have their roots in the Ballard narrative or have at least borrowed details from it. The "Genealogy" section in this chapter also includes stories that are not variants of the Ballard story but highlight divine interest in having genealogy and temple work completed.

Generosity Testing

Generosity testing makes up a small category of stories: 2 percent. Most of the stories are set in the late 1800s through the early 1900s. They echo the biblical account of the Widow of Zarephath, found in 1 Kings 17:10–16. The prophet Elijah asks the widow for food. She and her son have only a handful of grain and a bottle of oil remaining in their home; they are planning to eat what small amount they have and then wait for starvation to take them. Elijah responds: "Fear not; go and do as thou hast said: but make me thereof a little cake first, and bring it unto me, and after make for thee and for thy son. For thus saith the LORD God of Israel, The barrel of meal shall not waste, neither shall the cruse of oil fail."[11] She obeys and is blessed with a perpetually full grain barrel and oil vessel. Some of the stories in this collection mirror the biblical story exactly, while in other versions the reward for generosity comes in the form of advice or making a loaf of bread rise. These stories highlight the biblical injunction "Be not forgetful to entertain strangers; for thereby some have entertained angels unawares."[12]

The Generosity Testing story cycle also has a unique feature for Three Nephites stories: retribution. In a few cases, individuals fail the test and are punished as a result. While there are only six stories in Wilson's collection that fall into this category (and two of those are almost exact replicas), they are fascinating because they are a departure from the overarchingly positive feel of the story collection.[13] They do, however, provide a glimpse into some early church members' understanding of the role of the Three Nephites. For example, in a 1921 vision, Lerona Abigail Wilson said she learned the following:

> The Three Nephites who tarried and John the Revelator are coming among the people. They will appear in the temples, the churches, the homes, and the places of business, even in the secret places, for no one can hide away from them. It will be given to some of the people to know them. In some instances they will make themselves known. They will sometimes appear as beggars, as laborers, and as journeymen. They will put a mark upon the places they visit, not only upon the homes, but upon the fields and possessions of the people—a mark for preservation or destruction. They will find whether men are using their priesthood to the honor and glory of God, or to their own condemnation. Not any of us will escape inspection. They will visit us whether seen or unseen. They will not be seen in all the places they visit. I was shown the condition in which some of the people will be found, in the lowest and most degrading of vices which have crept in among our people—vices that have a hold upon our young people, and are creeping in among our married people. These are talked about and held up among women's clubs in so-called high society. These sins are getting such a hold upon the people that the Lord has to take matters in his own hands or few would be saved.[14]

While this description of the Three Nephites would not resonate with most modern members of the Church of Jesus Christ of Latter-day Saints, it should not be assumed that all the stories modern Latter-day Saints share are positive or kind. In a 1995 article titled "Mormon Folklore—Faith or Folly?" published in *Brigham Young* magazine (whose readers are almost exclusively practicing members of the faith), Bert called attention to the unsavory elements of LDS lore. He was troubled by the many story cycles within Latter-day Saint culture that

> reflect delight in the terrible retributions that befall individuals, both in and out of the Church, who act in sacrilegious ways or who persecute or defame the Church. In a mock ceremony, for example, a man consecrates a bottle of liquor and immediately falls paralyzed to the floor.[15] A minister of another religion will not cease speaking ill of Mormons and dies of throat cancer. Another minister delivers a fiery speech in which he denounces Joseph Smith; after the services he walks out and falls dead on the lawn. In Mexico, a town mistreats the missionaries and is destroyed by an earthquake. And in one story, known in virtually every mission field,[16] missionaries leave their garments at a laundry; the proprietor of the laundry hangs them in the window for public derision; the missionaries, following Biblical injunction, shake dust from their feet and curse the establishment; the laundry burns to the ground, the proprietor inside.[17]

Bert taught that folklore is a cultural mirror. And mirrors, he wrote, "are sometimes unpleasant things. They reveal us as we are, not as we ought to be or pretend to be."[18] Retributive stories typically tap into what some have dubbed "the Mormon Persecution Complex." Members of the faith typically share these stories when they are feeling ostracized or humiliated—for example, after a missionary has spent the day being rejected while proselyting. They are part of LDS lore generally; however, they are not typically part of Three Nephites lore specifically.[19]

Bert's disappointment with his culture's retributive stories was evident throughout "Faith and Folly," and yet he seemed to be finding his way to our thesis about his Three Nephites collection: that the Three Nephites stories model for members what it means to be a disciple. He writes, "We *should* have learned from the Nephite stories that just as these old disciples lovingly serve others in their times of need, so ought we do the same."[20] It's unclear if some of the retributive stories that Bert was lamenting in the 1990s are still in circulation among members today. What is clear is that within our collection of 1,686 stories only 6 contain this element and only 1 of those was told after the year 2000. They are very rare.

The Three Nephites model what disciples of Christ do: comfort, rescue, heal, and protect. Looking at a graph outlining how Nephites spend their

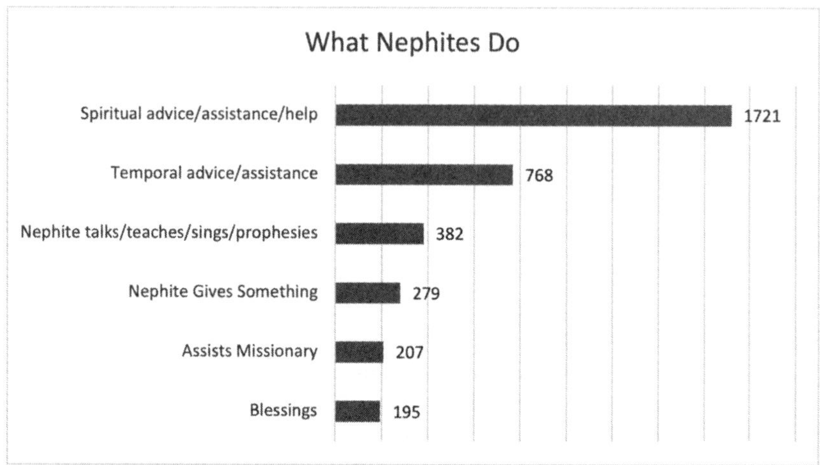

Figure 6. This bar graph illustrates what the Three Nephites did in the stories collected. There are more acts of service (1,721) than there are stories in the collection (1,686). They often rescue *and* heal, protect *and* comfort in one narrative.

time, there are more acts of service than there are stories in the collection. They often rescue *and* heal, protect *and* comfort in one narrative.

Jesus promises the three ancient apostles who chose to remain on earth until his return that they will "have a fulness of joy" "because of the thing which ye have desired of me, for ye have desired that ye might bring the souls of men unto me, while the world shall stand."[21] For Christians, the connection between service and joy is made clear in the Bible when Jesus says: "If ye keep my commandments, ye shall abide in my love; even as I have kept my Father's commandments, and abide in his love. These things have I spoken unto you, that my joy might remain in you, and that your joy might be full. This is my commandment, That ye love one another, as I have loved you."[22] Just as the Three Nephites were promised joy because of their decision to serve others, modern Latter-day Saints heard a similar message from their prophet and apostle Russell M. Nelson in 2016. He taught, "Joy is a gift for the faithful. It is the gift that comes from intentionally trying to live a righteous life, as taught by Jesus Christ."[23]

Bert frequently referred to folklore as "an unfailing mirror of what is most important in a society."[24] However, he worried that "what the nonspecialist sees in that mirror will be what the scholar chooses to collect and study."[25] If nonspecialists look into the mirror of this Three Nephites collection and see that, for members of the Church of Jesus Christ of Latter-day Saints, service is a reflection of their deep devotion to God, they will not be misled.

Mirrors are also used for evaluation. We look in mirrors to make sure the reflection matches the vision we have of ourselves. For Latter-day Saints, the collection can play the evaluative role of mirror. Have we allowed the Three Nephites to serve as behavioral models to follow?[26] Certainly this collection is an accurate reflection of Latter-day Saint priorities, mirroring the many members who dedicate their lives to serving in temples, in communities, in families, and around the world. Church members find joy in religious practice not because they expect divine visitors to ease their path but because they, like the three ancient apostles, have chosen to try to dedicate their lives to God by loving their neighbors.

Stories

COMFORTING

Runaway Bride

My next-door neighbor's mother was going to get married to this man, but she kept having all these doubts. She was actually at the wedding chapel getting ready in her wedding dress. The ceremony was going to begin and she jumped in her fiancé's truck and started driving and she got a flat tire and a man came up and helped her fix her tire and was talking to her a little bit—helped her fix her tire, directed her to some people who could help her out with her problems and kind of told her about the Mormon church. Then he disappeared. She didn't know where he went, and she believes he was one of the Three Nephites. She joined the church, found her true love, and got married in the temple.

—Amber Williams, 20. BYU sophomore from Orem, Utah. Collected by JoLynne Creason in 1999. #1577

A Shoulder to Cry On

My parents, Paula and John, were at the temple and had asked a prayer on their children. Meanwhile, at home, my sister's boyfriend had made unchaste demands of her and when she refused, he decided that he no longer loved her, and stormed off. She was extremely upset and went outside to wander around, alone in the dark wooded area around our home. As strange as it sounds, in this dark, secluded area, a man came to her and asked how she was doing. She wasn't in the least afraid of him and told him she wasn't doing very well at all. He walked with her a while, comforting her, then sent her into the house. She felt very peaceful until her parents came home to help her.

—Paula Hoopes, 53. Mountain Vista, California. Estimated time the story occurred: 1977. Collected by Janece Hoopes in 1987. #0889

Mourn with Those Who Mourn

Your letter dated June 18th came to hand, we were glad to hear from and learn that you were all well and looking forward to our visit on the 24th. We have trusted to our memory for the following particulars of the past events. In the fall of 1863, I worked for Bishop Milles making molasses, my first work in Utah. I got for my pay produce. We lived in the house owned by the Bishop's wife's father. Our furniture consisted of boxes and one raw hide bottom chair loaned to us and our bake bottle. We had two candles given to us by my sister Marvells Milles, the Bishop's wife. At this time our daughter Mary Ann Young West took worse—she had been sick during our journey across the plains with diarrhea. We went to bed early to save candles and fuel, during the night she wanted to get out, we persuaded her to go to sleep again but before going to sleep, she called us all by name and said, goodnight. In the morning, I found her dead in my arms. October 22, 1863, two days afterwards, she was buried in Provo Cemetery, Provo, Utah. Bishop Milles took us to the cemetery in his carriage just ourselves. She was put away without one word of prayer, which we both felt very keenly after we arrived home, towards evening. . . . Mother and I were feeling very sorrowful at our loss, and the way our child was put away, we were thinking over our past lives and trying to call up anything we had done to suffer this loss here with no one to comfort us. While in this frame of mind, a gentleman walked in our room and sat down in the rawhide chair and commenced talking to us. We thought him one to cheer us up, he gave us some word of comfort and said he had come to cheer us up. During his talk, which lasted out two minutes, we felt a different feeling, all our troubles seemed to vanish. He seemed well acquainted with our history, and blessed us in the name of God.

In leaving us I noticed that he walked backwards toward the door. I followed him and looked out in the street to see which way he went, but could not see him. He stood about 6 feet high and very erect, had on a grey suit of homemade cloths, he wore a long beard and very grey. We shall never forget the joy and peace of mind and comfort his words and presence caused us. As soon as I saw the Bishop, I thanked him for his kindness to us but more especially for sending us so good a man to comfort us. Thinking him a teacher I gave him a description of this man. He said, "Brother West we have no teacher in the ward that answers you[r] description." He said that we had been highly favored with a visit of one of the Nephites that was to tarry on the earth till the Savior comes.

—Rachel Humphreys, 23. BYU senior and Missionary Training Center teacher. Provo, Utah. Taken from a letter in her family history dated 1893. Collected in 1996. #1487

Breaking the News

A man and his daughter were flying in a private plane from Washington to Utah when bad weather caused them to crash. Both the husband and daughter were killed. Before news of the crash had reached the man's wife, she received a phone call. There was a man on the phone who told her of the crash and comforted her saying that her husband and daughter had been called on special missions in the spirit world. The man never gave his name, but the woman has always believed him to be one of the Three Nephites.

—Sharon Orton, 22. College senior, Yakima, Washington. Time the story occurred: 1950. *Sharon heard this story from her sister; the woman it happened to. Sharon believes this story to be true.* Collected by Douglass Wright in 1969. #0368

Christmas Miracle

A few years ago, my friend Tylyn was sick over the Christmas holiday. It was super sad, because she had to spend Christmas day in the hospital instead of at home with her eight kids. She was pretty depressed by this and was feeling pretty sorry for herself that day.

On Christmas morning she woke up feeling miserable because she wasn't with her family. She felt tired, sick, and dirty. While she waited for her family to come visit her, she had three nurses come into her room. They asked her if she would like them to wash her hair for her.

These male nurses told her that they visit the patients on Christmas morning and serve them in some way. So, she welcomed their hospitality, and they washed her hair for her, something that Tylyn could not do for herself. After they had brushed her hair for quite some time, the three nurses left her feeling so much better than she did thirty minutes prior.

Less than an hour later, the nurse who had been tender to her since her stay in the hospital came into her room. Tylyn's nurse told her "Merry Christmas," and asked her how she was feeling. Tylyn told her how much she appreciated the nurses that came in and washed her hair and brushed it for her. She explained how she was feeling better since that happened.

The nurse looked at her confused and then said, "Who came in here?" Tylyn responded, "You know, the group that goes around on Christmas morning, washing and brushing everyone's hair." The nurse was very puzzled and explained to Tylyn that she had never heard or seen anything like this happen on Christmas morning. She didn't even know who the nurses were that she was talking about.

Tylyn considers this to be her Christmas miracle. When she told me the story, she told me that she believed these three men were the three Nephites.

—Melissa Pitts, 52. Edmond, Oklahoma, Christmas. Time the event occurred: early 2000s. *Melissa isn't sure if she believes the story.* Collected by Lauren Pitts in 2018. #1671

Berth on a Train

When I was born, my father was overseas on the island of Calidonia [*sic*] as a radar-technician, monitoring flight patterns in the South Pacific. I've never been quite sure if this occurred while my father was in Calidonia, but there was an occasion for my mother to take me as a young child to rendezvous with him. And she had to take some passage of train in coach seats, and I was not at all well and appeared very sickly. And of course, in her dilemma, there was a very kindly and refined looking gentleman who came up to her and inquired of her well-being and mine as a sick child, whereupon he offered her his berth, which was not just a coach seat, but an actual berth where she and I could have comfort—where she could care for me and have warmth and isolation—a more comfortable situation. His manner and the spirit that surrounded him, told her that she was dealing with one of the Three Nephites referred to in the Book of Mormon.

—Jerry Gleyere Frederickson. Mercer Island, Washington. Happened to his mother. She related the story at fiftieth wedding anniversary. *He recalled the following impressions when he heard it at the event: "I thought that very, very interesting and rather wonderful that it came up again, and that it came up with the same simplicity and faith and the same bidding sense of gratitude that I remember being told as a child, this story. And the years had not dimmed her sense of rightness, nor was it even questioned there [at the family reunion where she told it again], and the fact that she told it again for the benefit of not only myself and my siblings, but also our children. The story is very, very much a part of me and I have no reason, nor desire to question it."* Told to his daughter, Whitney Ann Larsen, in Springville, Utah. 1993. #1278

RESCUING

A Cycling Save

During the summer when I was twelve or so, I was riding my bike through a gully. It was a beautiful day and I was riding at a good clip on the dirt trails. I remember passing some scrub oak before I turned to cross what was normally at this time of the year a dry stream bed, except this time it was a raging river. Before I could stop, I was in the middle and began to be swept downstream. I remember grabbing a branch with one hand and my bike with the other. Looking back, I am sure if I had let go of my bike, I could have eventually gotten out. But the bike was important to me and I remember thinking about how much trouble I would be in if I lost my bike in the river. As a result, I hung on and cried out for help. Without warning a man reached in and pulled my bike and me out of the river and just as immediately he was gone. Because I was holding on to a branch of dense scrub oak it was almost as if I was just plucked from the river because it would have been impossible to get my bike through the scrub oak. I also don't remember him talking to me; I just remember being on dry ground and him not being there.

—Gary S. Carter, 55. Hospital administrator. Belle Mead, New Jersey. Estimated time the event occurred: 1960. Collected by Thomas Gary Carter in 2000. #1550

Runaway Truck

A group of men boarded an old pickup one day and went to the hills to see if they could catch enough trout for a fish dinner. The pickup was old and not in the best condition, but it had never given much trouble. At the base of the steepest hill was a complicated wooden gate. The gate consisted of several slats, heavily barred across a log structure. It took two men several minutes to open the thing. Finally, the men got through and closed the gate behind them. After enjoying several hours of fishing, they decided that, by the size of their catch and the time, it was time to go home. With no sense of danger, they set out. At the crest of the hill just mentioned, however, the brakes on the truck inexplicably gave out. Such an occurrence wouldn't have been so disastrous because the steep incline soon gave way to smoother terrain, but there was, in front of them, that immense wooden gate, which, if they crashed into it at that speed, could hardly mean anything but instant death. The truck was hurtling down the incline, but as they neared the gate a man suddenly stepped from somewhere and began to undo the gate's fastenings. That he could open it in time was totally impossible, but somehow, by the time the pickup arrived at the gate, it was open. The men managed to slow the truck down, and finally to stop it; when they returned to the gate to thank the man who had saved them, he was nowhere to be seen. In fact, no one could recall having seen any vehicle near the gate or having seen the man approach it.

—Collected 1962 by Lana Hill. #0171

A Respite from the Storm

Grandma and her sister took a group of primary kids on a picnic. They lived in Montana and while they were at the picnic a big storm came up. It was really scary; there was thunder and lightning and they had this group of primary children, so they were really frightened. And the storm came so suddenly that they didn't have a lot of time to do anything. Out of nowhere, either two or three men happened upon them and helped them and the children to this cabin that was nearby. And the kids and grandma and her sister were able to get dry and warm. And then after the storm they were able to hike out and take the kids back to the church. And the men just disappeared. Like suddenly, they weren't there. Anyway, Grandma told her brothers about it, and they tried to find the cabin based on where they were, and they could never find it. So that was kind of our family legend about the Three Nephites because that's who they decided the men were.

—Christy Sanders, 48. Registered Nurse, Burns, Oregon. Estimated time of action: 1930s. Collected in 2018 by Shelby Woodland. #1665

Rescued on the Appalachian Trail

Sean was hiking with his dad on the Appalachian Trail. They were surprised by a storm that they were unprepared for. They tried to make it farther on the trail, but Sean realized that his dad wasn't doing well and decided to set up camp for the night. It was snowing and they didn't have enough warm clothes. Sean set up the tent and tried to get his dad warm, but his dad was not making sense and was not acting like himself. Sean tried to start a fire but couldn't get one started with the wet wood. He was praying and starting to panic as it got dark, and his father showed more signs of hypothermia.

Four men came hiking into their camp. Sean asked them to help him with his dad. They got a fire started and got his dad warmed up. He talked to them around the fire for a while. He asked their names and one man said that his name was John, but the others never answered that question. They set up their tent and stayed in the same camp.

In the morning when Sean and his father woke up, the men were gone. Sean's father stopped at a trailside ranger station later that morning. He wanted to get contact information from the ranger about the men who had saved his life so he could thank them. The ranger said that Sean and his father were the only ones on that section of the trail that night. No one else had a backcountry permit and no one else had passed by on the trail that morning or had passed by the station below the night before. So Sean and his dad concluded that the men were the Three Nephites traveling with John and had come when Sean had prayed and saved his father's life.

—Lisa Johnson, 45. Adjunct English instructor. Collected in 2017 by Julie Swallow. #1518

Ocean Rescue

This story is about my mother. Her name is Joyce and it happened while she was going to college, either her freshman or sophomore year at BYU Hawaii. I don't know what year that was, but she's fifty-four now. She went to the beach with her friends on the island of Oahu somewhere on the north shore, and they went swimming. She found herself way out from the shore. All the people were tiny little dots on the sand, and she was stuck in the big swells, and they were going up and down; part of the time she couldn't see the land. She started to panic and get very scared because she was getting sucked out into the ocean. Out of the blue, this little Hawaiian dude swims up beside her. He wasn't on a surfboard or anything and they were way out in the ocean. He just swims up beside her and asks her, "Do you need to get back?" and she said "YES!" So he says, "Alright I'll help you," and he grabs her with one arm to make sure she doesn't get away and they start swimming back toward shore and he pretty much drags her through because he was a pretty good swimmer. He tells her, "When you start getting into where the waves are crashing, you're gonna have to duck under each time or else we'll get tossed by the wave." They got up where the waves were breaking on the beach, and each time a big wave came, they'd duck under the water and then the wave would pass over them and they'd come back up and he'd swim closer. Finally, he got her to shore and pulled her up on the sand and helped her lay down and she was exhausted and catching her breath. When she was back to normal and she looked around for the guy, he was gone. Just as soon as he appeared and helped her to shore, he disappeared and was gone, and she never saw him again and she doesn't know his name but she swears that he was one of the Three Nephites and he could have been I guess. I guess we'll never know.

—Frederick, 22. Sophomore in college, working at Apex Marketing. McMinnville, Oregon. Collected in 1999 by JoLynne Creason. #1546

A Nephite in Zion National Park

We were on a family trip to Zion's, and we decided we'd go hike the East Rim Trail. We thought we'd researched it enough that we knew where the starting point was. Turns out that the place where we were supposed to start this hike is another two miles past where we started.

David dropped us off, and he was going to meet us at the other end because it ends at Weeping Rock, which is clear in the middle of the park.

We started just ambling off to the north up this slick rock canyon. And it wasn't too bad for probably a mile; it wasn't too bad. But then it started getting really steep.

By this point, we were starting to question if we were in the right place. It was only supposed to be a two-hour trail. We decided we were going to start rationing our water and our food because we were worried we were going to possibly be lost and out there overnight.

By the time we were able to finally climb out on top of the plateau, we were figuring we might be getting in bad trouble. We were getting kind of scared. And the only thing we knew was that the trail still had to be to the north of us. And so we said a prayer.

We both were really not feeling the best about our decisions.

We kept slogging on north and finally we came up on a trail, and we noticed out of the corner of our eyes a guy running up the trail.

He had long dark hair. Darker skin. And it wasn't just because of being out in the sun and being tan, he had a definite Mediterranean look to him.

When he spotted us coming onto the trail out of the brush, he stopped and chatted with us for a second. He said his name was Buzz. We told him that we were attempting to be on the East Rim trail and that we thought we should go this way, but he said, "Oh no no no. That's a dead end. If you want to go on the East Rim trail, you've got to go back that way." And so we were thinking, "Oh hallelujah we are saved."

We turned and headed that direction, and we were walking for a long time and I thought, "Oh he must not understand where we wanted to go." But we finally we got back to where there was another break in the trail and we didn't have a clue which way we should go. We actually started to go the wrong way again and he comes up from behind us and says "No no no, you want to turn around and go this way." And we get back on it and we start going on the right way, and he's going down that way too, just running on ahead of us.

Supposedly, the only thing we can assume (because we don't know) is that he takes offshoots and goes for a little ways and then comes back because we're following his footprints.

And at this point we notice on the sole of his shoes there was a Star of David. And I don't know of any shoe company that has a Star of David as their trademark. It wasn't a Nike symbol, it wasn't Adidas. It had a Star of David in the sole of his footprint.

We saw his footprints go off one way, but he said, "Get on this trail and stay on this trail" that last time. And so we get to a point where we don't see his footprints anymore and we're going, "Well okay, what direction do we go? Do we keep going this way?" And we said he said to stay on this trail. And so we start going and all of a sudden he's coming up from behind us again and he says, "Yep you're on the right track," and by this point we start hearing people ahead of us, and there's people around that are coming to just the top of the Weeping Rock trail.

Well, he comes up behind us and says, "You're doing great and you're almost there. You're going the right direction, you're almost there." And he goes on and we said, "Thanks Buzz," and he said, "Anytime," and he just keeps going.

We come down a little farther and all of a sudden, up ahead of us, coming around a corner is David. We're easily four hours beyond our time frame.

And David said, "We knew you were coming because a guy just ran past us and told us, 'Oh the people you're looking for are almost here.'" And we're going, "What?" He said, "yeah, this guy with long brown hair and he was running and just running like he was fresh as a daisy, just running," and we're going, "Buzz knew you were looking for us?" And he said, "Who's Buzz?"

And obviously we don't know for sure if that was one of the Three Nephites, but it sure felt like it, with how every time we reached a decision point he was right there.

The Star of David, his coloring, his appearance, is what made us think at first, Guardian Angel. And then, a couple of days later, we started thinking, "What is the possibility of that having been one of the Three Nephites?" Years later, with all of the canyoneering Steven did down there, Steven told us "I met your Buzz." And we said, "What?" And he said, "Buzz. From when you went on your hike." And we said, "Yeah." And he said, "He spends all of his time running through Zions Park and you guys are not the first ones to tell stories about him helping people find their way back that have been lost." And that solidified it for us. And I realize this is conjecture and opinion on our part, but I know from the internal feelings that we have that it was such a spiritual experience for us in that . . . for us we have no doubt that he was one of the Three Nephites.

—Bruce and DaraLee Jackson. Bruce, a large instrument specialist at Brigham Young University, was 67 at the time of collection, and Daralee, retired bus driver, was 64. They *"recognize there is a possibility the account doesn't detail an encounter with one of the Three Nephites, there's no doubt in [Daralee's] mind that the account is true and that one of the Three Nephites saved her and her husband that day."* Laila Jackson, age 19, collected the story from her grandparents in September 2020. Of the collecting experience she wrote: "*Retelling the story provoked many emotions within the informants. There were multiple points in which Bruce stopped to chuckle and toward the end when DaraLee took up the telling, she began to cry. There was a reverence and undoubtable air of belief circulating during the story's telling.*" #1686

Serendipitously Detained

My teacher's mom and dad were visiting Temple Square, and just as they were preparing to exit the gates, a man approached her mother and laid his hand on her arm and simply said, "Wait." After about a minute he let go and said, "Ok, you can go now." Her parents puzzled over this occurrence as they left and drove away. It was not long before they came upon the scene of an accident that had occurred about a minute before their arriving. My teacher's mother believes that the man who approached her was one of the Three Nephites and saved her from being in that accident.

—Female, 22. The teacher of her Young Women's class shared this story about her parents. Collected 1998. #1658

Spiritual Rescue

My father was not a member at the time that my mother and he got married. He had promised to investigate the church as long as my mother would be open minded and investigate his church. He was a strong Methodist. My father is a very smart and logical man, and he was not very open-minded in investigating the church. My mother had always had a testimony that the church is true; however, her parents were not very active, and she did not learn very much about the gospel while growing up. Consequently, she could not answer many of my father's many questions, or refute his seemingly sound logic against the church. She was feeling very frustrated one day and wondering if she should just join the Methodist church in order to keep the family together and restore peace between them. At that moment someone came to the door. He introduced himself and asked if her name was Deanna Hale Proudfoot and if her son was David Proudfoot. She said yes, and he said that he was just assigned as her new home teacher. He said that he came by to invite her and David back to church, as he had not seen them there in a while. My mother was so touched by his kindness and sincerity, and she knew that that was where she needed to be, so she made a new resolve to stay in the church and told him that she would be there. She closed the door and remembered that she never got his name, so one instant later [she] opened the door again, and no one was there. One could see up and down the whole street from her door, and there was no sign of anyone or a car.

—Deanna Proudfoot, 58. Homemaker. Tigard, Oregon. 1989. *Deanna believes that the man in the story is either an ancestor or one of the Three Nephites.* Collected 1997 by Karyne Proudfoot. #1600.

Rancher Rescue

As the story goes, why this rancher one winter was out looking for some cattle that had strayed. And as he was out looking, why he was caught in a very severe blizzard, so much so that he became lost. And he wanted to give up the search for the cattle and try to find his home if he could, because the snow was becoming so bad. He was lost after a certain period of time, though, and was wandering about off of his horse. Suddenly he came upon a man who was standing out in the blizzard. He walked up to the man, and the man said to follow him, he'd show him how to go to safety. So this rancher followed the man for a period of time, and finally they came to an overhanging cliff or a cave-like sort of a thing, and it provided shelter from the storm. And when they got there, why the man saw that the cattle he was looking for were actually hiding underneath that cliff and they were safe. And the man said that it is safe for you to stay here for the storm. So he walked under the cliff, and when he got under he turned around to talk to the man, and he had disappeared.

—Ray Garrison. Heard the story at a church meeting. It took place "during the pioneering days of the Church." Collected in 1964 by William A. Wilson. #199

Rescue at the Water Park

It was this last Sunday in testimony meeting, July 6, and a girl got up in my ward to share her testimony. She said she was about seven or eight and remembers having this very scary experience in a wave pool at a nearby water park. She got too deep and started to panic and was kind of drowning and flailing around in the water. And she was looking around and saw people around her and was trying to get their attention. And people were looking at her and either thought she was playing or something and weren't helping. She even tried to get the lifeguard to look at her and to help her and even the lifeguard didn't pay attention. And she felt somebody come up behind her and pick her up under the arm pits, she said, and place her up on the side. And then they got out behind her. And she said it was a young man. And so then as she was coughing and spitting up water, she turned back around to thank him and there wasn't anybody there. And so, she then off handedly mentioned, "I think it might have been one of the Nephites."

—Vashti Musig, 26. BYU Salt Lake Center front desk worker. Sandy, Utah. *Vashti is unsure how she feels about the story, but said the girl speaking seemed to believe she had encountered a Nephite.* Collected in 2019 by Julie Swallow. #1663

PROVIDING

Gift of Groceries

There was a woman who lived in Logan, and her husband recently died. She was left with four or five young kids. Naturally, the experience was very upsetting for her. She didn't know what to do and felt overwhelmed by her responsibilities. She was very worried because she had no income and could not buy groceries to feed her children. She prayed and prayed for help, but she never told anyone about her difficulties. One day she left her home for a few hours. When she came back, she found ten bags of groceries on her counter. She asked her neighbors if they had brought them, but they told her that they had seen three men in white clothing carry the groceries into her house.

—Camilla Allen, 20. Preschool teacher. Provo, Utah. Collected in 1997 by Leanna Fry. #1631

Cake Replenished

A student told me that his mother was giving a large wedding shower for a close friend. Unfortunately, she ran out of cake. She felt bad about that but accepted it. A little later, she went out to her laundry room to get something. She was really surprised because there, on the dryer, was another big sheet cake. So, as it turns out, everyone got cake! The mother said a Nephite left it. It had to be that.[27]

—Jacqueline Thursky. High School Teacher. Collected in 1990 by Lin Tsai. #1365

Miraculous Repairman

When my great-grandmother got married, they decided to hold their reception within their home in Utah. They got married during a really warm week, and just prior to their wedding and reception their air conditioner broke down. Apparently, an air conditioner repair man came to the home and fixed the problem and left within a short time. My great-grandmother said that no one had called for a repair man, nor had the man left any bill, they simply never saw the man again. My great-grandmother always believed that the man was one of the Three Nephites.

—Camden Womeldorf, 21. Student, Roseville, California. Of this story he said: "*I think that a lot of people would look at my great-grandmother, and anyone who believes in this or other similar stories, as someone with naivety or childish faith, but I think that her simple hope and faith is something that we could all strive for.*" Collected in 2016 by Camden Womeldorf. #1516

Mysterious Welder

In the summer of 1985, The Church of Jesus Christ of Latter-day Saints staged an outdoor pageant (a large-scale drama) in Independence, Missouri. I was a member of the cast. The rehearsals of the final week were plagued with rainstorms. Just two days before opening night, a freak windstorm blew through Independence, damaging our life-sized sets and destroying the light trees (large metal poles with stage lighting attached). The production staff and crew had to work furiously to make repairs in time for our opening performance.

They got it all done on time. Before the show started, the cast and crew held a testimony meeting in the chapel adjacent to the pageant grounds. One man got up to bear his testimony about the repairs. He and the others working on the light trees were at a welding shop. A man walked up and asked for a job. The owner of the shop said he couldn't talk to him because he was working on an emergency, and they would be working all night. The man stood watching for a while, and then he started helping. This stranger was the world's perfect welder. Every movement he made was efficient. He made no mistakes. He worked with the pageant crew through the whole night. They finished the work in the early hours of the morning. After the welding was done, the stranger was gone. Nobody saw him leave.

After telling this story, and bearing his testimony, the speaker sat down. The next person to speak said that he was going to search the scriptures to find out if the Three Nephites are welders. I really think the mysterious welder might have been one of the Three Nephites.

—Rebecca McKee. Independence, Missouri. 1985. Collected in 2017 by Rebecca McKee. #1530

WARNING

Stranger Warns Missionaries

Two missionaries met a lady and set up an appointment to teach her for the first time. They didn't talk to her much, they just made the appointment and then left.

The next day they were walking to the appointment and on the way an older man stopped them. They had never seen the man before, but he called them by their full names. This shocked the missionaries because he even used their first names which missionaries use very little on their missions. The man talked with them a while and then warned them not to go to the appointment with this lady, made sure they understood the importance of what he said, and said goodbye to them and left. The missionaries looked at each other a second then looked around the corner to see where the man had gone, but they didn't see him anywhere.

Both the missionaries knew that for some reason they really trusted the man and felt a good spirit about him, so they didn't go to the appointment. A few days later they passed by the lady's house and noticed it looked vacant and there was a for sale sign in front of it. They never found out what would have happened if they had gone to their appointment and neither one of them ever saw the man again.

—Matt Gold. Brigham Young University student studying illustration. Provo, Utah. Matt heard the story and he and some other friends who were preparing to go on missions were talking. *"Matt said he thought his friend brought it up to illustrate the idea that missionaries will be helped in their work if they are willing to listen and know when they are being helped. Matt said he thought the man could be one of the Three Nephites and his friend who told the story didn't say one way or the other."* Collected by Todd Robison, 1992, at BYU. #1306

Don't Cross That Bridge

There was a young couple on their way to the temple. This couple lived a considerable distance from the nearest temple and had been traveling several days in order to go to the temple. One night as they were driving there was a horrible rainstorm. As they were driving they noticed a man alongside the road who was waving them down. They pulled over and the man told them that there was a bridge just ahead that had been washed out because of the rain. The man then told them how to go around to a safer crossing. The couple thanked the man and continued on their way. They found a small hotel to stay in a few miles down the road.

The next morning they decided to call the police to see if the bridge had been repaired and the police told them that they were the first ones to tell them anything about it. They then began on their way. As they were driving they noticed that there were no houses of any kind around where the man had stopped them the night before. The couple decided that there was no possible way that the man could have just been there by accident. They were sure that the man was one of the Three Nephites who saved their lives.

—Joyce K. Foley. Told in Ogden, 1990. *She does not remember who told her the story. Told to Lisa Foley, her daughter, who asked if she knew any Nephite stories because she was collecting them for her class at USU [Utah State University].* #1394

I Was Going to Tell You

This experience of an appearance of one of the Three Nephites to my grandfather was told to me by my grandfather many times. He was raised in [the] early history of Utah, about 1880. He had many faith-promoting experiences and we as his grandchildren would always be interested in hearing them. On this occasion he told of how he lost three fingers on one of his hands and four of his toes, and he said if he would have listened it wouldn't have happened.

One night as he was coming home from sacrament meeting, he went out to put the team of horses away and feed the cows and check the stock before coming in. As he looked out [in] the field he saw a man riding a horse. He said he didn't realize the man was white and the horse was white until it came closer. He didn't pay any attention in fact; he just thought it was somebody also riding in the neighborhood until the horse came closer and closer. He said that as it approached him he felt something different, like a strange power that was coming over him, and as he rode closer he began to get nervous, very nervous. He said the man on the horse seemed like he was going to ride right over him, so when he was about three hundred feet from him he happened to have a pitchfork in his hand and so he raised it and said: "If you come any closer I'll kill you!" The man on the horse stopped, turned around, and rode away.

He said he didn't think about it maybe for more than a week. Then he said a considerable time later, up in the mountains he was getting logs for his lumber mill. He was there by himself and he was almost finished for the day. He was trimming one of the last logs and the ax slipped as he was trimming one of the branches and he cut off his big toe plus three of the little toes.

"Well," he said, "with something like that you try not to panic. The only horses you've got are hitched up to the wagon, you're all alone, and you can't take the wagon down because you have to have your feet to guide it." He was only thinking of one thing and that's getting down and taking care of that foot.

He unhooked one of the horses from the team, and he says as he went to get on the one horse he bent over. He was very weak, and he said it was at that moment he realized that it was going to be between the Lord and him if he made it to safety. He said as he knelt down he asked his Father in Heaven to stop the bleeding. As he straightened up, the bleeding stopped immediately, and he just kind of stayed there for maybe five minutes to gain some strength to get up on the horse. He rode on down to Star Valley in Afton, Wyoming, and got a doctor.

Sometime later he was in his sawmill and was taking the bark off a tree. He was skinning the logs and was adjusting one of the logs. He was pretty close to the blade of the saw and his hand got caught under the log and it went through the saw and it cut off two or three small fingers on his right hand. He wondered at the time how he would be able to continue on in the lumber business since he was losing limbs right and left. He said after this happened he was more careful in taking care of himself.

He was coming home from sacrament meeting one evening and he said it was a very spiritual meeting, and he was home and out taking care of the stock. This same man on the horse appeared to him but he wasn't scared this time. He didn't identify himself but he said right there to him, "I tried to warn you earlier but you wouldn't let me. I was going to tell you that you would be crippled in your foot and hand."

—Gary O. Gardner from Idaho. *This was told to him "as a faith-promoting story" about his grandfather.* Collected by James D. Bowne in Utah County, 1969. #242

PROTECTING

A Safe Walk Home

Clara Prudence Alexander Clyde is my great-grandma. She was born in Wanship, Summit County on May 10, 1867. When she was married, she moved to Heber and was married for three years and then her husband was called on a mission to the New England states.

At this time, she was the State MIA [Mutual Improvement Association] President. This particular night, Clara was walking home alone from the MIA.[28] It was a cold winter evening and quite late. She lived at the far end of town and she felt quite uneasy, without her husband there.

As she was walking, just a little way down the street she saw a surrey, five or six men were standing around it, they had come from Park City, and were drinking and yelling out obscene remarks to her.

She became very frightened, and stopped and said a prayer. No sooner did she finish, than she felt a tap on her left shoulder. Startled, she turned to see a man in an overcoat and a hat. He called her by name and said, "Clara, I see you have some trouble, would you like me to walk you home?" She felt a calm easy feeling come over her. He put out his arm, she took it, and they walked home, talking all the way.

When she got to her door, she turned to thank him, but he was gone. Nothing was there but his footprints where he had last stood in the snow.

—Heidi Daybell collected this story from herself about her ancestor. It was submitted in 1979 to the USU archives. The story takes place in 1902. Here is how she describes learning the story: *"My Grandma Daybell, Clara's daughter, told this story to me when I was seven years old. My mom and dad and grandma and I were going for a Sunday drive. I was so impressed with this story, it just gave me shivers."* #785

TRAVELING MERCIES

Mystery Tow Truck

There was this guy who was driving with his family. He and his family were Mormon. It was getting kind of dark, and the man began to get drowsy. He fell asleep at the wheel for a moment and crashed his car into a pole, bending the pole over the hood. So, it was beginning to get really dark and there was no one on the road, so the man made sure everyone was alright and got out to see if he could fix his car. When he saw that the pole was bent over his hood, he tried to bend it back, but it was way too heavy. The man and his family were miles away from any town, and there was no one on the road, so they decided to say a prayer so help would come. Moments later, a man who happened to be driving an old tow truck stopped and asked them if they needed help. He got out, bent the pole back from the car, hooked up the car, and towed the family to the nearest mechanic. The next day the man wanted to find the owner of the tow truck to thank him and pay him his dues, so he searched the nearest tow truck business, but the manager said he never had a tow truck like the one the man described. The man continued to search all of the tow truck businesses in the town, but none of them carried the tow truck he was looking for or knew the man he described. Finally, he went to a tow truck business on the outskirts of town. He described the tow truck driver to the manager, but the manager said he'd never seen him. Then the man saw the old tow truck that the mysterious tow truck driver used to tow his car and told the manager excitedly, "That's it! That's the tow truck he used!" The manager looked perplexed and asked, "Are you sure?" The man replied, "Yes, I am positive. It's the very one!" The manager took the man over to the tow truck and lifted up the hood. The truck had no engine. Then he said, "This truck hasn't been running for twenty years." The man concluded that the tow truck driver who answered his prayer and helped his family must have been one of the Three Nephites.

—Derek Lange. Collected in 2017 by Derek Lange. #1534

Startled Awake

There were two girls, probably about nineteen or twenty years old. They were driving through Montana, I believe. They were on their way back to college after Christmas break. It was snowy and bad weather out. No one else was to be seen on the road. They hadn't seen anyone for hours, and they were getting sleepy. They were both trying their hardest to stay awake. When all of a sudden, they see two men, white shirts and ties, dark suits, looking like Mormon missionaries. These men looked like they were trying to get them to stop. When they turned around and reached the spot, the men were gone. Not even footprints in the snow.

—Jessica Stecker, 20. Yakima, Washington. *Jessica heard this story as a twelve-year-old at a party, where everyone expressed "deep belief and a state of awe" in reaction to the story.* Collected in 1998 by Jessica Stecker. #1628

Mexico City Story

A family took a trip to Mexico City. In the confusion of travel, one of the children, a little boy, got lost, and missed the bus. He was gone for two or three days, during which a man fed him, cared for him, and provided him with a place to sleep. On the last day, the man escorted the child to a hotel. As the little boy walked in, he saw his parents walk out. He turned to thank the man and he was gone.

Later, when the boy was given a patriarchal blessing, it said that he had come in contact with one of the Three Nephites.

—John Aldrich, 23. Idaho Falls, Idaho. Collected in 1993 by Glenda Day. #1279

Roadside Assistance

This is a story that a friend related to me in Virginia during a family home evening.

Her family took a trip to Jerusalem, and they decided to take a drive to a sight that they heard was interesting. They got in their car, about five people in a little tiny car they rented there. The only way to get to this place was to drive along the tops of the sand dunes where the so-called roads are. As they were driving, they saw that the road was getting less and less traveled-looking. Then they got stuck about four hours from civilization. This is the Jerusalem desert, very dangerous and very hot. They tried and tried to get the car unstuck. They decided to pray. They prayed that they would receive the Lord's help in returning safely. A few minutes later, three people were walking towards them. These people were in excellent health and didn't show normal signs of what the desert would do to someone out walking through the desert. They said hello and assessed the situation. They lifted the little car up and with the help of the father and one of his sons, they turned the car in the other direction and back onto the road. The car was slightly off the road because they were trying to turn around. These three gentlemen turned and continued walking down the hill. When Adrienne, my friend, tried to run after them down the hill following their tracks, she saw that the tracks did not continue. The whole family ran down to take a look and saw that the tracks just ended.

—Brian Christensen, 24. Publication specialist, Arizona. *Believes it to be a true story.* Collected in 1995 by Jeff Niekamp. # 1422

Lost in the Airport

A few years ago, I was traveling with my parents and sister to Europe. We were in the Chicago International Airport, and our plane was about to board and leave. We, however, were completely lost and had no idea what terminal we were in or how to get to our gate. Because the airport is so big, they have an indoor train that runs between the gates and terminals. Somehow, we ended up with our baggage in a corner of the airport that was under construction. Hardly any people were there and only a few workers. Meanwhile, all of us are silently praying in our minds that we will make it in time to our flight.

Out of nowhere, this man most likely in his 50s, dressed in a business suit and carrying a briefcase, approaches us. He states that we are lost and points us in the right direction. We told him thank you and headed in that direction. When we turned around to see where he had gone, there was no trace of him left.

My family and I still marvel at that incident because he didn't even ask if we were lost. It was as if he knew what the problem was and knew exactly where to direct us.

—May Pysnak, 20. Student, Bountiful, Utah. Early 2010s. *May and her family came to the conclusion that the man in the airport had been sent as an answer to their prayer.* Collected in 2016 by May Pysnak. #1507

Miraculous Mechanic

When I was sixteen, we were driving up to a concert up Parley's Canyon, and it's before cell phones or anything, and we had to be at least five miles between exits—car broke. And so we sat there for twenty minutes, nobody stopped to help, there's no phones, so we decided we should probably cut across the freeway, all five lanes, and try to hitchhike the other way back home. Brilliant plan, I know, I know. So we just decided, we just get ready to go, and this guy says, "Hey, wait, I think I can fix your car."

I didn't see him pull up, I don't know where he came from. He had a toolbox, he had big, long white braids, and that headband thing. No tattoos, kind of like plain dress—jeans, t-shirt, and looked off. And we were like, "Oh crap, we're gonna get murdered or raped or something." But he seemed really serene and didn't seem like he fit. But he opened up the hood and an hour later, he [had] fixed the car. He's like, "There you go, ladies, you're on your way." And we were dumb, we didn't think anything of it, so we jumped back in the car, we're like, "Bye!" Didn't see him get into a car. No idea where he came from.

So we went to the concert, came home, and I told my dad, "Car broke, some guy fixed it for us, totally fine." And the entire alternator had been rebuilt on the side of the freeway with no parts, no idea how he did it, and he's like, "That is so weird." And I remember the thought that came to my head was, "Oh my gosh, that's one of the Three Nephites."

—Sherry Hardy, 47. High school teacher and ceramist, Wasatch Front, Utah. 1987 or 1988. Collected in 2018 by Erica Smith. #1666

Mechanics in White

Our family had set off on a long trip across the country that morning. I was driving. We were several hours into our trip and had just come to a particularly barren stretch of highway when our tire blew out. It was summer, and we were right in the middle of the Arizona desert, so needless to say, it was hot enough to fry an egg on the asphalt. To my dismay, as we looked for it, the spare was already on one of our other tires! So here we were in the middle of the desert on a hot summer's day, with no help in sight, no spare tire, and nothing to do but wait. Everyone in the car was getting pretty grumpy.

Suddenly, we saw a white car coming over the horizon. I could have sworn it hadn't been there just a few minutes ago. But here it was. It parked behind us quite a ways, and three guys got out. They were dressed in white mechanic's suits! Now if you ask me, that's pretty strange, because why would mechanics ever wear white? Seeing as how they deal with grease and oil all day. But it wasn't our place to ask, we were just grateful for the help! They quickly walked up, replaced our tire, and went on their way before we could even ask who they were or thank them. Come to think of it, we didn't even see them carrying a spare tire. But when we checked it, our original tire was good as new. Don't ask me how.

As they walked back to their car, I could have sworn I heard one of the guys call another one of the other guys something that sounded like, "ite." Maybe it was the Three Nephites.

—Nicholas "Grant" Garcia, 23. Student. Utah. Collected in 2018 by Nicholas "Grant" Garcia. #1668

Rescued in a Blizzard

When I was going to USU, I used to own an old Plymouth.

I drove this car over to Garden City to see my girlfriend who worked at a confectionary [*sic*] stand. I would hang around until 1:00 am and then drive home through Logan Canyon.

One particular night when I was visiting her, it had started to snow. I started out for home, and stopped at a gas station in Garden City, and the attendant told me to stay because the snow had started to drift in the canyon. I had taken that Plymouth through fairly deep snow, and I decided to try to make it through. I drove about forty-five minutes ploughing through two-foot drifts and sliding all over the road. It seems like I was in the darkest part of the canyon when I lost control and buried the Plymouth in the snowbank. Now I was faced with a decision: stay in the car, which, incidentally, had no heater, or try to make it back to Garden City. I decided to try and make it back. I got out of the car and started walking. It was not long until I was soaked clear through. I was trudging through waist deep snow. It was actually so dark I had to hold my hands out in front of me to guide me. After a while I was completely numb and starting to nod off, a sure sign that it was just about over. Just when I was resigned to that fact, I saw some headlights coming. A man in a car picked me up and took me on to Garden City and then drove away in the night. Now I don't know about this. I have thought about it a lot and driven myself bananas trying to figure out how he drove through that blizzard. No one else could have done [it,] and I know that it was a miracle that he made it through that canyon. I have wondered sometimes if he could not have been one of the Three Nephites.

—Kent Poulsen, 50. Land developer. American Northwest. Collected in 1984 by Eric P. Watts. #1611

Fixing a Flat

Emiline and her husband were driving through the deserts of St. George. There was nothing to be seen and no one within a hundred miles of them. They entered the desert with the intent of crossing straight through, when all of a sudden, right in the middle of this vast span of nothingness, their car broke down—they had a flat tire. These two were both old and weak and were unable to change the tire. They prayed to God for help, and right after they finished praying, they saw a car moving closer towards them, coming in the same way that they had come. The car stopped and three men got out. They didn't say anything. They just got out of their car, fixed the tire, got back in their car, turned around, and drove out of the desert the same way they had come in. Emiline attributes this miracle to the Three Nephites.

—Kimberly Young, 23. Junior at BYU from Blackfoot, Idaho. Collected in 1998 by Kimberly Young. #1616

Free Towing Service

This happened in the outskirts of Missoula, Montana, where we were driving up a mountain to visit a ghost town, and the roads were muddy from all the snow melting on the trail. The farther we moved forward, the more dangerous it became. We eventually came to the conclusion that we had better turn back while we still could. When my mother slowed down to turn around, we got stuck and could not move. We did not have anything to dig the snow with except for a plastic cup, so there I was trying to dig our car out with a tiny cup. No matter how many times we pushed the car or how much I dug out some snow, the car would not budge. Soon my mom called the Latter-day Saint missionaries to get us out. They thought it was funny to hear that we were stuck in the middle of a mountain in a minivan, but I did not want to keep effortlessly digging. I eventually said a little prayer to get us some help right away. As soon as I finished my prayer, this tow truck drove right towards us. The man driving the truck had the most unusual facial features. It's hard to describe it, but no one in the modern day would look like him. He asked us if we needed some help, and boy did we. He hooked our car to his truck, told my mom to not push on the break [*sic*], and then got us out of our situation. He then guided my mom doing a four-point turn without getting stuck again. What was surprising was how calm and gentle he was guiding my mother. He told her that everything would be ok even though she was scared that she would drive over the edge. When we were in a position to drive ourselves again, she asked him how much money he wanted, and he only asked for $50 then told my parents that we would have never gotten ourselves out of the snow no matter what and that we were lucky. He drove away as soon as she gave him the check; then we followed. When we took the turn on the trail, the tow truck was gone. At first, we thought that maybe he was way ahead of us. Then we realized that the tow truck had disappeared when we took another turn and saw the long straight line down with no other turns. The missionaries were on the bottom of the mountain and told us that they never saw a tow truck and said that maybe it was one of the Three Nephites. Although we will never know who it really was, but the check never got cashed.

—Benjamin Vance, 25. BYU Copy Center employee from Billings, Montana. Collected in 2020 by Benjamin Vance. #1685

Car Dies on the Freeway

My whole life I've been taught about the Three Nephites. I think everybody knows the story of the Three Nephites and how they're on the earth today and I never thought much about it. So, when I was in college I ran out of money, so I had to stop school for a semester, and go find a real job to put myself through school. I came down to Salt Lake and found a job. I was working for Beehive Thrift and Loan, and I was in an apartment and I had a friend who also had come from Montana who was living in a different apartment complex. I was out by West Valley City and she was in North Salt Lake. We were talking and I don't know why, but we both felt really strongly that I needed to come and stay with her for the night.

I kept thinking, "Wow. I don't have any money for gas. I don't know what I'm going to do but . . ." She kept saying, "Suzie you have to come and help me, you have to" and I said, "Well, you know, Leanne I don't have any money." She said, "I promise you, I know you'll make it here." I'm a single girl, I'm young, about thirty, forty pounds lighter [than my friend]. I get in my little Volkswagen Bug, and I'm driving along and I come to the Sixth North exit off the freeway. I'm speeding along and I put my blinker on and I whip around and it makes a quick round-a-about, and I'm in the middle of the round-a-bout, not quite yet to Sixth North but I'm on the middle of that ramp and my car dies. And this is busy Salt Lake traffic. I'm thinking, "Oh my gosh what do I do? Heavenly Father what do I do? I don't know what to do." I can't get out and walk out on the freeway. Luckily, there wasn't any traffic—which is really odd—and I said, "I can't leave my car here. I can't try to roll it back down cause I'm on a round-a-bout going up." I get out of my car, and this car comes whipping up the ramp and almost runs into me. And they swerve, and then pull around and stop and I'm thinking, "Oh man, help." And then I see that its three guys. They rolled down their window and one of them pops his head out and hollers back to me, "You need some help?" And I go, "Yeah I do." They said, "Well what's going on?" They got out of their car and I said, "I ran out of gas, and I have to get over to my friend's apartment. They're like, "We'll give you a ride to your friend's apartment where does she live?" And all of a sudden I just felt really, really calm. I felt okay, I felt like they'd truly get me to where I needed to go. So I get into the car with these three young men, they had clean cut missionary haircuts and normal clothes. They took me to get a gas container and we went and filled it up. They took me back and we filled my car up and they made sure my car started, and they said, "Is there anything else we can do for you?" I said, "I wish I had money to pay you." They said, "We don't want payment." One of them said, "Are you Mormon?" "I am." One of the others looked at me and said, "The only thing we ask is that you become the best that you can." And they got in their car and drove off. And the weird thing is that we hung out in that area all the time and I never heard from them again. And so I say, they were the three Nephites. Because I had had a blessing that said I would be watched over and protected while I was down here.

—Suzie Willmore, 48. Office manager and mother from South Jordan, Utah. *Suzie believes that her account of meeting the Three Nephites is true. It is a personal experience narrative that occurred in 1978. As the informant is my mother, I would have little reason to doubt the authenticity of the collection as well.* Collected by Kiel Willmore, 22. South Jordan, Utah. 2008. #1583

Burying the Axe

The story that I'm going to share was told to me by a friend that I grew up with. His name is David Sevy. The story is about his grandfather in a town called Koosharem, Utah, south of Richfield. He said that his grandfather was in the mountains one day, chopping wood. He mistakenly missed the wood and cut his foot very badly with the axe. He was up there all by himself. He had no way to get back to the town. He was bleeding quite severely and was quite concerned about how to take care of himself. It became obvious to him that in no way was he going to be able to take care of the problem himself.

He said, he looked up and he saw a man coming toward him. The man said, he should bury his axe head in the ground by swinging the axe, so the blade of the axe would go down in and be buried in the ground. His grandpa said, as soon as he did that with his axe, the bleeding stopped. The man walked away and was never seen again. His grandpa was firm in his conviction that he was one of the Three Nephites who had come by to help him at this time.

—(FIFE Archive) Eric Rasmossen, 30. Computer scientist. Logan, Utah. Collected in 1990 by Lin Tsai. #1361

David Lamoreaux's Healing by the Three Nephites

When David Burlock Lamoreaux was a young boy he was seriously hurt while out cutting trees. All alone in the forest, one of the trees fell and hit him on the forehead punching a hole clear through to his brain. For some reason it didn't kill him and so he stumbled home and fell on the door. His parents heard the noise and found him laying in a pool of blood. They brought him in and nursed him back to health. He tells the story how one night he was having a real hard time, and there came a knock at the door, when they opened it, there was two young men who stated they had come to take care of David through the night because they knew the family was tired. During the night they anointed him with oil and blessed him that the pain would leave. David said the pain left and never did come back the rest of his life. Well, the next morning when his parents were preparing breakfast for the two men they found that they had disappeared. They went outside and looked around but they had gone. David later received a confirmation that they were two of the Three Nephites that they had blessed him to save his life. Later David and his brother Andrew returned with Parley P. Pratt when he came off his mission and returned to Nauvoo.

—Male, 51. "*This story is not taken lightly . . . it is believed to be one of the most spiritual events that occurred to our forefathers. It would never be openly discussed with strangers for fear that it would be chalked up as 'another Three Nephites story'.*" Collected by Male in 1996.[29] #1485

Blessed for Recommitting

This sister-in-law of mine, her father was really sick, and he was in the hospital. He had been married in the temple years before, but he had fallen away. He was a heavy cigar smoker, and coffee drinker, and some booze, too.[30,]

He was laying in his bed in the hospital and three men appeared, dressed in white. One of them asked him if he remembered the vows he had made in the temple. He said, "Yes."

One of them said, "Brother Christianson, are you keeping those vows?"

He said, "No."

Then one of the men said, "If we prolong your life, will you fulfill the obligations you made in the temple?"

He said yes, and then the three men went right through the wall! He immediately called the nurse and asked her if she had seen the men. She told him she had been right at the nurse's station and had not seen anyone in the hall for quite a while.

He recovered and went and talked to the stake president. He said he felt he had been visited by the Three Nephites. He lived seven or eight more years; he was an old man when this happened. He was very righteous; he really straightened up.

—(U of U [University of Utah] archives) Mrs. J. Schow, 40. Taylorsville, Utah. *Mrs. Schow strongly believes the story.* Collected in 1973 by Cynthia A. Techmeyer. #1040

Roadside Rescue

"The Three Nephite[s] story," which I have heard came from my high school. While I was in the ninth grade, my older sister who was a senior at the time, told me this story. Her friend Darryl Mauerman worked as a runner for WordPerfect. He was making a run to Salt Lake when he fell asleep at the wheel, veered across the median, and hit a car head on. Both he and the passenger in the other car were going to die. The traffic began to pile up, and one of the witnesses trying to calm the situation said that a man with a black bag emerged on the scene, treated both of the victims so that they were stabilized, and vanished in thin air before anyone got his name. Even efforts in the newspaper trying to figure out the identity of this man were in vain. It was one of the Three Nephites.

—J. Colby Clark, 22. BYU student. Orem, Utah. Estimated time of action: 1988. Collected in 1997 by J. Colby Clark. #1606

Blessed before Surgery

In the year 1917, my grandfather's appendix ruptured, and he was taken to the hospital. While there, his bowels became obstructed, and surgery was needed to fix the problem. The doctor told him that success was very slim and most likely he would have to live the rest of his life not being able to do the things he wanted to do. Right before the surgery, an unknown man entered the hospital, gave my grandfather a blessing, and told him that it was not his time to go and that he had work to do on this earth. After that, the man left and never was seen again. The doctor came in right after and did some pre-surgery tests. The test results indicated that surgery was not needed anymore. The doctor told my grandpa that his recovery was a miracle. My grandpa always wondered if this mysterious man could have been one of the Three Nephites.

—Susan Callister, 47. Economic consultant. Bountiful, Utah. 1917. Collected by Sara Becker in 2001. #1622

A Nephite for a Surgeon

On Thursday, May 11, 1961, in Dr. Valentin's Book of Mormon in Spanish class, one fellow related the following story that was supposed to have happened to the grandmother of a friend of his. This was supposed to have taken place in about 1931 back when medicine was not as developed as it is today.

She became very ill with severe pains in the area of her stomach, and the doctors were unable to discover the cause of her pains. As time went on and she grew worse, they decided to operate to see if they could find the source of her illness.

The evening before the scheduled operation, the doctors checked in on her to make certain she was comfortable, and then they left for the evening.

She fell asleep, but she was awakened a short time later when a man she had never seen before entered her room. She felt very confident and relaxed in his presence. He asked her what was the matter, and she told him of the intense pains that had been bothering her. This man performed an actual operation on her and removed a small, black-colored growth from her stomach, which she was allowed to see. To close the incision, he just pressed the sides of the wound together, and it healed. Immediately, the pains left this woman's body, and she felt wonderful.

The man left, and the next morning when the doctors came to see her, she was in excellent health. Upon examining her after hearing her story, they could find no trace of any mark that would indicate that an incision had ever been made.

—1931. Collected in 1961 by Judy Morrison. #0174

A Baby Saved

A young mother in her early twenties slowly rocked her sick baby. He had been ill for the past three days, and as the mother swayed back and forth, she thought of the child's condition and her own isolation. The baby had been conscious only once this morning, and now he was burning with fever. She ran a cool, moist handkerchief over its almost invisible brow. Something would have to be done very soon or her most precious possession would be taken from her forever.

Her husband had been gone since Monday to cut timber, and he wouldn't be home until the weekend. The woman knew she was too far from her neighbors to get help, and besides, transportation was [as] scarce as doctors. She uttered another prayer. She had been praying with each breath—it was the last thing she could do. But to her, a single woman without her husband's priesthood to help her, her prayers seemed futile. Then suddenly the infant went into tremendous convulsions, splitting the silence with hideous screams and deafening sounds that made the young mother tremble. Then the child fell silent. His tiny stomach no longer moved with the rush of incoming air.

There was a knock at the door. Mechanically the woman said, "Come in." A very nice-looking old man with slightly red hair entered, and with no greeting, went directly to the child. He administered to it, and, as he prayed, the woman noticed a soft glow around the man's head. After a beautiful prayer, the baby awoke and smiled. The mother thanked the stranger and invited him to have lunch with her, but he insisted on leaving. As the woman saw him to the door, she noticed he had brought no horse or carriage. But the old man joyfully said it was a nice day for a walk. When he was partially down the dirt road, the woman shut the door intending to watch this wonderful man till he was out of sight; however, when she drew the curtains, the man was vanished, and he was never heard from or ever seen again.

—Paul Scherbel, 21. BYU student from Big Piney, Wyoming. 1870–1890. *Paul does not believe this story, but he is still a faithful member of the Church of Jesus Christ of Latter-day Saints.* Collected in 1969 by Paul Scherbel. #0309

Recipe for Healing

Matt had a great-grandfather or great-great-grandfather, he couldn't remember which, that was seriously burned. Matt couldn't remember how he was burned, but only that it was so bad he couldn't work. The family was poor and was even worse off without the income his great-grandfather's job provided. After a few weeks or so, a stranger came up to Matt's great-grandmother and talked to her about her husband. He then gave her some healing ointment and showed her how to make it. The only instructions he gave her was to use it wisely and never to write the recipe down or tell it to anyone. She could make all she wanted to help her husband and anyone else in the family or community that might need it, but she could never reveal the secret. After using the ointment on her husband, he did recover very rapidly and went back to work. She also used the ointment for others too, but, as far as Matt knows, she never did break her promise to keep it secret. Matt said that his great-grandmother never saw or heard of the stranger again after that day.

—Matt Gould, 19. BYU sophomore from Portland, Oregon. *Matt told the story's collector that he truly believes the story.* Collected in 1992 by Todd Robison. #1289

Mysterious Newspaper on a Fence Post

In the early 1900s in Wyoming, there was a rancher. One day while out rounding up the horses out in the fields, the ranchers noticed that there was some paper blown up against one of the fences and that it was bothering the horses. The man then got off his horse and looked at the newspaper and came to find that it was a paper from England that had been printed one day earlier. The information on the paper was an important list of this man's family history. He knew that it was impossible for a paper to travel so quickly from England, so he asked his church leader what he thought about it, and he was told that it must have been put there by one of the Three Nephites.

—(FIFE Archive) Leslie Anjewerden. Salt Lake City, Utah. Early 1900s. Collected in 1990 by Lisa J. Foley. #1388

Newspaper Wrapper Provides Needed Information

I can't remember whether it was my grandmother or my great-grandmother, but she and her sisters were going to Wilford, Idaho, up by Sugar City where we went to the graveyard. They were going up there to visit some of the rest of their family. They were coming from Logan [Utah] and going up there and on the way—people used to carry their lunches along with them—and they had been down to Logan doing genealogy work on—it must have been grandma Messervy because they had been working on the Messervy line—and they hadn't been able to find anything on this line. And as they were on this train, there was a gentleman there that was eating his lunch, and in a little while why he got up and left and his lunch had been wrapped in a newspaper and as he left, he left the newspaper there. They hadn't seen him leave, but they picked up the newspaper to see what it was, and it was a French newspaper that was dated just the day before, and it had in it a list of the genealogy of these Messervy ancestors that they were looking for.

—Barbara Hill. Extraction missionary. Smithfield, Utah. Collected in 1982 by Jeanne Hill. #773

Blessed with Health to Do the Work

Another incident that is very special to my family is something that happened to my grandfather, Alma Helaman Hale. John Boynton was one of the first apostles of the church, his sister married my great-grandfather. And then he was excommunicated because he didn't agree with polygamy and a few other things. But he still held his testimony and was interested in genealogy, and my grandfather, Jonathan, and his family came here with the saints. Uncle John kept sending records to them to have temple work done here. They had this Samuel Roskelly, who was a church recorder, working diligently on these to get them ready for temple work. He became ill and his eyesight was poor so he said he would have to take the records back to Grandpa Hale and he wouldn't be able to finish them. That was breaking our family's heart, so they had a fast day throughout the whole family as to what to do with those records. Brother Roskelly was going home from the temple one night when he said suddenly at his side appeared a man dressed in white on a white horse. He talked to him a minute. The man told him he would like to see the Hale records done and brother Roskelly told him what his health problem was. This messenger promised him that if he would take the records back and complete them, his eyesight and his health would be good to the end of his use for it. Then the personage disappeared. So Brother Roskelly went to Grandpa Hale and described the man, and Grandpa Hale said, "That's my father." So they took the records back. It took Brother Roskelly three more years to finish them, but his eyesight was the best it had ever been.

—(FIFE archive) Kay Merrill Olsen. Blackfoot, Idaho. *Kay only shared this story after being reassured that the collector was an active and faithful member of the LDS Church.* Collected in 1984 by Deborah Morris. #1355

Inspire to Do Temple Work

My sister-in-law, Myra York Hancock (lives over here on Ninth East), her father was in my home; when we was married fifty years, he was invited to our home as one of our guests. They sang songs and played music, and finally I turned and I said, "Grandpa York, it's your turn, now, to do something." So he stood up, and he says, "I want to insist and urge you all to rush your Temple work." He says, "I want to tell you an experience that I had years ago." He says, "I was out to the field ploughing," and he says, "I stooped over to scrape the mud off the plowshare—" He spoke a little broken. "And," he says, "when I raised up there was a man standing by me with a long white beard. And I said, 'Who are you, and what do you want?' And he told me that he was Daniel Webster, and asked me to do his temple work."

He says, "I trembled, I cried, and I promised." And he says, "He vanished. I was out away from the road. I looked. I couldn't see him nowhere." He says, "I was so overcome I couldn't go on and plow no more, and I went home, put my horses in the barn, went in and told my wife." He said, "She says, 'Oh, Pa, I think you stooped over and was a little dizzy.'"

"So," he says, "time went on, and I studied it over, and I wondered, well how could I do his temple work? I don't know anything about his records or where they could be found. I didn't know what to do." And he says, "More than a year went by. One day it was raining; I couldn't work in the field." And he says, "My wife turned, and she says, 'Gus, I wish you'd go out and climb up on the house when it quits raining, and saw that apple tree limb off.' She says, 'It brushes back and forth, back and forth on the roof and it makes me nervous.' "So," he says, "I did. I went out and sawed the apple tree limb off and threw it out in the kern [currant] bushes. Then," he says, "I thought well I mustn't leave the limb there, so," he says, "I went over to pick the limbs out of them kern bushes, and," he says, "when I raised up, I saw the same man. And he told me again, 'You didn't keep your promise.' And I said, 'Where will I find those records?' He said to go to Otis Terry's place on Provo Bench. So," he says, "I promised again. I lost no time. I went and hooked up my team, my wife got into the wagon with me, and I drove to Provo, and I talked to them and told them what I'd come for. They says, 'They's some old trunks in the basement; we'll go and look 'em through.'" He says, "Within two hours I had all those Temple records complete."

He says, "I drove back home, and I said to my wife, 'We'll go straight to the Manti temple. We'll lose no time.' And she said, 'Well, we can't Pa. I've got to cook up a little something to take.'" And he said they had one little log room over there that the Terry family kept a-purpose to have a place to stay when they went to do temple work. So he said while his wife was cooking something to take with them, he laid down on the couch. Then she called to him, she said, "'Pa, everything's ready, now, to go.'" When he went to raise up he was helpless; he couldn't raise. He tried, and he says, "It come to my mind at once it was a trick of the Devil. So," he says, "I called to my wife and told her to go to the nearest neighbor and get him to come and hook up the team to the wagon and drive up to the porch. I still remained Helpless. The man drove right up and helped me into the wagon. I reached to take the lines out of his hand, and I couldn't. I had no use of my hands. My wife drove the team till we got to Manti." And he said that terrible paralyzed feeling never left him till he went into the Temple.

And he says he saw every one of those people come through and march through, in one door and out of another, as fast as he did the work. They camped and stayed right there until he'd finished up that record complete. And I heard him bear that testimony, tell that story. And anyone to of took one look at him would a-knowed every word of it was the truth. And that was Gustus York.

Q: He felt that it was one of the Nephites?

A: Yes, he did. He felt sure that it was.

—Mrs. Jesse L. Barker, 77. Salt Lake City, Utah. Estimated date of action: 1936. Collected in 1946 by Hector Lee. #1173

A Book of Names

The mother of Mrs. Simmons (the owner of the Manti furniture store) had an interesting visitor. For several years she had been doing work in her family genealogy and had reached a point in her work where she was stopped by being unable to trace her lineage any further back. One day a man came to her home and asked for a meal. Professing not to be a beggar, this man gave her in return for the meal a book. This book proved to contain information which she needed to extend her family genealogy. No one saw this man come and no one saw him go. It is believed by some that he was one of the Three Nephites. I could get no definite information as to why it was believed that this man may have been other than an ordinary human except for the fact that he left information that was greatly desired.

—Mr. James Tatton, 83, and Mrs. Louisa C. Tatton, 82. Manti, Utah. Collected in 1946 by Mr. and Mrs. Harold Fox. #1222

GENEROSITY TESTING

Answer to Prayer

One morning Mrs. Albert Skinner was at home with her family of several small children. The grandchildren had been left without parents and the grandparents were giving them a home. To raise the children was a hard task because the grandparents were living in dire poverty. They had given up their home in the town of Beaver, Utah, to move out onto a dry land farm on a flat commonly known as the Buckhorn flats. Their home was the only one within several miles around. This day Mr. Skinner had gone to Parowan, Utah, to try to sell a load of wood in order to buy food and clothing for his children. It was quite early in the morning and the family had just finished a meager breakfast of bread and milk. A knock came to the door and upon answering it, Mrs. Skinner saw an old man dressed in shabby but very clean clothes. "Lady," he said, "could you give me a bite of something to eat? I have gone almost two days without food and I am very hungry."

Mrs. Skinner answered, "I haven't very much that I can fix for you, but if you will come in, I will be only too glad to warm some milk for you and give you some bread to eat with it." The man offered to work for his food, but as there was no small tasks to be done, he came into the house and talked to Mrs. Skinner while she prepared him what little food she had. The channel of their conversation soon turned to prayer. She told him how she had prayed for sufficient money and food to raise her grandchildren properly. As a general rule, she had fear of men who passed by her home on the road, especially if her husband was away, but this time she had no fear, whatsoever.

The old man ate the meal and seemed to enjoy it very much, meager as it was. When he was through, he spoke to her, "God bless you; you have been very kind. I hope that your prayers will be answered. May I have a drink of cool water?" She told him that there was a flowing well east of the kitchen a little ways from the house, and that he could get a refreshing drink there. Having said this, she stepped back into the house. As she closed the door, she remembered that there wasn't a cup at the well, so she took one from the cupboard and stepped outside with it. The man was not anywhere around. She looked in all directions, around the house and in all the sheds but he was not there. There were no trees, houses, or sheds for miles around and one could see for miles in every direction over the straight flat country. There wasn't a person in sight. What could this mean? Had she been visited by one of the Three Nephites? Questions filled her mind. She could not be positive as to the answers because there was no way of knowing the truth. Mrs. Skinner never told the experience as a fact, but as something very different and more beautiful than had ever happened to her. When Mr. Skinner came home late that day, he had sold all of his wood and had sufficient food and money for several days. She knew then that her prayers had been answered, perhaps because of her kind deed or perhaps for other reasons. She did not know and there was no way of finding out.

—Mrs. Wilson A. Moore. Salt Lake City, Utah. Collected in 1939 by Anna Burton. #1241

Entertaining an Angel

We were neighbors to the Birrells, and I grew up with Rachel. When she was about six or seven years of age, her family moved out to Hi[gh] land Park on Stratford and Chadwick Avenue. At that time, their house was the only one on Chadwick Avenue. It was at that time that the Hiland Park Ward was just being organized, and there wasn't a house on any side of them. Our family went out there to visit them and I remember them telling this story:

Mr. Birrell, father of Rachel, used to have to get up early in the morning and go to work. His wife used to get up and get his breakfast and then go back to bed and rest awhile. One hot summer morning she decided to stay up and was finishing some ironing, so that she, her daughter, and her mother could go to Liberty Park for a ward reunion that was to be held.

The Birrells had a large screen porch on the back of the house, that they used for a kitchen during the hot summer months. They also ate their meals out there because it was much cooler than the house. It was still before seven o'clock when an old man came to the door and asked for some food. The man was neatly dressed and was wearing a linen duster. Mrs. Birrell asked the man to come in and sit on the porch where it was cool, while she fixed him something to eat. As he sat down to rest, the old man remarked, "Your husband has to leave very early to go to work, doesn't he?" Mrs. Birrell presumed that he had seen her husband leave. As he ate, Mrs. Birrell observed that his garments were visible under his coat sleeves, and that they were pearly white. At first Mrs. Birrell had thought this stranger was just an ordinary tramp and had become hungry. Being slightly affected mentally, she thought, he had asked for food at the first house he came upon. Mrs. Birrell told the man about how hard they were working to pay for their nice home. He said, "You won't need to worry. If you'll just live as you should you'll be all right, and your home will be paid for."

They talked for about ten minutes, and then she offered him a cup of coffee. He refused and said that she would be better off too if she didn't drink coffee either. As the man was about to leave, Mrs. Birrell's small daughter, Rachel, came in to the room. He called Rachel by name, and then said to her, "Honor thy father and the mother, in order that thy days might be long on the earth." The young girl, being frightened by a stranger speaking in that manner, turned and fled back into the room from which she had come. The man said that he was also going to the reunion that afternoon, and that he would see them there. Then he left.

As soon as the man had gone, Rachel came into the kitchen and asked her mother who the old man was. Her mother said she didn't know, but that she was going to look to see which way he went. She went to the window and looked out, but the old man was nowhere to be seen. At that time, Mrs. Birrell's mother came from her bedroom. She asked who had been there so early. Then Mrs. Birrell said, "I believe that old man was one of the Three Nephites." And her mother said, "I do wish you had kept him here until I could see him, for you know that in your Patriarchal Blessing you were told you would entertain angels unaware."

—T. Edgar Lyon. Salt Lake City, Utah. Collected in 1939 by Anna Burton. #1242

A Blessing for a Dime

This happened around, my dad was born around 1903 and there were four siblings around the time this happened, so I'd say it was around, I'm not sure the year, maybe 1910. Somewhere in that area. There was a road that goes from the old highway, it goes through Logan into Wellsville, which is highway 91, and it goes from 91 up to Nibley. And they lived about two miles up that road that goes to Nibley. The road ran east and west, and so the house is on the south side of the road, and it had kind of long drive way going into the house, and then behind the house there was a single-car garage. To the east of that or to the west of that there was a barn and sheds and stuff like that. My grandfather come walking out of the back where the shed was and as he looked up a man was walking down the road and into the driveway.

And he went out to meet him in front of that single-car garage. The man came up to meet him and said, "Do you have ten cents?" My grandfather said "yes," and he handed him a dime and he turned back, then he turned back to the guy and he was gone. My aunt, who was the fourth sibling, was just little girl playing behind the house between the garage, and she witnessed the whole thing. Now several years later we had a family reunion in Woods Cross at the school.

There was only about 2 or 3 left at this time—there was 13 kids in the family. And so my aunts and uncles went up on the stage and all the siblings were in the recreation hall and we asked them questions about different things that went on. And I asked the question, "What happened at this time at this event?" And my Aunt says, "It did happen." My Aunt Louise stood there and watched the whole thing. And then that statement, as he looked at my grandfather he says, "From now on your needs of want, you'll never need to worry about it ever again. You or your posterity." Years later, before I went on my mission, I got a patriarchal blessing, and in my blessing it says, which I've always been kind of concerned about it says, "Friends will be raised up to care for your needs." So I feel that is part of that promise that was given to my grandfather.

—Rex Zollinger, Mechanist, 80 years old. *Shared the story during Fast and Testimony meeting. He first heard the story when he was around 10 years old. He then asked family members about it at a family reunion when he was 40. Of the story he said, "This wasn't broadcast everywhere. It just happened to be that somebody mentioned about this thing happened at that time so it's kinda kept kinda quiet. Nobody really said anything. So that's why I was so curious to ask at that time at that reunion, 'Did this really happen?' and people told me it did happen."* Collected in 2020 by Julie Swallow. This story is referenced in the introduction. #1681

Yeast Is Activated

The legend is told of a woman who was making bread and could not get it to rise. She had no other food in the cabin to feed her family except a small amount of milk, cheese, and the bread she was making. She tried all she could to get the bread to rise, but it was to no avail.

There came a knock at her door, and when she answered it there was an old, gray-haired man standing there. She invited him in and offered him the crust of a stale loaf of bread and the only piece of cheese she had in the cabin.

When he finished the meager meal, she offered him the bed to rest his feet on before he continued his journey. When he left, she went back to the kitchen and found the loaves of bread had risen.

She ran to the door to thank the man whom she believed was one of the Three Nephites, but he had disappeared completely with no trace that he had been there.

—(FIFE folklore archive) Debby Brey. Logan, Utah. Collected in 1974 by Debby Brey. #1411

Spared from the Flu and Famine

It was when that other war was on and we had the flu so bad. And he said, "I've heard that you've had a Nephite come here." And I said, "We did." And he said, "I've brought this lady down here—she's a widow—and I brought her down here," he says, "to see you because I want you to tell her just what he looked like." And I said, "Well—" I described him, and told just exactly what he looked like, to her. And she said, "That was him." And she asked me how he was dressed, and I told her, and she said, "Well, that was him." But he went to this lady's house where they had a party, or was going to have a party. He knocked at her door because she was going to have trouble with the flu, and he thought he could prevent it, and make things so they'd be all right. And he knocked at the door, and she says, "I haven't time to bother with you tonight. I've got to have my—my crowd's a-coming and I haven't time." So he crossed the street to this widow lady's. And this widow lady had quite a large family. And she never had very much in the house to eat. He said to her, "Please, may I lay down just a few minutes and rest?" She said, "I'll say you can." And the little children stood around and watched him, and he laid down. And then she went out to tend to some work that she was doing, and the little children watched him. In a little while he got up, and he said to her, "I bless you and bless your ground, bless every thing," he says, "here. And not one of you shall die with the flu, not one of you. But this lady across the street—I wanted to go there so bad—will lose some." He says, "But you will never want for food—never any more." And then, she said, she went after he had gone and everything was filled up. Her flour bin was filled, and there was butter; there was everything you could ask for. And she says, "I've never wanted for a thing. I don't know where it comes from, but it's put in my house when I'm away to work." And she says, "I've never wanted for anything since he came that day."

—Mrs. Irvin Fisher, 72. Bountiful, Utah. Collected in 1946 by Hector Lee and Miss Monza Higgs. #1148

Remember the Old Man When the Rocks Come Down

I feel I am walking on sacred ground when I even think or talk or write about my wonderful mother. She was so far different from any other person in the world. I believed everything she said or taught us children.

It's been so long ago, so I'll not be able to remember every detail of her account of believing she'd seen one of the Three Nephites who had been promised by the Savior that they could remain without tasting death until Jesus came again.

It was, I think, in the year 1923. One day a strange and old man came to the door and asked mother for a drink of water. Of course, she quickly reached for a glass and water for him, and as she came back to the door with the drink, she picked up some fruit (possibly a pear or a peach or two) and offered them to the stranger, with the glass of water.

After he had taken his drink, he accepted the fruit with the comment, "I don't usually eat (food or fruit), but I will because of you." (I think this is about the wording, but I don't remember exactly the words.) Then he said, "The women in town are so busy fanning themselves, they wouldn't even take time to give an old man a drink. They'll remember the old man when these rocks come rolling down."

Then the stranger was gone. Mother looked up and wondered, "Who was that man? Where did he come from? Where did he go?" She ran to the front of the house and looked in all directions for him, but he was nowhere to be seen.

A day or two later, a terrible thunderstorm hit the canyon, and the big cliff that hung out over the canyon fell and crashed as the terrible flood waters carried the monstrous rocks, stones, trees and rubbish down the canyon onto the little town of Willard without warning. It had just got dark.

The people who lived on the west side of the highway, mainly Gus Perry and family; Irven Perry and family; Artimus and family and others came fleeing to father's house for protection from the flood and thunder, lightning and drenching rain. They screamed that all of their animals, cows, horses, etc. had been taken away by the flood. It seemed no one ventured out into the storm to see what was happening. The noise and roar was so awful. The lightning and thunder was beyond description.

When things quieted down and folks dared go out to see what had happened, the town of Willard was deeply buried in a deep mass of rocks, mud, and water. There were broken trees and houses. Later we learned that two ladies from Willard had been drowned.

I was only eight or nine years of age and I wondered if we'd ever get back to school again! When we did, we walked in the center of the highway with banks of rocks and mud, many feet high, in the air on each side of the dugout road.

The strange thing about the flood was that our house was in the center of the canyon sloping down, and the massive flood and rocks and mud separated just as it got to our house where all the people had come for protection. And then closed in to cover the farms etc. all over town.

I'm sure we all did some praying to God for protection during those hours of horror.

Of course, it was mighty hard in those days to clean up the rubbish, trees, huge rocks, mud, etc. from off the gardens and farms and property. Father, or "Pappa" is what we children called our father, worked so hard. His farms were several and all had been flooded. I remember Mother commenting that possibly the flood and the tremendous work involved had something to do with father's heart condition and his early death about a year later.

—(FIFE folklore archive) Richard P. Young, 50. Computer specialist. Tooele, Utah. 1927. Collected in 1991 by Marie Fullmer. #1377

Weeds from the Wanderer

My aunt Rosina had always made it a point never to turn a person away from her door. One week she had had so many tramps and visitors and so forth that she felt she couldn't feed anyone else. She saw a man coming who looked as if he might be a salesman, so she told her daughter just to tell him that she didn't have time to talk to him, and so when the man come to the door she sent him on without finding out what he wanted. It worried my aunt, and she asked her daughter what he wanted but she didn't know. Since that time the Bermuda grass has come up so thick in her yard she can't get it out, and she says it is because she sent that man away.

—Mrs. Juanita Brooks, 35. St. George, Utah. 1939. #1064

Zeniff Destroyed

On August 8, 2017, Russell, his sons Clayton (13) and Eli (7), and Eric Eliason and his son Samuel (14) were driving on remote dirt Zeniff Road outside Snowflake, Arizona. Eric and Samuel had come down from Utah to visit. Russell was driving us to a hunting spot when he stopped for us to look at some crumbling adobe ruins of a few houses and a spring well. Next to the dried up well was a stone structure that looked like it was designed for a historical marker plaque. It looked like no plaque had ever been placed.

Russell said: "This is what is left of the town of Zeniff—an old Mormon pioneer settlement named after king Zeniff in the Book of Mormon. They did well for a while because they found this spring. But then the spring dried up and they all left. Old timers say that there was a wandering stranger who came through town and asked for water, but he was turned away. So, the stranger cursed the well so that it dried up, and then he disappeared.

Eric asked, "So, was he one of the Three Nephites?"

Russell: "That is the implication in the stories I hear—a Nephite or some destroying angel. People around here feel that the people of Zeniff were given a test from God. They failed."[31]

—Russell Smith. Mesa, Arizona. Collected in 2017 by Eric A. Eliason. #1517

EPILOGUE

Bringing Latter-day Saints Beliefs about Miracles into Focus

A Call for Academic Self-Correction

JULIE SWALLOW

Three Nephites stories often leave listeners with the question, Was that an experience with the divine? Similarly, we hope this book leaves readers with a sense of curiosity and wonder, particularly if those emotions lead them to ask more questions of, listen more intently to, and act with more compassion toward people of faith. We encourage readers to reflect on what it means to experience something divine and how those experiences shape our communities. Most importantly, we would like readers to consider how they can further the work of the Three Nephites both academically and personally.

Academics, students, and folklore enthusiasts can all participate in gathering more stories about the Three Nephites. Perhaps most importantly, we encourage researchers to begin collecting stories in Latter-day Saint communities outside of the United States. Membership in the church has grown more rapidly outside of the United States than inside it since the late 1990s. Bert's collection, started in the 1960s, tapered off at about the same time this transition in membership took place. Figures 7–10 indicate where the stories in his collection took place and where the stories were collected. We suspect that Three Nephites stories exist in Latter-day Saint faith communities around the world, but more research is needed to confirm our beliefs.

We also believe that further research needs to be done into where the stories are told, why they are told, and how they are received. In over two decades of teaching and collecting these stories at Brigham Young University, we've seen a change in both why the stories are told and how they are received. When Jill and Eric began teaching in the mid-1990s, most Three Nephites stories that students collected for their classes, including proclaiming-the-

Figure 7. This map shows where stories took place around the world. Fifty-four percent of stories happened in the United States, whereas other stories were found in the Middle East, Europe, Australia, Canada, and Central and South America.

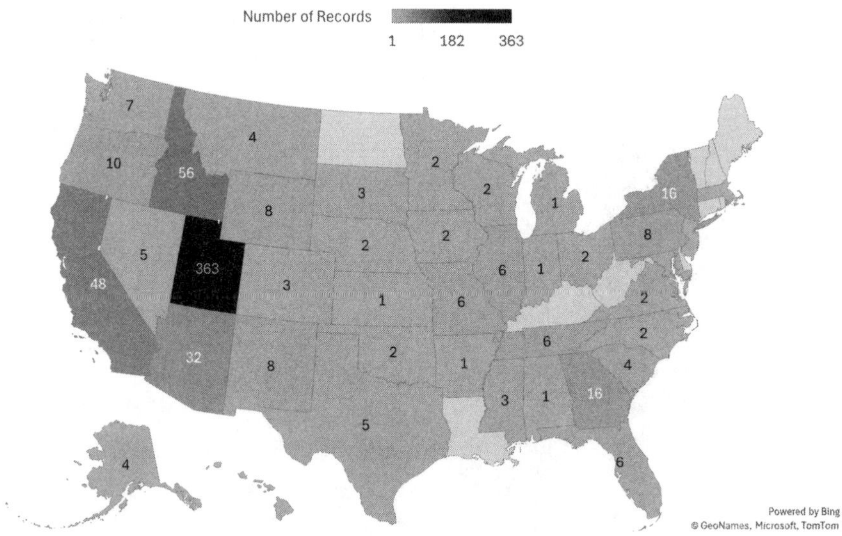

Figure 8. Following the previous figure, this map shows where in the United States the stories collected took place. Research found that most stories happened in Utah as compared to other states.

Figure 9. This map shows where stories were collected as they were told. Seventy-nine percent of stories were collected in the United States, whereas other stories were collected in Australia, the UK, Central America, and Canada.

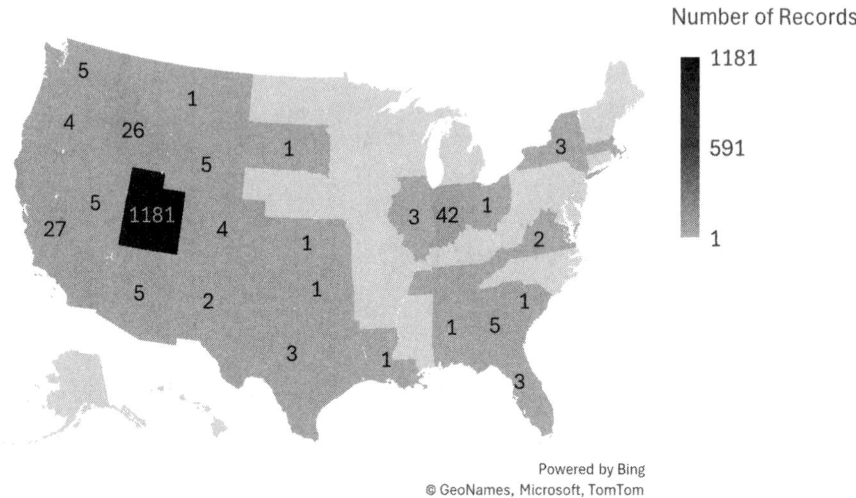

Figure 10. Following the previous figure, this map shows where in the United States the stories were collected. Research found that most stories were collected in Utah as compared to other states.

gospel stories, were told from a "friend of a friend" point of view, or there was no assumed connection between the teller and anyone who experienced the story events firsthand. The stories were often told in group settings with the intention of being both funny and disbelieved; they often highlighted the gullibility of Latter-day Saints. The Three Nephites stories, like urban legends, became almost too well known, so the recognizable plots and patterns served as a joke, something to be mocked or parodied.

Yet sometime in the past decade, things have shifted. The stories are often the personal experiences either of the teller or of the teller's family. Those telling the stories express more belief and more reverence for the recounted events. They are also more careful about where and to whom they tell the story. For example, in the contextual data for a story about David Lamoreaux's healing included in chapter 5 ("That Your Joy Might Be Full"), it is explained that "this story is not taken lightly by my family, it is believed to be one of the most spiritual events that occurred to our forefathers. It would never be openly discussed with strangers for fear that it would be chalked up as 'another Three Nephites story'" (#1485).

We wonder if this perceived shift is tied to changing generational attitudes about sharing sacred things or if it reflects something else taking place within Latter-day Saint communities. We added a few stories to Bert's collection because we wanted to demonstrate that the stories are still in active circulation. However, a study of Three Nephites stories currently being submitted to the William A. Wilson archives might clarify whether there is truly a transition away from the silly toward the sacred as we suspect.

Polishing the Mirror

Finally, we suggest that more emphasis be placed on gathering personal narratives highlighting the acts of service that members of the church provide for one another. Latter-day Saints do believe in miracles. They will attest that God watches over them and answers prayers. But more often than not, they find their prayers answered through the divinely inspired kindness of other people.[1] By extension, members feel they are doing God's work as they strive to meet the needs of those around them, often relying on spiritual guidance to do so. An equally large collection of stories about these kinds of "every day" miracles placed next to this volume would provide a much more accurate reflection of Latter-day Saint culture and belief. Two such collections placed side by side would, as Bert hoped, give people a "better understanding and appreciation of what [Latter-day Saints] feel and believe most deeply."[2]

In 1989 Bert called on scholars to turn their attention to these stories:

> Mormon supernatural stories do indeed exist in rich abundance (sometimes too rich for my taste). And they do play the roles I have described. But they are only part of a larger, more important, whole. The picture I have drawn here is not inaccurate; it is simply incomplete or, perhaps better, not quite in focus. It is, therefore, an uncertain mirror for truth. Fortunately, scholarship is a self-correcting process. The task for future Mormon folklore study will be to enlarge the picture, and to bring the images reflected in it into sharper focus."[3]

Unfortunately, the academic self-correcting process has been slow. To understand why church leaders can attest that "many miracles happen every day in the work of our Church and in the lives of our members,"[4] scholars will need to understand that, for LDS Church members, miracles happen in the rendering and receiving of everyday human kindness.

Eugene England, an LDS scholar and dear friend of Bert's, sent a letter to him in 1998 detailing service that his ward was providing for one individual in need:

> When we moved here our neighbor, Elmer Henderson was in the late stages of MS [multiple sclerosis]. Our priesthood quorum organized itself to care for him. Each day one of us would read to him for a few hours, each night one of us would help him bathe. A member had built a motorized sling to lift him from his wheelchair into the tub, which a single person could operate with a little training, and that is what we used so he could have a full body bath each day, which helped immensely in avoiding bedsores. This went on for about five years until he died.[5]

When Bert shared this story in 2007 at the Leonard J. Arrington Mormon History Lecture Series, he once again called on scholars to continue gathering supernatural stories while at the same time putting greater effort into gathering service stories. Both are required to understand "what makes Mormons tick."[6] We are beginning this self-correcting process and ask others to join us; this work will serve not only as an homage to William A. Wilson's legacy but also as a means of polishing the mirror of Latter-day Saint folklore studies.

Ministering

These acts of human kindness are promoted through LDS Church policy and practice. Prior to 2018, every member had a monthly home visit that included a gospel message from another nearby member through the home teaching or visiting teaching programs. In 2018, the home and visiting teaching programs were replaced with "ministering." The Church of Jesus Christ.org web page defines the program as follows: "Ministering is Christlike caring for others. It is motivated by our desire to follow the commandment to love our neighbor and includes serving people out of concern for their spiritual and temporal well-being."[7] Prophet Russell M. Nelson called it a "newer, holier approach to caring for and ministering to others."[8] Speaking of this new program Jean B. Bingham, then the Relief Society general president, promised that as members lovingly serve each other, "miracles will happen."[9]

Curiously, the word "ministering" has direct connections to the actions of the Three Nephites in the Book of Mormon. In 3 Nephi 28, the prophet and historian Mormon, after whom the book is named, states that the Three Nephites "did go forth upon the face of the land, and did minister unto all the people, uniting as many to the church as would believe in their preaching; baptizing them, and as many as were baptized did receive the Holy Ghost."[10] Then he promises that they "shall minister until all the scattered tribes of Israel, and unto all nations, kindreds, tongues and people, and shall bring out of them unto Jesus many souls, that their desire may be fulfilled, and also because of the convincing power of God which is in them."[11] Readers of the Book of Mormon know of Mormon's lonely and desperate situation as he records the destruction of his people. So it is particularly poignant to read these words in his chapter explaining the whereabouts of the Three Nephites: "Behold, I have seen them, and they have ministered unto me."[12] While there is no evidence to suggest that the name of the new program is connected to 3 Nephi 28, it does seem clear that Latter-day Saints are being asked to do what the Three Nephites do: Minister to those in need.

If this book inspires better scholarship in the realm of religious folklore and more acts of kindness everywhere, it will be an appropriate tribute to our friend William A. Wilson: scholar, humanitarian, and devout Christian. And after working closely with this collection over several decades, I believe that reading the tales of service rendered by the Three Nephites encourages people to "go and do likewise."[13]

Appendix

The following is an example of one of the original data tracking worksheets Bert created for Hannele and me to use while reading through his collection of Nephite stories. As mentioned in the prologue, those filled-out worksheets were lost in an office move. However, while combing through some of Bert's digital files a few years ago, I found a version of the worksheet we used in the 1990s. The casual font was selected by Bert, and we have left it as he created it. It would have been helpful to have this while I was creating the spreadsheet we used for this book but, upon comparison, we captured most of what he has listed here as well as some additional characteristics.

#______________

Collection________

Genre: L M

Gender

Collector: M F

Informant: M F

People in Story: M F B Fa U

Time (@=Estm. P,1,2,3,4 H=Horsepower M=Modern)

Of collection:

Of action in story:

Informant heard story:

Collector submitted story:

Place

of collection:

of action in story:

Belief

Collector: Y N

Informant: Y N

Original Teller: Y N

Age of informant at time of C: (C T A M O)___

Age of Collector_________

People in Story_________

Age of person from Whom Learned_____

Where Story Learned

Family/home; Job;

Friends/Social gathering;

Church talk; Church class

Seminary/Institute; Mission

Testimony meeting; BYU Religion Class

Other:

From Whom Story Learned

Parent; Sibling; Relative;

Friend; Church Teacher;

Seminary/ Institute Teacher;

Church Leader;Church Speaker

Companion; Religion Prof;

Other

NOTES:

Recurring Features

Number of Nephites 1 2 3 U

Remarkable Appearance____

Remarkable Disappearance_____

No Tracks in snow/dust/sand____

Remarkable speed/transportation____

Nephite is a Hitchhiker_____

Transportation___H A F

Nephite Described H E B S L V Brd

Age Y M O

Remarkable Knowledge or Can Read Mind__

Removes Socks and/or exposes Feet___

Dress S A W O

White Clothes/Robes_____

Leaves Feeling G S O

Eats but Food Remains_____

Other___ (If so see note)

Recurring Themes

Appears as Answer to Prayer____

Asks for Help (Food etc)_____

Rewards G F

Emotional Assistance_______
Physical Assistance_____
Assists the Traveler_____
Provides Food________
Works (on farm,ploughing etc)_______
Money Given_________
Saves from Disaster_____
Protects Someone/Something_____
Medical Advice/Assistance________
Gives Temporal Advice/Info_____
Spiritual Advice/assistance_______
Urges GW TW TA
Gives Genealogy Assistance_______
Newspaper Given______
Appears in Temple_______
Gives Blessing other than for sickness____
Administers to and/or heals the sick_____
Prepares way for Missionaries______
Teaches/Preaches the Gospel____
Converts Smne?____
Assists Missionaries____ E S B
Street Meeting____ S FS C O
Missionary Experience______
Gives Warning____ (Second Coming Y N)
Predicts Future______
Answers Perplexing Question______
Urges gathering Food Supply_______
Just Talks______
Intervenes in Arab-Israeli Conflict_______
Leaves Something Behind_______
Food Mentioned in Story_______
H or A Mentioned in Story_______
Word of Wisdom Mentioned_______
Chastity Mentioned_______
Indians mentioned in Story_______
Other:

Guide to Abbreviations

COLUMN #1
Under People in Story Fa=Family
U=Unclear

Time P=Pre 1900's, 1=1900-1925
2=1926-1950 3=1951-1976
4=1977-Present

Under Age of Informant Etc.
C=Child (0 - 12)
T=Teen (13 - 19)
A=Adult (20 - 39)
M=Middle Age (40-64)
O=Old Age (65+)

COLUMN #2
Of Nephites U=Unclear/uncertain

Transportation H=Horse A=Automobile F=Foot

Nephite Described H=Hair E=Eyes
B=Build S=Skin L=Limb V=Voice Brd=Beard

Age Y=Young M=Middle Age O=Old

Dress S=Shabby A=Average W=Well O=Other

Leaves Feeling G=Good S=Strange O=Other

Rewards G=Generosity F=Faithfulness

Urges GW=Genealogy Work TW=Temple Work
TA=Temple Attendance

Assists Missionaries E=Elders S=Sisters B=Both

Street Meeting S=Sings FS=Finds Scripture
C=Calms Crowd O=Other

Glossary

degree of glory: "Differing kingdoms in heaven. At the Final Judgment, each person will inherit an eternal dwelling place in a specific kingdom of glory, except those who are sons of Perdition."[1] Celestial glory is "the highest of the three degrees of glory that a person can attain after this life. Here the righteous will dwell in the presence of God the Father and His Son Jesus Christ."[2] Terrestrial glory is "the second of the three degrees of glory in which people will dwell after the Final Judgment."[3] Telestial glory is "the lowest of the three degrees of glory in which people will dwell after the Final Judgment."[4]

elder: "The title given to all holders of the Melchizedek Priesthood. For example, male missionaries are addressed as elders. Also, an Apostle is an elder, and it is proper to speak of members of the Quorum of the Twelve or Quorums of the Seventy by this title."[5]

fast and testimony meeting: "A Sunday, usually the first one of each month, on which Latter-day Saints abstain from food and drink for two meals and donate the equivalent cost, or more, to the Church to assist the poor and needy. The money donated is called a fast offering. The sacrament meeting on each Fast Sunday, called fast and testimony meeting, is devoted to the voluntary expression of testimony by members."[6] A testimony is the sincere spiritual belief of what is true in church teachings; verbally expressing that testimony is referred to as "bearing your testimony" in Latter-day Saint parlance.

First Presidency: "The First Presidency is the highest governing body of the Church. Along with the Quorum of the Twelve Apostles, members of the First Presidency are special witnesses of Jesus Christ. They seek the

Lord's guidance as they oversee the affairs of the Church."[7] The head of the First Presidency is the church president. Although all members of the First Presidency and the Quorum of the Twelve Apostles are "prophets, seers, and revelators," the president of the church exclusively uses the title "Prophet" and is exclusively able to receive revelation that applies to the entire church. The other two members of the First Presidency are the first counselor and the second counselor.

genealogy: Also called "family history," genealogy is "the process of discovering and learning more about our family members and gathering and preserving information about them. It is also performing saving ordinances for them in temples of the Church of Jesus Christ of Latter-day Saints."[8]

General Conference: "General conference is the worldwide gathering of the Church of Jesus Christ of Latter-day Saints. Twice a year, during the first weekend of April and the first weekend of October, Church leaders from around the world share messages, or sermons, focused on Jesus Christ and His gospel."[9]

gold plates: "Plates made of gold upon which the ancient American prophet Mormon abridged the record of his people. Joseph Smith translated the writings on the golden plates into what became the Book of Mormon: Another Testament of Jesus Christ."[10]

inactive: Latter-day Saint parlance referring to someone who has been baptized, and may still believe and self-identify as Mormon, but who does not attend church, or participate much in the life of their congregation. Since keeping covenants is central to the religion, "active members" often pray for and reach out to "inactives" (more formally known as "less active members") in hopes of bringing them back to church.

investigator: Latter-day Saints use the term "investigator" to refer to nonmembers who are learning about the church and are interested in converting.

laying on of hands: Latter-day Saints beliefs about the laying on of hands are similar to many other religions that incorporate the practice. In order to bestow a blessing or any degree of priesthood authority, an authorized individual—either a clergy member or a lay Latter-day Saint male, who has been ordained to the priesthood—places their hands upon the head of one receiving the blessing or authority and prays to bestow that blessing or authority on them. Sometimes a small amount of olive oil that has received a similar blessing, referred to as "consecrated oil," is applied to the head of the person receiving a blessing.

missionary: "Those who volunteer to serve missions are missionaries. Missionaries can be young adults or senior missionaries. Missionaries can be single men between the ages of eighteen and twenty-five, single women over the age of nineteen, or retired couples. Missionaries work with a companion of the same gender during their mission, with the exception of couples, who work with their spouse. Single men serve missions for two years and single women serve missions for eighteen months."[11] Senior missionaries are married couples of the age of forty or older with no children younger than eighteen or who depend on them. There is no upper age limit for senior missionaries.[12]

Missionary Training Center: Often referred to as the MTC, missionaries begin their missions here. They learn about teaching the gospel and, if they need to learn a language, they begin language training here as well. Missionaries spend between two and nine weeks here before going to the area where they have been called to serve. While there is a large training center in Provo, Utah, there are ten other training centers around the world in locations from New Zealand to Guatemala.

Nephi: The founder of the Nephite people, from whom the Three Nephites get their name. Nephi wrote the first two books in the Book of Mormon (1 Nephi and 2 Nephi), wherein he depicted himself as a faithful prophet and servant of God. Nephi's brother Laman was the founder of the Lamanite people, who would eventually wipe out all the Nephites, excluding the Three Nephites.

ordinance: "In the Church, an ordinance is a sacred, formal act or ceremony performed by the authority of the priesthood. Some ordinances are essential to our exaltation. They include baptism, confirmation, ordination to the Melchizedek Priesthood (for men), the temple endowment, and the marriage sealing. With each of these ordinances, we enter into solemn covenants with the Lord. Other ordinances, such as naming and blessing children, consecrating oil, and administering to the sick and afflicted, are also performed by priesthood authority. While they are not essential to our salvation, they are important for our comfort, guidance, and encouragement."[13]

patriarchal blessings: "A patriarch is a priesthood holder who is ordained to give special patriarchal blessings to members of the Church."[14] "Each patriarchal blessing is sacred, confidential, and personal. Therefore, it is given in private except for a limited number of family members who may be present. A person who receives a patriarchal blessing should treasure its words, ponder them, and live to be worthy to receive the promised blessings in this life and in eternity."[15]

prophets: Inspired men called to speak for the Lord, both living and ancient. Examples from the Bible are Moses, Isaiah, Noah, and Peter. In modern day, the Church of Jesus Christ of Latter-day Saints believe the president of the church to be the prophet—the only person on earth who receives revelation for the whole church.

quorum: "In the Church of Jesus Christ of Latter-day Saints, the word *quorum* refers to a group of men who hold a specific priesthood position. The highest quorum in the Church is the First Presidency, followed by the Quorum of the Twelve Apostles. There are also eight Quorums of Seventy that help administer the Church throughout the world. Local congregations, or wards, have quorums for each of the following priesthood offices: deacon, teacher, priest, and elder. There is also a quorum for high priests on the stake level."[16]

Relief Society: The women's organization in the Church of Jesus Christ of Latter-day Saints. When men meet in priesthood quorums on Sunday, women hold Relief Society meetings.

restored gospel: The Church of Jesus Christ of Latter-day Saints believes that the gospel as taught by Christ gradually became misunderstood and mistaught over the centuries that followed. As such, the priesthood—understood by Latter-day Saints to be the authority to act in God's name—was removed from mortal hands. The founding of the Church of Jesus Christ of Latter-day Saints in the early nineteenth century was a gradual return of long-lost gospel concepts to humanity from God, through the prophet Joseph Smith. Most importantly, the priesthood was given to men once more, allowing important ordinances to be fulfilled.

sealing: "An ordinance performed in the temple eternally uniting a husband and wife, or children and their parents."[17]

seminary: "Seminary is a worldwide, four-year religious educational program for youth ages 14 through 18. It is operated by the Church of Jesus Christ of Latter-day Saints but is open to teenagers of all faiths. In seminary, students and their teachers meet each weekday during the school year to study scripture. The curriculum is organized in a sequential or chapter by chapter manner. Instruction concentrates on a different volume of scripture each year, rotating between the following four courses: Old Testament, New Testament, Book of Mormon and Doctrine and Covenants and Church History. By the time a student graduates from seminary, he or she will have completed the study of all of the standard works of scripture."[18]

stake: "Congregations of the Church of Jesus Christ of Latter-day Saints are organized geographically, and members attend worship services near their home. Each member belongs to a stake, which is similar to a Catholic diocese. The leader of a stake is called the stake president. Each stake is comprised of several smaller congregations called wards or branches.

There are usually five to twelve wards and branches in a stake. In areas where the Church is new, members are organized into districts instead of stakes."[19]

temple: In Latter-day Saint doctrine, temples are literally the house of God. There, worthy members complete ordinances to enter into covenants with God. The two primary ordinances are sealing ordinances and the endowment. Sealings are the eternal bindings of families on earth and in heaven: "temple marriages" are weddings held in the temple wherein a man and a woman (and their prospective children) are sealed together for eternity. The endowment is a ceremony wherein members are taught information vital to entering the Celestial Kingdom (see "degrees of glory"). Temples also allow living members to perform ordinance ceremonies for the dead: Living members perform ordinances as physical stand-ins for deceased family members and ancestors of church members.

translated beings: "Persons who are changed so that they do not experience pain or death until their resurrection to immortality."[20]

Twelve Apostles: "An ordained leader in the Melchizedek Priesthood in the Church of Jesus Christ of Latter-day Saints. Apostles are chosen through inspiration by the president of the church, sustained by the general membership of the Church, and ordained by the First Presidency and the quorum of the Twelve apostles by the laying on of hands. They serve as general authorities—as distinguished from local and regional officers—holding their office as apostle for the duration of their lives. The senior apostle is the President of the Church."[21]

ward: A local congregation.

women's conference: Women's conference is an annual event in Utah where Latter-day Saint women from all over the world may come to listen to presentations and attend workshops on various spiritual and practical matters relating to their religion.

Word of Wisdom: A set of dietary recommendations that faithful Latter-day Saints follow, forbidding the use or consumption of alcohol, tobacco, coffee, and tea. The Word of Wisdom can be found canonized in LDS scripture in Doctrine and Covenants section 89. See https://www.churchofjesuschrist.org/study/scriptures/dc-testament/dc/89?lang=eng.

Notes

Prologue

1. William A. Wilson, "Freeways, Parking Lots, and Ice Cream Stands: Three Nephites in Contemporary Mormon Culture," in *The Marrow of Human Experience: The Essays on Folklore by William A. Wilson*, ed. Jill Terry Rudy and Diane Call (University Press of Colorado, 2006), 239.

2. We have made the decision to refer to Dr. William A. Wilson as Bert throughout this book to highlight our affection and esteem for him and because it is how he liked to be addressed. He was a brilliant scholar and our decision not to refer to him as Dr. Wilson should not diminish that. Anyone wishing to quote passages of this book in scholarly publications may choose to replace all references to our affectionate use of the name Bert with [Dr. Wilson].

3. Denise Wilson Jamsa, "A Daughter's Biography of William A. Wilson," in Rudy and Call, *Marrow of Human Experience*, 286.

4. William A. Wilson, interview by Denise Wilson Jamsa, November 19, 1996, tape 6b, William A. Wilson Archive, Harold B. Lee Library, Provo, Utah.

5. Audio recordings and transcriptions of Denise Jamsa's interviews with her father, Bert Wilson, are available in the William A. Wilson Folklore Archives at BYU, Provo, Utah. Jamsa is also working on a book dedicated to her father's biography, which we are looking forward to.

6. William A. Wilson, interview by Denise Wilson Jamsa, October 19, 2003, tape 6b, William A. Wilson Archive, Harold B. Lee Library, Provo, Utah; George Schoemaker, "'On Being Human': The Legacy of William A. Wilson," Westminstercollege .edu, archived June 21, 2004, at the Wayback Machine, https://web.archive.org/web/20040621213144/http://people.westminstercollege.edu/faculty/dstanley/folklore/Edited%20Final%20Draft/fiu1lschoemaker.htm.

7. Amber M. Nichols, "Richard M. Dorson: 1916–1918," archived June 10, 2008, at the Wayback Machine, https://web.archive.org/web/20080610120942/http://www.mnsu.edu/emuseum/information/biography/abcde/dorson_richard.html; Jan Harold Brunvand, "Obituary: Richard M. Dorson (1916–1981)," *Journal of American Folklore* 95, no. 377 (1981): 347.

8. Wilson, "Freeways," 238–39.

9. See the appendix for a sample of the worksheet.

10. Wilson, "Freeways," 247–48.

11. Wilson, "Freeways," 250.

12. Wilson, "Freeways," 246.

13. Wilson, "Freeways," 239–46.

14. William A. Wilson, "'Teach Me All That I Must Do': The Practice of Mormon Religion," in Rudy and Call, *Marrow of Human Experience*, 256.

15. Wilson, "Teach Me," 256.

16. Wilson, "Teach Me," 256.

17. This is an amalgamation of two similar paragraphs in two of his essays: William A. Wilson, "What's True in Mormon History? The Contribution of Folklore to Mormon Studies," in Leonard J. Arrington Mormon History Lecture Series, no. 13 (Utah State University Press, 2008), 24–25; and Wilson, "Teach Me," 260. The railroad worker Bert refers to in this paragraph was his father.

18. See "First Presidency" in the glossary; William A. Wilson, "Mormon Folklore: Faith or Folly?" *Brigham Young Magazine*, May 1995, 48.

19. In 1981, President Spencer W. Kimball announced the Three-Fold Mission of the Church. President Thomas S. Monson added the fourth mission in 2009. The current mission statement for the Church of Jesus Christ of Latter-day Saints can be found at https://www.churchofjesuschrist.org/learn/about-us?lang=eng.

20. The phrase "anxiously engaged" is found in the Latter-day Saint scripture Doctrine and Covenants 58: 27–28. It reads, "Verily I say, men should be anxiously engaged in a good cause, and do many things of their own free will, and bring to pass much righteousness; For the power is in them, wherein they are agents unto themselves. And insomuch as men do good they shall in nowise lose their reward." Latter-day Saints understand the word "anxiously" in this context to mean "diligently" or "eagerly engaged" rather than connoting unease or anxiety.

21. Wilson, "Teach Me," 260.

Introduction

1. 3 Nephi 28:2.

2. John 21:22; 3 Nephi 28:4–9.

3. 3 Nephi 28:30–31.

4. 3 Nephi 28:35–36.

5. Holland is currently a member of the Twelve Apostles. A member of the First

Quorum of the Seventy is considered a General Authority in the Church of Jesus Christ of Latter-day Saints.

6. Latter-day Saints use words like "telestial status" and "terrestrial state" to refer to different levels of holiness achievable in the afterlife. See "degree of glory" in the glossary for a more comprehensive explanation. Jeffrey R. Holland, *Christ and the New Covenant: The Messianic Message of the Book of Mormon* (Deseret Book, 1997), 305–306.

7. Holland, Christ and the New Covenant, 306.

8. LDS cosmology espoused by individuals such as Joseph Fielding Smith can be complicated. For more information about these ideas, see Joseph Fielding Smith, *Doctrines of Salvation: Sermons and Writings of Joseph Fielding Smith*, ed. Bruce R. McConkie (Deseret Books [c1954–1956]). The section titled "The Earth: Its Creation and Destiny" is a good place to begin.

9. Holland, Christ and the New Covenant, 306.

10. 3 Nephi 28:38–39.

11. Many of the stories in Bert's collection highlight the remarkable nature of their changed bodies, examples of which can be found under the subtitle "Nephites by the Numbers" in this chapter.

12. Mormon 1:13.

13. 3 Nephi 28:27–29.

14. This is also the time period (1835) when David W. Patten has an encounter with a dark spirit reported to be Cain.

15. Variations of this story abound. In many, someone sees three people they assume are hired hands completing the work.

16. The Hill Cumorah is a hill in Palmyra, New York, where Latter-day Saints believe Joseph Smith received the gold plates from the angel Moroni, who had buried the plates in the hill centuries prior. See "gold plates" in the glossary.

17. Orson Pratt and Joseph F. Smith, "Report of Elders Orson Pratt and Joseph F. Smith," *Millennial Star*, December 9, 1878, 772.

18. Pratt and Smith, "Report of Elders," 772.

19. Pratt and Smith, "Report of Elders," 773.

20. Brigham Young, "Extensive Character of the Gospel—Comprehensiveness of Divine Revelation, etc.," in *Journal of Discourses* 6 (1859): 283–95.

21. Brigham Young, "Extensive Character," 294–95.

22. Brigham Young, "Extensive Character," 295.

23. Orson Pratt, "Progress of the Work—Consecration—Preaching to Israel—The Times of the Gentiles—Sanctification of the Saints," in *Journal of Discourses* 2 (1855): 264.

24. John W. Taylor, "Ancient Prophecies Fulfilled in These Days—The Work of John and the Three Nephites—Preparation for the Coming of the Messiah," in *The Seventy-Third Semi-Annual Conference of the Church of Jesus Christ of Latter-day Saints* (Deseret News, 1902), 75.

25. Lynne McNeill, "Folklore: To Define or Not to Define: Why Is This a Question?" *Folklore Thursday* (blog), September 28, 2017 (site discontinued).

26. Lynne McNeill, *Folklore Rules: A Fun, Quick, and Useful Introduction to the Field of Academic Folklore Studies* (Utah State University Press, 2013), 16.

27. David Utter, "Mormon Folk-Lore," *The Folk-Lorist: Journal of the Chicago Folk-Lore Society* 1 (1892/1893): 76; William A. Wilson, "Freeways, Parking Lots, and Ice Cream Stands: Three Nephites in Contemporary Mormon Culture," in *The Marrow of Human Experience: The Essays on Folklore by William A. Wilson*, ed. Jill Terry Rudy and Diane Call (University Press of Colorado, 2006), 237.

28. William A. Wilson, "Austin and Alta Fife," in *Utah History Encyclopedia*, ed. Allen Kent Powell (University of Utah Press, 1994).

29. Wilson, "Freeways," 238.

30. Wilson, "Freeways," 238; Austin E. and Alta (Stevens) Fife, *Saints of Sage and Saddle* (Indiana University Press, Bloomington, 1956); Hector Lee, *The Three Nephites: The Substance and Significance of the Legend in Folklore* (University of New Mexico Press, 1949).

31. Tom Mould and Eric Eliason do an excellent job of tracing the history of Three Nephites scholarship, discussing how it parallels the history of Mormon folklore study itself and explaining why folklore attracts so many LDS scholars, in the introduction to their book *Latter-day Lore: Mormon Folklore Studies*. It is well worth a read. Wilson, *Marrow of Human Experience*, 238.

32. Church of Jesus Christ of Latter-day Saints, "Are John the Beloved and the Three Nephites Actually Still on the Earth? If So, What Are They Doing?" *Ensign*, November 2017, https://www.churchofjesuschrist.org/study/new-era/2017/11/to-the-point/are-john-the-beloved-and-the-three-nephites-actually-still-on-the-earth-if-so-what-are-they-doing?

33. Church of Jesus Christ of Latter-day Saints, "Lesson 134: 3 Nephi 28," in 2017 Book of Mormon Seminary Teacher Manual, accessed January 31, 2024, https://www.churchofjesuschrist.org/study/manual/book-of-mormon-seminary-teacher-manual-2017/introduction-to-third-nephi-the-book-of-nephi/lesson-134-3-nephi-28.

34. 3 Nephi 28:27–28.

35. Church of Jesus Christ, "Lesson 134."

36. Clyde J. Williams, "The Three Nephites and the Doctrine of Translation," in *The Book of Mormon: 3 Nephi 9–30: This Is My Gospel*, ed. Charles D. Tate and Monte S. Nyman (Salt Lake City, 1993), 249. Also at chrome-extension://efaidnbmnnnibpcajpcglclefindmkaj/https://archive.dev-bookofmormoncentral.org/sites/default/files/archive-files/pdf/nyman/2015-12-09/nyman_3_nephi_9-30_this_is_my_gospel.pdf.

37. Janice Kapp Perry, "I'm Trying to Be Like Jesus," in *Children's Songbook* (Church of Jesus Christ of Latter-day Saints, 1989), 78.

38. Ammon made himself servant to an enemy king, protected his sheep by chopping off the arms of would-be thieves, and eventually preaches the gospel to the king and converts a nation. Captain Moroni led the people to battle against a much larger

army, reminded the people of God, and created the title of liberty. He is different from the prophet Moroni; Captain Moroni was the later prophet's namesake.

39. Eric Eliason, in discussion with the author, October 2017.

40. David Hufford, *The Terror That Comes in the Night: An Experience-Centered Study of Supernatural Assault Traditions* (University of Pennsylvania Press, 1989).

41. See "temple work" in the glossary.

42. This story is not in the Wilson collection. It was collected by the William A. Wilson archivist, Christine Blythe, for her archival exhibit on the Three Nephites. The archive is located in BYU's Harold B. Lee Library.

43. William A. Wilson, "What's True in Mormon History? The Contribution of Folklore to Mormon Studies," Leonard J. Arrington Mormon History Lecture Series, no. 13 (Utah State University Press, 2008), 24.

44. See chapters 3 and 5.

45. See Jill's chapter, "Proclaiming-the-Gospel Stories," to learn more about a popular cycle of stories in which sister missionaries are protected by large men, often in "warrior" dress.

46. Barbara Walker, Introduction to *Out of the Ordinary: Folklore and the Supernatural* (Utah State University Press, 1995), 2.

47. Doctrine and Covenants 63: 9.

48. See "First Presidency" in the glossary.

49. Joseph Fielding Smith, "Preservation and Multiplication of Life—Dangers of Sign Seeking—Man Established in the Truth by Faithfulness and the Spirit of God," in *The Seventieth Semi-Annual Conference of the Church of Jesus Christ of Latter-day Saints* (Deseret News, 1900), 40.

50. Neil L. Andersen, "Spiritually Defining Memories," *Ensign*, April 2020, https://www.churchofjesuschrist.org/study/general-conference/2020/04/15andersen.

51. Tom Mould, *Still, the Small Voice: Narrative, Personal Revelation, and the Mormon Folk Tradition* (Utah State University Press, 2011), 77–78.

52. The full story, "A Blessing for a Dime," can be found in chapter 5, "That Your Joy Might Be Full."

53. To read the full account, see story #1662 in William A. Wilson's Three Nephites collection housed in the Harold B. Lee Library at BYU, Provo, Utah.

54. William A. Wilson, "Documenting Folklore," in *Folk Groups and Folklore Genres: An Introduction*, ed. Elliot Oring, 225–54 (Utah State University Press, 1986).

55. All graphs in this book represent our specific definitions of the terms. We invite scholars who are interested in specific aspects of this project to access the collection in the William A. Wilson Folklore Archives located in the Harold B. Lee Library on the BYU Provo campus and run their own calculations.

56. This story is a retelling of a story told to Eric Eliason by one of his students, which he then shared with me.

57. Wilson, "What's True," 6.

58. Dennis Lythgoe, "Mormon Folklore Gives a Look into a Unique Culture,"

Deseret News, December 24, 2006, https://www.deseret.com/2006/12/24/19992439/mormon-folklore-gives-a-look-into-a-unique-culture.

59. Wilson, "What's True," 9.

60. Wilson, "What's True," 12.

61. In 1987, when he wrote "Freeways, Parking Lots, and Ice Cream Stands," Bert indicated that Three Nephites stories involving Arab-Israelis seemed to be dying out, but he felt they would have resurgence whenever there were heightened tensions in the Middle East. However, they no longer seem to be actively circulating. It's unclear whether or not the dramatic events in Israel and Palestine during 2023 and 2024 will inspire a resurgence of stories in LDS culture in which Israel experiences divine protection.

62. Numbers given by the LDS Church History Library upon request. Request #CH109660.

63. A. E. Fife, "The Legend of Three Nephites among the Mormons," *Journal of American Folklore* 53, no. 207 (1940): 6.

64. Holland commented on this characteristic: "Twice they [the Three Nephites] were cast into a den of wild beasts, only to play with them as a child would a suckling lamb, receiving no harm. Such is not surprising when we remember that they (and therefore these animals?) now existed in a terrestrial state. When the earth is returned to its paradisiacal glory, the lamb will lie down with the lion, and all will be able to so play." Wilson, *Christ and the New Covenant*, 207.

65. The following was typed above this entry: "Published version written in Clarissa Young Spencer, 'No Footprints,' in *The Improvement Era*, Vol. 34 (February, 1931), pp. 231–232. Retold by Fife, JAFL, Vol. 53 (January–March, 1940), No. 12. Fife did not locate the original version and erroneously called the author Mrs. Jerome D. Spencer. She was the wife of John D. Spencer. Cf. #1048."

66. See "fast and testimony meeting" and "restored gospel" in the glossary.

67. William A. Wilson, "The Paradox of Mormon Folklore," in *BYU Studies Quarterly* 17, no. 1 (1976): 42; emphasis added.

68. William A. Wilson, "Paradox," 42; emphasis added.

69. Wilson, "What's True," 2; emphasis added.

70. Erin Hallstrom, "What I (Don't) Know," *LDS Living*, May/June 2017, 14.

71. Dan Davis, in discussion with Julie Swallow, August 2024.

Chapter 1. "Vanishing Hitchhiker" Nephites

The epigraph to this chapter is from Jalāl al-Dīn Muḥammad Rūmī, "Zero Circle," in *Ten Poems to Change Your Life*, by Roger Housden (Harmony Books, 2001), 43.

1. Jan Harold Brunvand, *The Vanishing Hitchhiker: American Urban Legends and Their Meanings* (W. W. Norton, 1981); Jan Harold Brunvand, *The Choking Doberman and Other "New" Urban Legends* (W. W. Norton, 1981); Jan Harold Brunvand, *The Baby Train & Other Lusty Urban Legends* (W. W. Norton, 1993).

2. David Stanley, *Folklore in Utah: A History and Guide to Resources* (Utah State University Press, 2004).

3. An "oikotype" is variant of any instance of folklore that displays characteristics specific to, and reflects distinctive features of, a locality, region, time period, or folk group such as ethnicity, religion, or avocational subculture. With just a few changes in the details of a narrative's text, such as the setting or a motif or two, a complex item of folklore that occurs with broad similarities across many distinctive cultures can be made to seem almost organically specific to a particular folk group in which the oikotype circulates. The term "oikotype" was coined by Swedish folklorist C. W. von Sydow. See "Folktale Studies and Philology: Some Points of View," in *The Study of Folklore,* ed. Alan Dundes, 219–42 (1948; Prentice Hall, 1965); Alan Dundes, "Geography and Folk-Tale Oicotypes: Carl Wilhelm von Sydow," in *International Folkloristics: Classic Contributions by the Founders of Folklore,* edited by Alan Dundes, 137–40 (Rowman & Littlefield, 1999).

4. Jan Harold Brunvand, "The Killer in the Backseat," in *The Vanishing Hitchhiker: American Urban Legends and Their Meanings* (W. W. Norton, 1981), 52–53.

5. Ethan Dunn, "Friend & Foe: Two Facets of the Vanishing Hitchhiker Legend Cycle," senior seminar project, submitted to the William A. Wilson Folklore Archive, Special Collections, BYU Library, November 20, 2018.

6. William R. Bascom, "Four Functions of Folklore," *Journal of American Folklore* 67, no. 266 (1954): 333–49.

7. Vladimir Propp, *Morphology of the Folktale*, 2nd ed., trans. Laurence Scott (University of Texas Press, 1968).

8. A good comprehensive treatment of the changes this movement wrought on the field can be found in Richard Bauman, *Folklore, Cultural Performances, and Popular Entertainments: A Communications-Centered Handbook* (Oxford University Press, 1992).

9. Ian Brodie, correspondent, personal conversation with author, November 2022.

10. Bill Ellis, "The Frackville Angel," in *Aliens, Ghosts, and Cults: Legends We Live* (University Press of Mississippi, 2001), 99–116.

11. In the 1920s, Swedish folklorist Carl Wilhelm von Sydow first coined the term "memorate" to refer to a personal narrative about the teller's own claimed supernatural encounter. Since then, many folklorists have dug into and raked over this topic, arguing about the meaning of the term and how best to use it. Von Sydow himself began to regard the many beings and beliefs found in stories contemporaneous to him as "ficts," or fanciful bogeymen used to manage children. But in recent decades most folklorists are more likely to rely on storytellers' own understandings of what is real and factual, at least for the purpose of distinguishing genres from each other, if not always for traditional knowledge's possible insight into the ostensible realities of supernatural beings and a real but (usually) unseen world. Today the term not only refers to ghosts, goblins, and fairies of yore but also to cryptids like Bigfoot and aliens who abduct. Dundes, "Geography and Folk-Tale Oicotypes," 137–40; Lauri

Honko, "Memorates and the Study of Folk Beliefs," *Journal of the Folklore Institute* 1, nos. 1/2 (1964): 5–19; Linda Dégh and Andrew Vázsonyi, "The Memorate and the Proto-Memorate," *Journal of American Folklore* 87, no. 345 (1974): 225–39.

12. Jacques Vallee, *Passport to Magonia: From Folklore to Flying Saucers* (H. Regnery, 1969).

13. One might wonder if some of the fine-grained, attention-to-detail Bible story readings presented here might produce different outcomes if they relied on different Bible translations. This is indeed an important issue to consider in understanding and interpreting the Bible, especially in evaluating any claim that certain similarities exist between very different parts of the Bible. Translators' various theological assumptions and translation philosophies and intentions for readers can produce quite different wording when rendered into English from the Bible's Hebrew, Aramaic, and Greek—especially when there are many varieties of English into which they might be translated, such as modern or archaic vocabulary; formal and informal registers; British, American, or international Englishes, and so on. To mitigate against this, I consulted my collection of every currently in-print Bible translation. I did not consult every translation for every story but tried to range wildly between paraphrase, dynamic, equivalence, and word-for-word translations associated with various scholarly and faith traditions. The quotes from, and references to, stories presented in this chapter are sometimes compilations of the wording of several different translations. The ones I turned to most included the following: the New Revised Standard Version (NRSV) of the *Harper Collins Study Bible* and *Oxford Annotated Bible* for their up-to-date scholarship and reliance on the full suite of available ancient manuscripts, as well as their attention to cultural and historical issues; the New English Translation (NET) for its copious linguistic and grammatical notes and commitment to providing, in its marginal notes, every plausible alternate translation of the source languages' wording; the King James Version (KJV) and English Standard Version (ESV) for their familiar and dignified wording; the Catholic New American Bible (NAB) and the Jewish Publication Society's Tanakh (JPS) as a check on the Protestant Evangelical dominance in many translation projects such as the popular New International Version (NIV). Perhaps surprisingly, but certainly significantly, all of these translations seem to be pretty much in agreement in presenting the story examples shared in this chapter as initially ambiguous encounters that may or may not have had religious significance, or may or may not have involved divine or mortal beings, whose theological significance only became more apparent later in the events depicted, if it did at all. While it is certainly true that passages may be cherry-picked showing dramatic differences between various Bible translations, my own experience, and that of others I know who spend a lot of time with a wide variety of Bible translations, is being impressed that even the most different translations sure seem to convey pretty much the same information most of the time, in their broad strokes, as well as their small details.

14. The scholarly tradition approaching the Bible as literature foregrounds ancient genre forms and understandings as a primary lens of interpretation and appreciation. Examples include Leland Ryken, *How to Read the Bible as Literature* (Zondervan,

1985); Leland Ryken, *A Complete Handbook of Literary Forms in the Bible* (Crossway, 2014); and John B. Gabel, Charles B. Wheeler, Anthony D. York, and David Citino, *The Bible as Literature: An Introduction*, 5th ed. (Oxford University Press, 2005).

15. The scholarship at the intersection of folklore/orality with biblical studies is vast because their overlapping relevance is vast. See, for example, Alan Dundes, *Holy Writ as Oral Lit: The Bible as Folklore* (Rowman & Littlefield, 1999); Susan Niditch, *Oral World and Written World: Ancient Israelite Literature* (Westminster John Knox Press, 1996); Susan Niditch, *Folklore and the Hebrew Bible* (Wipf & Stock, 2004); David M. Carr, *Writing on the Tablet of the Heart: Origins of Scripture and Literature* (Oxford University Press, 2008); David M. Carr, *The Formation of the Hebrew Bible: A New Reconstruction* (Oxford University Press, 2011); Marcel Jousse, *Memory, Memorization, and Memorizers: The Galilean Oral-Style Tradition and Its Traditionists* (Cascade Books, 2018); Eric Eve, *Behind the Gospels: Understanding the Oral Tradition* (Fortress Press, 2014); Rafael Rodriguez, *Oral Tradition and the New Testament: A Guide for the Perplexed* (T&T Clark, 2014); James D. G. Dunn, *The Oral Gospel Tradition* (Eerdmans, 2013). For some ways the folklore studies/Bible scholarship nexus might illuminate various aspects of the Latter-day Saint experience, see Eric A. Eliason, "Orality, Literacy, and the Cultural World of the Bible, in Ancient Near Eastern Scholarship and Latter-day Saint Reception," in *The Bible and the Latter-day Saint Tradition,* ed. Taylor Petrey, Eric A. Eliason, and Cory Crawford, 254–68 (University of Utah Press, 2023).

16. Some evidence suggests that in the earliest days of the Restoration, reporting a personal visit from Jesus was a prerequisite to becoming an apostle. See D. Michael Quinn, "The Twin Charges of Apostleship," in *The Mormon Hierarchy: Extensions of Power* (Signature Books, 1997), 1–20. More recently, a desire to return to this idea has led to tension with, and disaffection from, the mainstream church for some, such as the followers of Denver C. Snuffer Jr. See Snuffer, *The Second Comforter: Conversing with the Lord through the Veil* (Mill Creek Press, 2006).

17. Westminster Assembly, *The Westminster Confession of Faith*, 1646, chapter 2, verse 1, https://www.ligonier.org/learn/articles/westminster-confession-faith.

18. Latter-day Saint apostle Jeffrey R. Holland apparently saw such scholarship having so much resonance with Restoration theology that he cited a few examples of it in his 2007 General Conference talk, "The Only True God and Jesus Christ Whom He Hath Sent." With gratitude, I reproduce below Elder Holland's footnote 17 as it is an excellent collection of references to scholarship noting embodied concepts of God in biblical Israel and among the earliest Christians:

> David L. Paulsen, "Early Christian Belief in a Corporeal Deity: Origen and Augustine as Reluctant Witnesses," *Harvard Theological Review* 83, no. 2 (1990): 105–16; David L. Paulsen, "The Doctrine of Divine Embodiment: Restoration, Judeo-Christian, and Philosophical Perspectives," *BYU Studies* 35, no. 4 (1996): 7–94; James L. Kugel, *The God of Old: Inside the Lost World of the Bible* (2003), xi–xii, 5–6, 104–106, 134–35; Clark Pinnock, *Most Moved Mover: A Theology of God's Openness* (2001), 33–34.

Elder Holland's conference address can be found at https://www.churchofjesuschrist.org/study/general-conference/2007/10/the-only-true-god-and-jesus-christ-whom-he-hath-sent?lang=eng.

19. Eric A. Eliason, "Spirit Babies and Divine Embodiment: PBEs, Bible Scholarship, First Vision Accounts, and the Experience-Centered Approach to Mormon Folklore," *BYU Studies Quarterly* 53, no. 2 (2014): 21–28; and Eric A. Eliason, "Angels among the Mormons," in *The Big Book of Angels*, ed. Beliefnet (Rodale Books, 2002), 96–104.

20. Gabriel Bunge, *The Rublev Trinity: The Icon of the Trinity by the Monk-Painter Andrei Rublev* (St. Vladimir's Seminary Press, 2007).

21. William G. Deaver, *Did God Have a Wife? Archaeology and Folk Religion in Ancient Israel* (Eerdmans, 2008).

22. "Elohim: Hebrew god," *Encyclopædia Britannica*, https://www.britannica.com/topic/Elohim.

23. For scholarship that seeks to flesh out a possible pre-cultural universal nature to many societies' reported experiences with potentially supernatural beings, see David J. Hufford, *The Terror That Comes in the Night: An Experience-Centered Study of Supernatural Assault Traditions* (University of Pennsylvania Press, 1989); Barbara Walker, *Out of the Ordinary: Folklore & the Supernatural* (Utah State University Press, 1995.)

24. Christopher James Blythe, "The Prophetess of Endor, Reception of 1 Samuel 28 in Nineteenth Century Mormon History," *Journal of Bible Reception* 4, no. 1 (2017): 43–70.

25. Ronald W. Walker, *Wayward Saints: The Godbeites and Brigham Young* (University of Illinois Press, 1998); Stephen Taysom, "'Satan Mourns Naked upon the Earth': Locating Mormon Possession and Exorcism Rituals in the American Religious Landscape, 1830–1977," *Religion and American Culture: A Journal of Interpretation* 27, no. 1 (2017): 57–94.

26. Frank F. Judd Jr. and Terrence Szink, "John the Beloved in Latter-day Saint Scripture (D&C 7)," in *The Doctrine and Covenants: Revelations in Context: The 37th Annual Brigham Young University Sidney B. Sperry Symposium*, ed. Andre H. Hedges, J. Spencer Fluhman, and Alonzo L. Gaskill (Brigham Young University, 2012), https://rsc.byu.edu/doctrine-covenants-revelations-context/john-beloved-latter-day-scripture-dc-7, accessed January 20, 2024.

27. For examples of memorates recounting visitations from deceased relatives, see the following examples found in the William A. Wilson Folklore Archive, L. Tom Perry Special Collections, Harold B. Lee Library at Brigham Young University: Alyssa Sims (collector), "Heavenly Visit from Deceased Relatives," FA 02, submitted 2021; Lesa Munyan (collector), "Dead Husband Visits Dying Wife," FA 03, submitted 2021; Veronica Wright, "Collection of Apparition Stories," FA 1 box 339, folder 3, item 4073, submitted 2008.

28. Ghost stories' implicit claim often seems to be that one possible interpretation is that the ghost is the disembodied spirit of a deceased person. While this may seem

so obvious to us in the West that it would not even need to be pointed out, it is by no means the only way to make sense of narrative reports of witnessing what looks like the image of someone who died. Even in a post-Christian context, this presumption assumes a host of Christian concepts: that humans have a spirit separate from their physical body, that this spirit looks human but is non-corporeal; or that it persists in existing after the body dies in some sort of afterlife. While narrative reports of encountering what looks like a person known to be dead occur in many cultures, they are not always understood to be ghosts. For example, in a classic ethnographic essay that underscores the culturally transmitted nature of beliefs that are so deep and pervasive that they can seem universal, anthropologist Laura Bohannon claimed that Africa's Tiv people have no conception of the afterlife and interpret what we would call a ghost as trickery brought about by witchcraft. Laura Bohannon, "Shakespeare in the Bush," *Natural History* 75 (1966): 28–33.

29. "US Religious Knowledge Executive Summary," Pew Research Center, September 28, 2010, https://www.pewresearch.org/religion/2010/09/28/u-s-religious-knowledge-survey/, accessed January 19, 2024.

30. Stanley Kripal, *The Flip: Who You Really Are and Why It Matters* (Penguin, 2020); D. W. Pasulka, *American Cosmic: UFOs, Religion, Technology* (Oxford University Press, 2019); D. W. Pasulka, *Encounters: Experiences with Nonhuman Intelligences* (St. Martin's Press, 2023).

31. On ethnobotany, see Richard Evans Schultes and Siri von Reis, *Ethnobotany: Evolution of a Discipline* (Timber Press, 1995); Wade Davis, *One River* (Simon & Shuster, 1997); Paul E. Minnis, *Ethnobotany: A Reader* (University of Oklahoma Press, 2000). On traditional ecological knowledge, see Fikret Berkes, *Sacred Ecology: Traditional Ecological Knowledge and Resource Management* (Taylor & Francis, 1999); J. T. Ingliss, *Traditional Ecological Knowledge: Concepts and Cases* (International Development Research Center, 1993); V. M. Toledo, "Ethnoecology: A Conceptual Framework for the Study of Indigenous Knowledge of Nature," in *Ethnobiology and Biocultural Diversity*, ed. John R. Stepp and associates (International Society of Ethnobiology, 2002). On the experience-centered approach, see Hufford, *Terror That Comes in the Night*; B. Walker, *Out of the Ordinary*.

32. David J. Hufford, "Beings Without Bodies: An Experience-Centered Theory of the Belief in Spirits," in *Out of the Ordinary: Folklore and the Supernatural* (Utah State University Press, 1995), 20–22.

33. Hufford, *Terror That Comes in the Night*, 12–17, 46.

34. This information is from the author's personal conversations with David Hufford in the late 1990s and early 2000s.

35. The author wishes to thank the anonymous reviewer who pointed out this connection.

36. Gregory A. Prince, *Power from On High: The Development of Mormon Priesthood* (Signature Books, 2019), 178–81.

37. Those active in the faith for decades have noticed both decreasing quantity and specificity of items in church guidance on preparedness, which includes food. This has

been noted in a popular magazine aimed at mostly North American Latter-day Saints. Haley Lundberg, "What's the Church's Current Recommendation on Food Storage?" *LDS Living*, March 21, 2022, https://www.ldsliving.com/what-is-the-churchs-current-recommendation-on-food-storage/s/10518.

38. Latter-day Saint preparedness culture has provided important influence in the emergence of the "prepper" movement/subculture, not just in the United States but worldwide, which can be seen in news stories such as the following from the United Kingdom: Sky News US Team, "Mormon Teaching of Food Storage Catching On: Many of the Food Banks That Do Internet Sales Are Based in Utah, Where the Church Is Based, and Has Strong Influence," *Sky News*, December 24, 2013, https://news.sky.com/story/mormon-teaching-of-food-storage-catching-on-10423573.

39. William A. Wilson, "Freeways, Parking Lots, and Ice Cream Stands: Three Nephites in Contemporary Mormon Culture," in *The Marrow of Human Experience: The Essays on Folklore by William A. Wilson*, ed. Jill Terry Rudy and Diane Call, 236–52 (University Press of Colorado, 2006).

40. Jack Reid, *Roadside Americans: The Rise and Fall of Hitchhiking in a Changing Nation* (University of North Carolina Press, 2020).

41. For a rich ethnographic evocation of Latter-day Saints' knowledge, cultivation, and interpretation of "promptings," see Tom Mould, *Still, the Small Voice: Narrative, Personal Revelation, and the Mormon Folk Tradition* (Utah State University Press, 2011).

42. 1 Kings 19:12.

43. If English speakers in general have Jan Brunvand's *Vanishing Hitchhiker* to thank for popularizing the term "urban legend" in common usage, folklorists might have him to thank for the widespread use of "FOAF" among folklorists.

44. Hebrews 13:1–2 (ESV).

45. Usually, prophetic warnings in scripture, as well as Three Nephites stories, come with the proviso that calamity can be avoided if the prophecy's recipients repent. Occasionally, the narrative suggests that even immediate repentance cannot stop destruction when wickedness has gone on too long. In this theme, this story echoes King Josiah's fate in 2 Kings 22:15–20.

46. Seminary is a religious education program for young Latter-Day Saints between the ages of fourteen and eighteen.

47. This story inverts the genre expectation that the story subject is driving and the Nephite is hitchhiking.

Chapter 2. The Worldwide End of the World

1. Doctrine and Covenants 133:37.

2. Isaiah 2; Malachi 4:5–6.

3. To understand Latter-day Saint views on the last days, see Christopher James Blythe, *Terrible Revolution: Latter-day Saints and the Apocalypse* (Oxford University Press, 2020).

4. 3 Nephi 28:7.

5. 3 Nephi 28:31.

6. Roger of Wendover and Matthew Paris, *Roger of Wendover's Flowers of History: Comprising the History of English from the Descent of the Saxons to A.D. 1235*, trans. and ed. J. A. Giles (Henry G. Bohn, 1849), 514.

7. Michael Allred, *Madman*, vol. 1 (Dark Horse Books, 2021; library ed.), 280.

8. 1 Nephi 13:12.

9. As scholar Zachary McLeod Hutchins has argued, "Nothing in the text identifies Nephi's man among the Gentiles as Columbus; he could be Columbus's cabin boy, Bartholomew de las Casas, Amerigo Vespucci, John Cabot, John Smith, or a thousand other Renaissance-era explorers." Zachary McLeod Hutchins, "I Lead the Way, Like Columbus," in *Americanist Approaches to the Book of Mormon*, ed. Elizabeth Fenton and Jared Hickman (Oxford University Press, 2019), 392.

10. See "Twelve Apostles" in the glossary.

11. Orson Hyde, *A Voice from Jerusalem; or, A Sketch of the Travels and Ministry of Elder Orson Hyde: Missionary of the Church of Jesus Christ of Latter Day Saints, to Germany, Constantinople, and Jerusalem* (Albert Morgan, 1842), 368.

12. Washington Irving, A History of the Life and Voyages of Christopher Columbus (John Murray, 1828), 1:177–88.

13. Orson Hyde, "Celebration of the Fourth of July," *Journal of Discourses* 6 (1859): 367–68.

14. George Lippard, *Washington and His Generals: or, Legends of the Revolution* (G. B. Zieber and Co., 1847), 394.

15. *The State* [Columbia, SC], "Superstition Helps Protect Structure," July 17, 1970.

16. Patrick Mason, *The Mormon Menace: Violence and Anti-Mormonism in the Postbellum South* (Oxford University Press, 2011).

17. Orson Pratt, "Redemption of Zion . . .," *Journal of Discourses* 17 (1875): 289–300.

18. "Vision of Arapine on the Night of the 4th of Feb 1855," Brigham Young Office files, Church History Library, Salt Lake City, Utah.

19. George Washington Hill, "An Indian Vision," *Juvenile Instructor* 12 (January 1877): 11.

20. J. Reuben Clark, Sermon, in *General Conference Report*, October 5, 1946, 88.

21. Ether 13:5.

22. Hyde, *Voice from Jerusalem*, 29.

23. William A. Wilson, "Freeways, Parking Lots, and Ice Cream Stands: Three Nephites in Contemporary Mormon Culture," in *The Marrow of Human Experience: The Essays on Folklore by William A. Wilson*, ed. Jill Terry Rudy and Diane Call (University Press of Colorado, 2006), 243.

24. 2 Kings 6:16–17.

25. Joseph Fielding Smith, *The Signs of the Times: A Series of Discussions . . . with Additional Information Taken From Events From 1942 to 1952* (Salt Lake City: Deseret Book, 1952), 228–229.

26. Wilson, "Freeways," 243.

27. This item seems to be referencing John Trumbull's painting *Declaration of Independence*, which was installed in the US Capitol rotunda in 1826. https://www.aoc.gov/explore-capitol-campus/art/declaration-independence.

28. This is the second of four stories about the pillar that Jepson recorded in the Wilson collection. The first account is "Pillar Marks Slavery Atrocity to Stand until Second Coming."

29. Tuba was a Hopi chief who converted to the Church of Jesus Christ of Latter-day Saints in 1876.

Chapter 3. Proclaiming-the-Gospel Stories

1. Bert Wilson describes a similar structure for all Three Nephites stories in "What's True in Mormon Folklore: The Contribution of Folklore to Mormon Studies," in *Leonard J. Arrington Mormon History Lecture Series*, no. 13 (Utah State University Press, 2007).

2. Narratologists study the building blocks, or grammar, of stories. See Arthur Frank, *Letting Stories Breathe: A Socio-Narratology* (University of Chicago Press, 2010), 200.

3. Frank, *Letting Stories Breathe*, 54.

4. This works for fiction as well because stories afford tellers and listeners vicarious experiences. See Maria Nikolajeva, *Reading for Learning: Cognitive Approaches to Children's Literature* (John Benjamins Publishing, 2014).

5. Wilson, "What's True," 9.

6. Richard Bauman, *Story, Performance, and Event: Contextual Studies of Oral Narrative* (Cambridge University Press, 1986), 2.

7. See Richard Bauman, *Verbal Art as Performance* (Waveland Press, 1984).

8. A. E. Fife, "The Legend of the Three Nephites among the Mormons," *Journal of American Folklore* 53, no. 207 (1940): 1–49; Hector Lee, *The Three Nephites: The Substance and Significance of the Legend in Folklore* (University of New Mexico Press, 1949).

9. Elliott Oring gives a useful approach to folk narrative genres of myth, legend, and folktale that develops these storytelling concepts in more detail; see Elliott Oring, "Folk Narrative," in *Folk Groups and Folklore Genres: An Introduction*, ed. Elliott Oring, 121–45 (Utah State University Press, 1986).

10. Elliott Oring, "Legendry and the Rhetoric of Truth," *Journal of American Folklore* 121 (2008): 133.

11. Oring, "Legendry," 133.

12. Tom Mould, *Still, the Small Voice* (University Press of Colorado, 2011), 89.

13. Ronald E. Bartholomew, "Nineteenth-Century Missiology of the Bedfordshire Conference," *Journal of Mormon History* 37, no. 1 (2011): 215.

14. Bartholomew, "Nineteenth-Century Missiology," 217; emphasis added. Writing specifically of the Bedfordshire Conference in nineteenth-century England, and related with other LDS mission areas and eras, Bartholomew identifies four distinctive

elements of this restoration theology: scriptural literalism, apocalyptic millenarianism, continuing revelation, and evangelism. Because proclaiming-the-gospel Three Nephites stories show how God's power and his messengers operate directly in the lives and work of Latter-day missionaries, scriptural literalism and apocalyptic millenarianism relate particularly to our study.

15. Latter-day Saints understand their commitment to proselytizing as a continuation of the Hebrew Bible's Abrahamic covenant and the New Testament Great Commission. Calling missionaries to full-time service emphasizes the ongoing expectation of church members to go about the world gathering the people of Israel before Christ's Second Coming.

16. Writing of Roman Catholic understanding of mission, Stephen Bevans, in his article "Roman Catholic Perspectives on Mission" (*Ecumenical Review* 66, no. 1 (2014), posits a "distinctively Catholic" approach that involves the ecumenical acts of "drawing on any truth that can help deepen an understanding of the entire church's great commission to proclaim and witness to Jesus Christ to all creation," an approach that includes specific statements issued by the Catholic Church since 1919 and sees baptism as a call bringing every Catholic Christian "to mission" (68, 70). The World Council of Churches' recent documents on mission and discipleship connect proclaiming Christ with acts of reconciliation: "In the passage [2 Corinthians 5:18–20], God is and acts as a missionary God. . . . When we share God-given reconciliation in Christ, we take part in God's mission and become ambassadors of reconciliation and unity with and for one another. This is mission." Risto Jukko, *Call to Discipleship: Mission in the Pilgrimage of Justice and Peace, WCC Commission on World Mission and Evangelism Documents 2018–2021* (World Council of Churches, 2021).

17. Dallin H. Oaks and Lance B. Wickman, "The Missionary Work of the Church of Jesus Christ of Latter-day Saints," in *Sharing the Book: Religious Perspectives on the Rights and Wrongs of Proselytism*, ed. John Witte Jr. and Richard C. Martin (Orbis Books, 1999), 247.

18. Oaks and Wickman, "Missionary Work," 247–48.

19. Histories of LDS missions tend to be geographically centered, and a comprehensive book remains to be written.

20. Rex Thomas Price, "The Mormon Missionary of the Nineteenth Century" (PhD diss., University of Wisconsin–Madison, 1991).

21. Jessie L. Embry, "LDS Sister Missionaries: An Oral History Response, 1910–71," *Journal of Mormon History* 23, no. 1 (1997); Matthew McBride, "'Female Brethren': Gender Dynamics in a Newly Integrated Missionary Force, 1898–1915," *Journal of Mormon History* 44, no. 4 (2018).

22. See the stories about preparing whole communities to accept the gospel in chapter 2.

23. Price, "Mormon Missionary"; Embry, "LDS Sister Missionaries."

24. Wilson, "What's True," 13.

25. 3 Nephi 28:18–22.

26. Wilson, "What's True," 14.

27. Wilson, "What's True," 15–16.

28. William A. Wilson, "The Study of Mormon Folklore: An Uncertain Mirror for Truth," in *The Marrow of Human Experience: Essays on Folklore by William A. Wilson*, ed. Jill Terry Rudy and Diane Call (University Press of Colorado, 2006), 182; William A. Wilson, "'Teach Me All That I Must Do': The Practice of Mormon Religion," in Rudy and Call, *Marrow of Human Experience*, 253.

Chapter 4. Mix-ups, High Jinks, and Jokes

1. Matthew 19:26.

2. "Behold! I Am a God of Miracles," Ronald A. Rasband, Church of Jesus Christ of Latter-day Saints, https://www.churchofjesuschrist.org/study/general-conference/2021/04/52rasband?lang=eng, accessed August 29, 2024.

3. Elliott Oring, *Jokes and Their Relations* (University Press of Kentucky, 1992), 2.

4. Elliott Oring, introduction to "The Seriousness of Mormon Humor," in William A. Wilson, *The Marrow of Human Experience* (Utah State University Press, 2006), 222.

5. William A. Wilson, "What's True in Mormon Folklore? The Contribution of Folklore to Mormon Studies" (2007). Arrington Annual Lecture. Paper 12. https://digitalcommons.usu.edu/arrington_lecture/12.

6. Dirkmaat said the word "testimony" using air quotes.

7. Gerrit Dirkmaat, "LDS Educators Conference—Gerrit J. Dirkmaat & J. Gordon Daines III," Conference address, Provo, Utah, July 8, 2019, https://www.youtube.com/watch?v=6yQxFWHhRGc.

8. Peter Narvaez, "The Folk Parodist," *Canadian Folk Music Journal* 5 (1927): 32–37.

9. Eric Eliason, in discussion with the author, October 2017.

10. Oring, introduction to "The Seriousness of Mormon Humor," 222.

11. Oring, *Jokes and Their Relations*, 83.

12. William A. Wilson, "The Seriousness of Mormon Humor," in *Marrow of Human Experience* (Utah State University Press, 2006), 234.

13. Wilson, "Seriousness of Mormon Humor," 235.

Chapter 5. That Your Joy May Be Full

1. William A. Wilson, "What's True in Mormon History? The Contribution of Folklore to Mormon Studies," in Leonard J. Arrington Mormon History Lecture Series, no. 13 (Utah State University Press, 2008), 256.

2. Wilson, "What's True," 256.

3. Wilson, "What's True," 257.

4. James E. Faulconer, foreword to *Postponing Heaven: The Three Nephites, the Bodhisattva, and the Madhi*, by Jad Hatem, trans. Jonathon Penny, ix–xii (Neal A. Maxwell Institute for Religious Scholarship, 2015).

5. Faulconer, foreword, xi.

6. Latter-day Saints believe that men ordained to the priesthood can call upon God's power to heal the sick and afflicted, typically administered through the laying on of hands.

7. In the early church, both women and men administered blessings to the sick. For more information about the history of priesthood blessings in the LDS Church, see "Priesthood Ordinances and Blessings," Church of Jesus Christ of Latter-day Saints, https://www.churchofjesuschrist.org/study/manual/family-guidebook/priesthood-ordinances-and-blessings?lang=eng.

8. See "First Presidency" in the glossary.

9. *Church News Archives*, "President Hinckley: Work for Dead Is Essential to Earth's Purpose," November 19, 1994, https://www.thechurchnews.com/1994/11/19/23256235/president-hinckley-work-for-dead-is-essential-to-earths-purpose.

10. Margaret McNeil Ballard, "Autobiography of Margaret McNeil Ballard, Wife of Henry Ballard. Utah Pioneer," unpublished manuscript, 1917, 20–21, https://archive.org/details/autobiographyofm00ball.

11. 1 Kings 17:13–14.

12. Hebrews 13:2.

13. In the Wilson collection, there are also four stories where someone feels they were tested and failed. That person feels guilt. Guilt seems like a self-punishment rather than an inflicted punishment, so I did not include these stories in retributive number.

14. Lerona Abigail Wilson Martin, *Life Sketches and Experiences of Lerona Wilson*, vol. 1, unpublished manuscript, typewritten by Alexander I. Wilson (1932), 101–102. Merrill-Cazier Special Collections & Archives, Folklore Collection. FOLK COLL 1 no. 355.

15. Latter-day Saints consecrate olive oil by praying over it, setting it apart to be used to bless the sick and afflicted. Consecrated oil is innately holy. Liquor, on the other hand, is explicitly prohibited by the Word of Wisdom and, as such, is seen as a spiritually harmful substance.

16. It should be noted that this article was written in 1995. There is no evidence to suggest that this story is still circulating among missionaries as it once was.

17. William A. Wilson, "Mormon Folklore: Faith or Folly?" *Brigham Young* magazine (May 1995), 54.

18. Wilson, "Mormon Folklore," 54.

19. Wilson, "Mormon Folklore," 54.

20. Wilson, "Mormon Folklore," 54; emphasis added.

21. 3 Nephi 28:9–10.

22. John 15:10–12 (KJV); emphasis in original.

23. Russell M. Nelson, "Joy and Spiritual Survival," October General Conference, 2016, https://www.churchofjesuschrist.org/study/general-conference/2016/10/joy-and-spiritual-survival?lang=eng.

24. William A. Wilson, "The Study of Mormon Folklore: An Uncertain Mirror for Truth," in *Marrow of Human Experience, The: Essays on Folklore by William A. Wilson*, ed. Jill Terry Rudy and Diane Call (University Press of Colorado, 2006), 196.

25. Wilson, "Study of Mormon Folklore," 196.

26. See passage from William A. Wilson's essay "Teach Me All That I Must Do: The Practice of Mormon Religion," in Rudy and Call, *Marrow of Human Experience*, 257. "Once one understands that service is a vital and central part of LDS belief, then those dramatic tales of divine intervention take on an entirely different character. They can be seen not simply as accounts of how God has helped individuals with their personal problems but as behavioral models urging individuals to help others as God has helped them."

27. This story resembles the biblical event at the wedding in Cana found in John 2 when Jesus turned water into wine because they were running out.

28. The Mutual Improvement Society was the precursor to what is now the Young Women's organization in the Church of Jesus Christ of Latter-day Saints. For more information, see https://www.churchofjesuschrist.org/study/history/topics/young-women-organizations?lang=eng.

29. The incident left David Lamoreaux "horribly deformed." He says that when this story is told in his family, "two things have been emphasized: first, this event occurred before the family had any contact with the Mormon missionaries or the LDS Church; and second, when David Burlock Lamoreaux served as Joseph Smith's bodyguard, he recounted this story to the Prophet, and it was Joseph Smith who identified the heavenly ministrants as two of the three Nephites" (from a letter written by Delmar L. Norton about his great-great-grandfather). See my note in the story above. The story submission makes it a bit unclear who received the letter and when. And, based on things included in the story submission, I think we should remove the names of the person who collected the story and who told the story. David Lamoreaux is a reasonably well-known figure in LDS history with a large posterity. The story won't identify the teller or collector. For example, another version of the story can be found online here: chrome-extension://efaidnbmnnnibpcajpcglclefindmkaj/http://aprilsancestry.com/files/DBL_LifeStory2.pdf.

30. See "Word of Wisdom" in the glossary.

31. Zeniff is a minor but pivotal figure in the Book of Mormon narrative (Mosiah 9) and a prescient namesake for this Arizona ghost town. Zeniff was the pioneering founder, and first of three kings, of a group of Nephites who returned to the Nephites' ancestral lands, long ago overtaken by Lamanites. As later in Arizona, the people of Zeniff ultimately abandoned their failed settlement in part due to their own wickedness.

Epilogue

1. See Church of Jesus Christ of Latter-day Saints, *Teachings of the Presidents of the Church: Spencer W. Kimball* (Church of Jesus Christ of Latter-day Saints, 2006),

81–82. "God often meets others' needs through our small acts of service. We need to help those we seek to serve to know for themselves that God not only loves them, but he is ever mindful of them and of their needs. . . . God does notice us, and he watches over us. But it is usually through another person that he meets our needs."

2. William A. Wilson, "'Teach Me All That I Must Do': The Practice of Mormon Religion," in *The Marrow of Human Experience: Essays on Folklore by William A. Wilson*, ed. Jill Terry Rudy and Diane Call, 260.

3. William A. Wilson, "Study of Mormon Folklore: An Uncertain Mirror for Truth," in Rudy and Call, *Marrow of Human Experience*, 182.

4. Dallin H. Oaks, "Miracles," *Ensign*, June 2001 https://www.churchofjesuschrist.org/study/ensign/2001/06/miracles?lang=eng#p79.

5. William A. Wilson, "What's True in Mormon Folklore? The Contribution of Folklore to Mormon Studies" (2007), 24. Leonard J. Arrington Annual Lecture. Paper 12, https://digitalcommons.usu.edu/arrington_lecture/12.

6. William A. Wilson, "What's True in Mormon History?" Leonard J. Arrington Mormon History Lecture Series, no. 13. Utah State University Press, 2007, 25.

7. Church of Jesus Christ of Latter-day Saints, "Ministering," Gospel Topics and Questions, Church of Jesus Christ of Latter-day Saints, accessed January 28, 2024, https://www.churchofjesuschrist.org/study/manual/gospeltopics/ministering?lang=eng.

8. Russell M. Nelson, "Ministering," Church of Jesus Christ of Latter-day Saints, transcript and video, https://www.churchofjesuschrist.org/study/general-conference/2018/04/ministering?

9. Jean B. Bingham, "Ministering as the Savior Does," April 2018 General Conference, Church of Jesus Christ of Latter-day Saints, https://www.churchofjesuschrist.org/study/general-conference/2018/04/ministering-as-the-savior-does?lang=eng.

10. 3 Nephi 28:18.

11. 3 Nephi 28:29.

12. 3 Nephi 28:26.

13. Luke 10:37.

Glossary

1. The Church of Jesus Christ of Latter-day Saints, "Degrees of Glory," in *The Guide to the Scriptures* (Church of Jesus Christ of Latter-day Saints, 2013), https://www.churchofjesuschrist.org/study/scriptures/gs/degrees-of-glory?lang=eng.

2. Church of Jesus Christ, "Celestial Kingdom," in *Guide to the Scriptures*, https://www.churchofjesuschrist.org/study/scriptures/gs/celestial-glory?lang=eng.

3. Church of Jesus Christ, "Terrestrial Kingdom," in *Guide to the Scriptures*, https://www.churchofjesuschrist.org/study/scriptures/gs/terrestrial-glory?lang=eng.

4. Church of Jesus Christ, "Terrestrial Kingdom," in *Guide to the Scriptures*, https://www.churchofjesuschrist.org/study/scriptures/gs/telestial-glory?lang=eng.

5. Church of Jesus Christ, "Elder," in *Guide to the Scriptures*, https://www.churchofjesuschrist.org/study/scriptures/gs/elder?lang=eng#p3.

6. The Church of Jesus Christ, "Fast Sunday," Newsroom, Church of Jesus Christ of Latter-day Saints, https://newsroom.churchofjesuschrist.org/article/fast-Sunday.

7. The Church of Jesus Christ, "General Church Leadership," Topics and Questions, Church of Jesus Christ of Latter-day Saints, updated February 9, 2024, https://www.churchofjesuschrist.org/learn/global-leadership-of-the-church?lang=eng.

8. Church of Jesus Christ, "Family History," Topics and Questions, https://www.churchofjesuschrist.org/study/manual/gospel-topics/family-history?lang=eng#p4.

9. The Church of Jesus Christ, "What Is General Conference?" General Conference, Church of Jesus Christ of Latter-day Saints, https://www.churchofjesuschrist.org/feature/general-conference?lang=eng.

10. Church of Jesus Christ, "Gold Plates," Topics and Questions, https://www.churchofjesuschrist.org/study/manual/gospel-topics/gold-plates?lang=eng.

11. Church of Jesus Christ, "Missionary Program," Newsroom, https://news-ie.churchofjesuschrist.org/topic/missionary-program.

12. The Church of Jesus Christ, "Serving as a Missionary," Senior Missionary, Church of Jesus Christ of Latter-day Saints, https://seniormissionary.churchofjesuschrist.org/srsite/ft/about-brightspot?lang=eng.

13. Church of Jesus Christ, "Ordinances," Topics and Questions, https://www.churchofjesuschrist.org/study/manual/gospel-topics/ordinances?lang=eng.

14. Church of Jesus Christ, "Patriarch," Topics and Questions, https://www.churchofjesuschrist.org/study/manual/gospel-topics/patriarch?lang=eng.

15. The Church of Jesus Christ, "Patriarchal Blessings," *General Handbook: Serving in The Church of Jesus Christ of Latter-day Saints* (Church of Jesus Christ of Latter-day Saints, 2023), https://www.churchofjesuschrist.org/study/manual/general-handbook/18-priesthood-ordinances-and-blessings?lang=eng.

16. Church of Jesus Christ, "Quorum," Newsroom, https://newsroom.churchofjesuschrist.org/article/quorum.

17. Church of Jesus Christ, "Sealing," Topics and Questions, https://www.churchofjesuschrist.org/study/manual/gospel-topics/sealing?lang=eng.

18. Church of Jesus Christ, "Seminary," Newsroom, https://newsroom.churchofjesuschrist.org/topic/seminary.

19. Church of Jesus Christ, "Stake," Newsroom, https://newsroom.churchofjesuschrist.org/article/stake.

20. The Church of Jesus Christ, "Translated Beings," in *The Guide to the Scriptures*, https://www.churchofjesuschrist.org/study/scriptures/gs/translated-beings?lang=eng.

21. S. Kent Brown, "Apostle," in *Latter-day Saint Essentials: Readings from the Encyclopedia of Mormonism*, ed. John W. Welch and R. Devan Jensen, 126–28 (Brigham Young University Press, 2002).

Works Cited

Prologue

Brunvand, Jan Harold. "Obituary: Richard M. Dorson (1916–1981)." *Journal of American Folklore* 95, no. 377 (1982): 347–53.

Jamsa, Denise Wilson. "A Daughter's Biography of William A. Wilson." In *The Marrow of Human Experience: Essays on Folklore,* by William A. Wilson, edited by Jill Terry Rudy and Diane Call, 283–92. University Press of Colorado, 2006.

Nichols, Amber M. "Richard M. Dorson: 1916–1918," archived June 10, 2008, at the Wayback Machine, https://web.archive.org/web/20080610120942/http://www.mnsu.edu/emuseum/information/biography/abcde/dorson_richard.html.

Schoemaker, George. "'On Being Human': The Legacy of William A. Wilson," Westminster college.edu, archived June 21, 2004, at the Wayback Machine, https://web.archive.org/web/20040621213144/http://people.westminstercollege.edu/faculty/dstanley/folklore/Edited%20Final%20Draft/fiullschoemaker.htm.

Smith, Joseph Fielding. *Doctrines of Salvation: Sermons and Writings of Joseph Fielding Smith*. Ed. Bruce R. McConkie. Deseret Books, [c1954–1956].

Wilson, William A. Interview by Denise Wilson Jamsa, November 19, 1996, tape 6b, William A. Wilson Archive, Harold B. Lee Library, Provo, Utah.

Wilson, William A. Interview by Denise Wilson Jamsa, October 19, 2003, tape 6b, William A. Wilson Archive, Harold B. Lee Library, Provo, Utah.

Wilson, William A. "Freeways, Parking Lots, and Ice Cream Stands: Three Nephites in Contemporary Mormon Culture." In *The Marrow of Human Experience: Essays on Folklore,* by William A. Wilson, edited by Jill Terry Rudy and Diane Call, 236–52. Utah State University Press, 2006.

Wilson, William A. "Mormon Folklore: Faith or Folly?" *Brigham Young Magazine* (May 1995): 46–54.

Wilson, William A. "'Teach Me All That I Must Do': The Practice of Mormon Religion." In *The Marrow of Human Experience: Essays on Folklore*, by William A. Wilson, edited by Jill Terry Rudy and Diane Call, 253–60. Utah State University Press, 2006.

Wilson, William A. "What's True in Mormon History? The Contribution of Folklore to Mormon Studies." Leonard J. Arrington Mormon History Lecture Series, no. 13. Utah State University Press, 2008.

Introduction

Andersen, Neil L. "Spiritually Defining Memories." *Ensign*, April 2020. https://www.churchofjesuschrist.org/study/general-conference/2020/04/15andersen.

The Church of Jesus Christ of Latter-day Saints. "Are John the Beloved and the Three Nephites Actually Still on the Earth? If So, What Are They Doing?" *Ensign*, November 2017. https://www.churchofjesuschrist.org/study/new-era/2017/11/to-the-point/are-john-the-beloved-and-the-three-nephites-actually-still-on-the-earth-if-so-what-are-they-doing?

The Church of Jesus Christ of Latter-day Saints. "Lesson 134: 3 Nephi 28." 2017 Book of Mormon Seminary Teacher Manual. https://www.churchofjesuschrist.org/study/manual/book-of-mormon-seminary-teacher-manual-2017/introduction-to-third-nephi-the-book-of-nephi/lesson-134-3-nephi-28.

Fife, A. E. "The Legend of Three Nephites among the Mormons." *Journal of American Folklore* 53, no. 207 (1940): 1–49.

Fife, Austin E., and Alta (Stevens) Fife. *Saints of Sage and Saddle*. Indiana University Press, 1956.

Hallstrom, Erin. "What I (Don't) Know." *LDSLiving*, May/June 2017, 14.

Holland, Jeffrey R. *Christ and the New Covenant: The Messianic Message of the Book of Mormon*. Deseret Book, 1997.

Hufford, David. *The Terror That Comes in the Night: An Experience-Centered Study of Supernatural Assault Traditions*. University of Pennsylvania Press, 1989.

Lee, Hector. *The Three Nephites: The Substance and Significance of the Legend in Folklore*. University of New Mexico Press, 1949.

Lythgoe, Dennis. "Mormon Folklore Gives a Look into a Unique Culture." *Deseret News*, December 24, 2006. https://www.deseret.com/2006/12/24/19992439/mormon-folklore-gives-a-look-into-a-unique-culture.

McNeill, Lynne S. *Folklore Rules: A Fun, Quick, and Useful Introduction to the Field of Academic Folklore Studies*. Utah State University Press, 2013.

McNeill, Lynne S. "Folklore: To Define or Not to Define: Why Is This a Question?" *Folklore Thursday* (blog). September 28, 2017 (site discontinued; used with author's permission).

Mould, Tom. *Still, the Small Voice: Narrative, Personal Revelation, and the Mormon Folk Tradition*. Utah State University Press, 2011.

Mould, Tom, and Eric Eliason, eds. *Latter-day Lore: Mormon Folklore Studies*. Salt Lake City: University of Utah Press, 2013.

Perry, Janice Kapp. "I'm Trying to Be Like Jesus." *Children's Songbook*. Church of Jesus Christ of Latter-day Saints, 1989, 78.

Pratt, Orson. "Progress of the Work—Consecration—Preaching to Israel—The Times of the Gentiles—Sanctification of the Saints." *Journal of Discourses* 2 (1855): 259–66.

Pratt, Orson, and Joseph F. Smith. "Report of Elders Orson Pratt and Joseph F. Smith." *Millennial Star* (Liverpool) 40, no. 40, December 9, 1878, 771–74.

Smith, Joseph Fielding. "Preservation and Multiplication of Life—Dangers of Sign Seeking—Man Established in the Truth by Faithfulness and the Spirit of God." In *The Seventieth Semi-Annual Conference of the Church of Jesus Christ of Latter-day Saints*, 40–42. Deseret News, 1900.

Taylor, John W. "Ancient Prophecies Fulfilled in These Days—The Work of John and the Three Nephites—Preparation for the Coming of the Messiah." In *The Seventy-Third Semi-Annual Conference of the Church of Jesus Christ of Latter-day Saints*, 73–76. Deseret News, 1902.

Utter, David. "Mormon Folk-Lore." *The Folk-Lorist: Journal of the Chicago Folk-Lore Society* 1 (1892/1893): 76.

Walker, Barbara. Introduction to *Out of the Ordinary: Folklore and the Supernatural*. Utah State University Press, 1995. 1–7.

Williams, Clyde J. "The Three Nephites and the Doctrine of Translation." In *The Book of Mormon: 3 Nephi 9–30: This Is My Gospel*, edited by Charles D. Tate and Monte S. Nyman. Deseret Book, 1993. Accessed on Gospelink on July 5, 2019.

Wilson, William A. "Austin and Alta Fife." In *Utah History Encyclopedia*, edited by Allen Kent Powell. University of Utah Press, 1994. https://www.uen.org/utah_history_encyclopedia/f/FIFE_AUSTIN_AND_ALTA.shtml.

Wilson, William A. "Documenting Folklore." In *Folk Groups and Folklore Genres: An Introduction*, edited by Elliot Oring, 225–54. Utah State University Press, 1986.

Wilson, William A. "Freeways, Parking Lots, and Ice Cream Stands: Three Nephites in Contemporary Mormon Culture." In *The Marrow of Human Experience: Essays on Folklore*, by William A. Wilson, edited by Jill Terry Rudy and Diane Call, 236–52. Utah State University Press, 2006.

Wilson, William A. "The Paradox of Mormon Folklore." *BYU Studies Quarterly* 17, no. 1 (1976): 40–56.

Wilson, William A. "What's True in Mormon History? The Contribution of Folklore to Mormon Studies." Leonard J. Arrington Mormon History Lecture Series, no. 13. Utah State University Press, 2008.

Young, Brigham. "Extensive Character of the Gospel—Comprehensiveness of Divine Revelation, etc." *Journal of Discourses* 6 (1859): 283–95.

Chapter 1. Vanishing Hitchhiker Nephites

Bascom, William R. "Four Functions of Folklore." *Journal of American Folklore* 67, no. 266 (1954): 333–49.

Bauman, Richard. *Folklore, Cultural Performances, and Popular Entertainments: A Communications-Centered Handbook*. Oxford University Press, 1992.

Berkes, Fikret. *Sacred Ecology: Traditional Ecological Knowledge and Resource Management*. Taylor and Francis, 1999.

Blythe, Christopher James. "The Prophetess of Endor, Reception of 1 Samuel 28 in Nineteenth Century Mormon History." *Journal of Bible Reception* 4, no. 1 (2017): 43–70.

Bohannon, Laura. "Shakespeare in the Bush." *Natural History* 75 (1966): 28–33.

Brunvand, Jan Harold. *The Baby Train & Other Lusty Urban Legends*. W. W. Norton, 1993.

Brunvand, Jan Harold. *The Choking Doberman and Other "New" Urban Legends*. W. W. Norton, 1981.

Brunvand, Jan Harold. *The Vanishing Hitchhiker: American Urban Legends and Their Meanings*. W. W. Norton, 1981.

Bunge, Gabriel. *The Rublev Trinity: The Icon of the Trinity by the Monk-Painter Andrei Rublev*. St. Vladimir's Seminary Press, 2007.

Carr, David M. *The Formation of the Hebrew Bible: A New Reconstruction*. Oxford University Press, 2011.

Carr, David M. *Writing on the Tablet of the Heart: Origins of Scripture and Literature*. Oxford University Press, 2008.

Davis, Wade. *One River*. Simon & Shuster, 1997.

Deaver, William G. *Did God Have a Wife? Archaeology and Folk Religion in Ancient Israel*. Eerdmans, 2008.

Dégh, Linda, and Andrew Vázsonyi. "The Memorate and the Proto-Memorate." *Journal of American Folklore* 87, no. 345 (1974): 225–39.

Dundes, Alan. "Geography and Folk-Tale Oicotypes: Carl Wilhelm von Sydow." In *International Folkloristics: Classic Contributions by the Founders of Folklore*, edited by Alan Dundes, 137–40. Rowman & Littlefield, 1999.

Dundes, Alan. *Holy Writ as Oral Lit: The Bible as Folklore*. Rowman & Littlefield, 1999.

Dunn, Ethan, collector. "Friend & Foe: Two Facets of the Vanishing Hitchhiker Legend Cycle." William A. Wilson Folklore Archive, L. Tom Perry Special Collections, Harold B. Lee Library at Brigham Young University, Provo, Utah, 2018.

Dunn, James D. G. *The Oral Gospel Tradition*. Eerdmans, 2013.

Eliason, Eric A. "Angels among the Mormons." In *The Big Book of Angels*, edited by Beliefnet, 96–104. Rodale Books, 2002.

Eliason, Eric A. "Orality, Literacy, and the Cultural World of the Bible, in Ancient Near Eastern Scholarship and Latter-day Saint Reception." In *The Bible and the Latter-day Saint Tradition,* edited by Taylor Petrey, Eric A. Eliason, and Cory Crawford, 254–68. University of Utah Press, 2023.

Eliason, Eric A. "Spirit Babies and Divine Embodiment: PBEs, Bible Scholarship, First Vision Accounts, and the Experience-Centered Approach to Mormon Folklore." *BYU Studies Quarterly* 53, no. 2 (2014): 21–28.

Ellis, Bill. *Aliens, Ghosts, and Cults: Legends We Live*. University Press of Mississippi, 2001.

Encyclopaedia Britannica. "Elohim: Hebrew god." Edinburgh: Encyclopædia Britannica, Inc. https://www.britannica.com/topic/Elohim.

Eve, Eric. *Behind the Gospels: Understanding the Oral Tradition*. Fortress Press, 2014.

Gabel, John B., Charles B. Wheeler, Anthony D. York, and David Citino, eds. *The Bible as Literature: An Introduction, Fifth Edition*. 5th ed. Oxford University Press, 2005.

Holland, Jeffrey R. "The Only True God and Jesus Christ Whom He Hath Sent." *Ensign*, November 2007, 40–42. ChurchofJesusChrist.org.

Honko, Laurie. "Memorates and the Study of Folk Beliefs." *Journal of the Folklore Institute* 1, nos. 1/2 (1964): 5–19. https://doi.org/10.2307/3814027.

Hufford, David J. "Beings Without Bodies: An Experience-Centered Theory of the Belief in Spirits." In *Out of the Ordinary: Folklore and the Supernatural*. Utah State University Press, 1995, 11–45.

Hufford, David J. *The Terror That Comes in the Night: An Experience-Centered Study of Supernatural Assault Traditions*. University of Pennsylvania Press, 1982.

Ingliss, J. T. *Traditional Ecological Knowledge: Concepts and Cases*. International Development Research Center, 1993.

Jousse, Marcel. *Memory, Memorization, and Memorizers: The Galilean Oral-Style Tradition and Its Traditionists*. Cascade Books, 2018.

Judd, Frank F., Jr., and Terrence Szink. "John the Beloved in Latter-day Saint Scripture (D&C 7)." In *The Doctrine and Covenants: Revelations in Context: The 37th Annual Brigham Young University Sidney B. Sperry Symposium*, edited by Andre H. Hedges, J. Spencer Fluhman, and Alonzo L. Gaskill, online edition 2012. https://rsc.byu.edu/doctrine-covenants-revelations-context/john-beloved-latter-day-scripture-dc-7. Brigham Young University.

Kripal, Stanley. *The Flip: Who You Really Are and Why It Matters*. Penguin, 2020.

Kugel, James L. *The God of Old: Inside the Lost World of the Bible*. Free Press, 2003.

Lundberg, Haley. "What's the Church's Current Recommendation on Food Storage?" *LDS Living*, March 21, 2022. https://www.ldsliving.com/what-is-the-churchs-current-recommendation-on-food-storage/s/10518.

Minnis, Paul E. *Ethnobotany: A Reader*. University of Oklahoma Press.

Mould, Tom. *Still, the Small Voice: Narrative, Personal Revelation, and the Mormon Folk Tradition*. Utah State University Press, 2011.

Munyan, Lesa, collector. "Dead Husband Visits Dying Wife." FA 03. William A. Wilson Folklore Archive, L. Tom Perry Special Collections, Harold B. Lee Library at Brigham Young University, 2021.

Niditch, Susan. *Folklore and the Hebrew Bible*. Wipf & Stock, 2004.

Niditch, Susan. *Oral World and Written World: Ancient Israelite Literature*. Westminster John Knox Press, 1996.

Pasulka, D. W. *American Cosmic: UFOs, Religion, Technology*. Oxford University Press, 2019.

Pasulka, D. W. *Encounters: Experiences with Nonhuman Intelligences*. St. Martin's Press, 2023.

Paulsen, David L. "The Doctrine of Divine Embodiment: Restoration, Judeo-Christian, and Philosophical Perspectives." *BYU Studies* 35, no. 4 (1996): 7–94.

Paulsen, David L. "Early Christian Belief in a Corporeal Deity: Origen and Augustine as Reluctant Witnesses." *Harvard Theological Review* 83, no. 2 (1990): 105–116.

Pew Research Center. "US Religious Knowledge: Executive Summary." Report posted September 28, 2010. https://www.pewresearch.org/religion/2010/09/28/u-s-religious-knowledge-survey/.

Pinnock, Clark. *Most Moved Mover: A Theology of God's Openness*. Baker Publishing Group, 2001.

Prince, Gregory A. *Power from on High: The Development of Mormon Priesthood*. Signature Books, 2019.

Propp, Vladimir. *Morphology of the Folktale*, 2nd ed. Translated by Laurence Scott. University of Texas Press, 1968.

Quinn, D. Michael. *The Mormon Hierarchy: Extensions of Power*. Signature Books, 1997.

Reid, Jack. *Roadside Americans: The Rise and Fall of Hitchhiking in a Changing Nation*. University of North Carolina Press, 2020.

Rodriguez, Rafael. *Oral Tradition and the New Testament: A Guide for the Perplexed*. T & T Clark, 2014.

Rūmī, Jalāl al-Dīn Muḥammad. "Zero Circle." Translated by Colman Banks. In *Ten Poems to Change Your Life*, edited by Roger Housden, 43. Harmony Books, 2001.

Ryken, Leland. *A Complete Handbook of Literary Forms in the Bible*. Crossway, 2014.

Ryken, Leland. *How to Read the Bible as Literature*. Zondervan, 1985.

Schultes, Richard Evans, and Siri von Reis. *Ethnobotany: Evolution of a Discipline*. Timber Press, 1995.

Sims, Alyssa, collector. "Heavenly Visit from Deceased Relatives." FA 02. William A. Wilson Folklore Archive, L. Tom Perry Special Collections, Harold B. Lee Library at Brigham Young University, 2021.

Sky News US Team. "Mormon Teaching of Food Storage Catching On: Many of the Food Banks That Do Internet Sales Are Based in Utah, Where the Church Is Based, and Has Strong Influence." *Sky News*, December 24, 2013. https://news.sky.com/story/mormon-teaching-of-food-storage-catching-on-10423573.

Snuffer, Denver C., Jr. *The Second Comforter: Conversing with the Lord through the Veil*. Mill Creek Press, 2006.

Stanley, David. 2004. *Folklore in Utah: A History and Guide to Resources*. Utah State University Press.

Taysom, Stephen. "'Satan Mourns Naked upon the Earth': Locating Mormon Possession and Exorcism Rituals in the American Religious Landscape, 1830–1977." *Religion and American Culture: A Journal of Interpretation* 27, no. 1 (2017): 57–94.

Toledo, V. M. "Ethnoecology: A Conceptual Framework for the Study of Indigenous Knowledge of Nature." In *Ethnobiology and Biocultural Diversity*, edited by John

R. Stepp, F. S. Wyndham, and R. K. Zarger, 511–22. International Society of Ethnobiology, 2000.

Vallee, Jacques. *Passport to Magonia: From Folklore to Flying Saucers*. H. Regnery, 1969.

von Sydow, C. W. "Folktale Studies and Philology: Some Points of View." In *The Study of Folklore*, edited by Alan Dundes, 219–42. 1948; Prentice Hall, 1965.

Walker, Barbara. *Out of the Ordinary: Folklore & the Supernatural*. Utah State University Press, 1995.

Walker, Ronald W. *Wayward Saints: The Godbeites and Brigham Young*. University of Illinois Press, 1998.

Westminster Assembly. 1646. *The Westminster Confession of Faith*. https://www.ligonier.org/learn/articles/westminster-confession-faith.

Wilson, William A. "Freeways, Parking Lots, and Ice Cream Stands: The Three Nephites in Contemporary Mormon Culture." In *The Marrow of Human Experience: Essays on Folklore*, by William A. Wilson, edited by Jill Terry Rudy and Diane Call, 236–52. Utah State University Press, 2006.

Wright, Veronica, collector. "Collection of Apparition Stories." FA 1, box 339, folder 3, item 4073, William A. Wilson Folklore Archive, L. Tom Perry Special Collections, Harold B. Lee Library at Brigham Young University, 2008.

Chapter 2. The Worldwide End of the World

Allred, Michael. *Madman*. Library ed. Vol. 1. Dark Horse Books, 2021.

Blythe, Christopher James. *Terrible Revolution: Latter-day Saints and the Apocalypse*. Oxford University Press, 2020.

Clark, J. Reuben. Sermon. *General Conference Report*. October 5, 1946, 88.

Hill, George Washington. "An Indian Vision." *Juvenile Instructor* 12 (January 1877): 11.

Hutchins, Zachary McLeod. "'I Lead the Way, Like Columbus': Joseph Smith, Genocide, and Revelatory Ambiguity." In *Americanist Approaches to the Book of Mormon*, edited by Elizabeth Fenton and Jared Hickman, 391–419. Oxford University Press, 2019.

Hyde, Orson. "Celebration of the Fourth of July." *Journal of Discourses* 6 (1859): 367–68.

Hyde, Orson. *A Voice from Jerusalem: or, A Sketch of the Travels and Ministry of Elder Orson Hyde: Missionary of the Church of Jesus Christ of Latter Day Saints, to Germany, Constantinople, and Jerusalem*. Albert Morgan, 1842.

Irving, Washington. *A History of the Life and Voyages of Christopher Columbus*. 4 vols. John Murray, 1828.

Lippard, George. *Washington and His Generals: or, Legends of the Revolution*. G. B. Zieber and Co., 1847.

Mason, Patrick. *The Mormon Menace: Violence and Anti-Mormonism in the Postbellum South*. Oxford University Press, 2011.

Pratt, Orson. "Redemption of Zion . . . " *Journal of Discourses* 17 (1875): 289–300.

Roger of Wendover, and Matthew Paris. *Roger of Wendover's Flowers of History: Comprising the History of English from the Descent of the Saxons to A.D. 1235.* Translated and edited by J. A. Giles. Henry G. Bohn, 1849.

Smith, Joseph Fielding. *The Signs of the Times: A Series of Discussions Sponsored by the Sisters of the Lion House Social Center.* 1942; Indiana University Press, 1970.

The State [Columbia, SC]. "Superstition Helps Protect Structure." July 17, 1970.

"Vision of Arapine on the Night of the 4th of Feb 1855." Brigham Young Office Files, Church History Library. Salt Lake City, Utah.

Wilson, William A. "Freeways, Parking Lots, and Ice Cream Stands: Three Nephites in Contemporary Mormon Culture." In *The Marrow of Human Experience: Essays on Folklore*, by William A. Wilson, edited by Jill Terry Rudy and Diane Call, 236–52. Utah State University Press, 2006.

Chapter 3. Proclaiming-the-Gospel Stories

Bartholomew, Ronald E. "Nineteenth-Century Missiology of the Bedfordshire Conference." *Journal of Mormon History* 37, no. 1 (2011): 206–245.

Bauman, Richard. *Story, Performance, and Event: Contextual Studies of Oral Narrative.* Cambridge University Press, 1986.

Bauman, Richard. *Verbal Art as Performance.* Waveland Press, 1984.

Bevans, Stephen. "Roman Catholic Perspectives on Mission." *Ecumenical Review* 66, no. 1 (2014): 65–71.

Embry, Jessie L. "LDS Sister Missionaries: An Oral History Response, 1910–71." *Journal of Mormon History* 23, no. 1 (1997): 100–139.

Fife, A. E. "The Legend of the Three Nephites among the Mormons." *Journal of American Folklore* 53, no. 207 (1940): 1–49.

Frank, Arthur W. *Letting Stories Breathe: A Socio-Narratology.* University of Chicago Press, 2010.

Jukko, Risto, ed. *Call to Discipleship: Mission in the Pilgrimage of Justice and Peace, WCC Commission on World Mission and Evangelism Documents 2018–2021.* World Council of Churches, 2021. https://www.oikoumene.org/resources/publications/call-to-discipleship.

Lee, Hector. *The Three Nephites: The Substance and Significance of the Legend in Folklore.* University of New Mexico Press, 1949.

McBride, Matthew. "'Female Brethren': Gender Dynamics in a Newly Integrated Missionary Force, 1898–1915." *Journal of Mormon History* 44, no. 4 (2018): 40–67.

Mould, Tom. *Still, the Small Voice.* University Press of Colorado, 2011.

Nikolajeva, Maria. *Reading for Learning: Cognitive Approaches to Children's Literature.* John Benjamins Publishing, 2014.

Oaks, Dallin H., and Lance B. Wickman. "The Missionary Work of the Church of Jesus Christ of Latter-day Saints." In *Sharing the Book: Religious Perspectives on the Rights and Wrongs of Proselytism*, edited by John Witte Jr. and Richard C. Martin, 247–75. Orbis Books, 1999.

Oring, Elliott. "Folk Narrative." In *Folk Groups and Folklore Genres: An Introduction*, edited by Elliott Oring, 121–45. Utah State University Press, 1986.
Oring, Elliott. "Legendry and the Rhetoric of Truth." In *Journal of American Folklore* 121 (2008):127–66.
Price, Rex Thomas. "The Mormon Missionary of the Nineteenth Century." PhD diss., University of Wisconsin–Madison, 1991.
Wilson, William A. "The Study of Mormon Folklore: An Uncertain Mirror for Truth." In *The Marrow of Human Experience: Essays on Folklore*, by William A. Wilson, edited by Jill Terry Rudy and Diane Call, 182–200. Utah State University Press, 2006.
Wilson, William A. "'Teach Me All That I Must Do': The Practice of Mormon Religion." In *The Marrow of Human Experience: Essays on Folklore*, by William A. Wilson, edited by Jill Terry Rudy and Diane Call, 253–60. Utah State University Press, 2006.
Wilson, William A. "What's True in Mormon Folklore: The Contribution of Folklore to Mormon Studies." Leonard J. Arrington Mormon History Lecture Series, no. 13. Utah State University Press, 2007.

Chapter 4. Mix-ups, High Jinks, and Jokes

Dirkmaat, Gerrit. "LDS Educators Conference—Gerrit J. Dirkmaat & J. Gordon Daines III." Conference Address, Provo, Utah. July 8, 2019. Video. https://www.youtube.com/watch?v=6yQxFWHhRGc.
Narvaez, Peter. "The Folk Parodist." *Canadian Folk Music Journal* 5 (1977): 32–37.
Oring, Elliott. Introduction to "The Seriousness of Mormon Humor." In *The Marrow of Human Experience: Essays on Folklore,* by William A. Wilson, edited by Jill Terry Rudy and Diane Call. Utah State University Press, 2006.
Oring, Elliott. *Jokes and Their Relations.* University Press of Kentucky, 1992.
Rasband, Ronald A. "Behold! I Am a God of Miracles." Church of Jesus Christ of Latter-day Saints. https://www.churchofjesuschrist.org/study/general-conference/2021/04/52rasband?lang=eng.
Wilson, William A. "The Seriousness of Mormon Humor." In *The Marrow of Human Experience: Essays on Folklore*, by William A. Wilson, edited by Jill Terry Rudy and Diane Call, 221–35. Utah State University Press, 2006.
Wilson, William A. "What's True in Mormon Folklore? The Contribution of Folklore to Mormon Studies." Arrington Annual Lecture. Paper 12. 2007. https://digitalcommons.usu.edu/arrington_lecture/12.

Chapter 5. "That Your Joy Might Be Full"

Ballard, Margaret McNeil. "Autobiography of Margaret McNeil Ballard, Wife of Henry Ballard. Utah Pioneer 1859." Unpublished manuscript. Typescript. 1917. https://archive.org/details/autobiographyofm00ball.
Church News Archives. "President Hinckley: Work for Dead Is Essential to Earth's Pur-

pose." November 19, 1994. https://www.thechurchnews.com/1994/11/19/23256235/president-hinckley-work-for-dead-is-essential-to-earths-purpose.
Church of Jesus Christ of Latter-day Saints. "Priesthood Ordinances and Blessings." https://www.churchofjesuschrist.org/study/manual/family-guidebook/priesthood-ordinances-and-blessings?lang=eng.
Faulconer, James E. Foreword to *Postponing Heaven: The Three Nephites, the Bodhisattva, and the Madhi*, by Jad Hatem. ix–xii. Translated by Jonathon Penny. Neal A. Maxwell Institute for Religious Scholarship, Brigham Young University, 2015.
Nelson, Russell M. "Joy and Spiritual Survival." October General Conference, 2016. https://www.churchofjesuschrist.org/study/general-conference/2016/10/joy-and-spiritual-survival?lang=eng.
Wilson, Lerona Abigail Martin. *Life Sketches and Experiences of Lerona Wilson*. Vol. 1. Typewritten by Alexander I. Wilson, 1932, 101–102. Merrill-Cazier Special Collections & Archive: Folklore Collection. FOLK COLL 1 no. 355.
Wilson, William A. "Mormon Folklore: Faith or Folly?" *Brigham Young Magazine* (May 1995), 46–54.
Wilson, William A. "The Study of Mormon Folklore: An Uncertain Mirror for Truth." In *Marrow of Human Experience: Essays on Folklore*, by William A. Wilson, edited by Jill Terry Rudy and Diane Call, 182–200. Utah State University Press, 2006.
Wilson, William A. "Teach Me All That I Must Do: The Practice of Mormon Religion." In *The Marrow of Human Experience: Essays on Folklore*, by William A. Wilson, edited by Jill Terry Rudy and Diane Call, 253–60. Utah State University Press, 2006.
Wilson, William A. "What's True in Mormon History? The Contribution of Folklore to Mormon Studies." Leonard J. Arrington Mormon History Lecture Series, no. 13. Utah State University Press, 2008.

Epilogue

Bingham, Jean B. "Ministering as the Savior Does." April 2018 General Conference. Church of Jesus Christ of Latter-day Saints. https://www.churchofjesuschrist.org/study/general-conference/2018/04/ministering-as-the-savior-does?lang=eng.
Church of Jesus Christ of Latter-day Saints. "Ministering." Topics and Questions, https://www.churchofjesuschrist.org/study/manual/gospeltopics/ministering?lang=eng.
Church of Jesus Christ of Latter-day Saints. *Teachings of the Presidents of the Church: Spencer W. Kimball*. Church of Jesus Christ of Latter-day Saints, 2006.
Nelson, Russell M. "Ministering." The Church of Jesus Christ of Latter-day Saints. Transcript and video, 2018. https://www.churchofjesuschrist.org/study/general-conference/2018/04/ministering?
Oaks, Dallin H. "Miracles." *Ensign*, June 2001. https://www.churchofjesuschrist.org/study/ensign/2001/06/miracles?lang=eng#p79.
Wilson, William A. "Study of Mormon Folklore: An Uncertain Mirror for Truth." In

The Marrow of Human Experience: Essays on Folklore, by William A. Wilson, edited by Jill Terry Rudy and Diane Call, 182–200. Utah State University Press, 2006.

Wilson, William A. "Teach Me All That I Must Do: The Practice of Mormon Religion." In *The Marrow of Human Experience: Essays on Folklore*, by William A. Wilson, edited by Jill Terry Rudy and Diane Call, 253–60. Utah State University Press, 2006.

Wilson, William A., "What's True in Mormon Folklore? The Contribution of Folklore to Mormon Studies" (2007). *Arrington Annual Lecture.* Paper 12. https://digitalcommons.usu.edu/arrington_lecture/12.

Wilson, William A. "What's True in Mormon History? The Contribution of Folklore to Mormon Studies." Leonard J. Arrington Mormon History Lecture Series, no. 13. Utah State University Press, 2007.

Glossary

Brown, S. Kent. "Apostle." In *Latter-day Saint Essentials: Readings from the Encyclopedia of Mormonism*, edited by John W. Welch and R. Devan Jensen, 126–28. Brigham Young University Press, 2002.

Church of Jesus Christ of Latter-day Saints. "General Conference." *The Church of Jesus Christ of Latter-day Saints.* https://www.churchofjesuschrist.org/feature/general-conference?lang=eng.

Church of Jesus Christ of Latter-day Saints. *General Handbook: Serving in the Church of Jesus Christ of Latter-Day Saints. The Church of Jesus Christ of Latter-day Saints,* August 2024. www.churchofjesuschrist.org/study/manual/general-handbook/title-page?lang=eng.

Church of Jesus Christ of Latter-day Saints. "Guide to the Scriptures." *The Church of Jesus Christ of Latter-day Saints.* https://www.churchofjesuschrist.org/study/scriptures/gs?lang=eng.

Church of Jesus Christ of Latter-day Saints. "Newsroom." *The Church of Jesus Christ of Latter-day Saints.* https://newsroom.churchofjesuschrist.org/.

Church of Jesus Christ of Latter-day Saints. "Senior Missionary." *The Church of Jesus Christ of Latter-day Saints.* https://seniormissionary.churchofjesuschrist.org/srsite/ft/about-brightspot?lang=eng.

Church of Jesus Christ of Latter-day Saints. "Topics and Questions." *The Church of Jesus Christ of Latter-day Saints.* https://www.churchofjesuschrist.org/study/manual/gospel-topics?lang=eng.

Index

JULIE SWALLOW is a teaching and learning consultant at Brigham Young University.

CHRISTOPHER JAMES BLYTHE is an assistant professor of English at Brigham Young University.

ERIC A. ELIASON is a professor of English at Brigham Young University.

JILL TERRY RUDY is an associate professor of English at Brigham Young University.

The University of Illinois Press
is a founding member of the
Association of University Presses.

Composed in 10.5/13 Minion Pro
with Avenir display
by Jim Proefrock
at the University of Illinois Press
Manufactured by Sheridan Books, Inc.

University of Illinois Press
1325 South Oak Street
Champaign, IL 61820-6903
www.press.uillinois.edu